Fragile Aid

The UNU World Institute for Development Economics Research (UNU-WIDER) was established by the United Nations University as its first research and training centre and started work in Helsinki, Finland, in 1985. The mandate of the institute is to undertake applied research and policy analysis on structural changes affecting developing and transitional economies, to provide a forum for the advocacy of policies leading to robust, equitable, and environmentally sustainable growth, and to promote capacity strengthening and training in the field of economic and social policy-making. Its work is carried out by staff researchers and visiting scholars in Helsinki and via networks of collaborating scholars and institutions around the world.

United Nations University World Institute for Development Economics Research (UNU-WIDER)
Katajanokanlaituri 6B, 00160 Helsinki, Finland
www.wider.unu.edu

Fragile Aid

Development Cooperation in Weak States and Conflict Contexts

Edited by

RACHEL M. GISSELQUIST
PATRICIA JUSTINO
AND
ANDREA VACCARO

UNU WIDER

A study prepared by the United Nations University World Institute for Development Economics Research-(UNU-WIDER)

OXFORD
UNIVERSITY PRESS

OXFORD
UNIVERSITY PRESS

Great Clarendon Street, Oxford, OX2 6DP,
United Kingdom

Oxford University Press is a department of the University of Oxford. It furthers the University's objective of excellence in research, scholarship, and education by publishing worldwide. Oxford is a registered trade mark of Oxford University Press in the UK and in certain other countries

Published in the United States of America by Oxford University Press
198 Madison Avenue, New York, NY 10016, United States of America

British Library Cataloguing in Publication Data

Data available

Library of Congress Control Number: 2025930997

ISBN 9780198960287

DOI: 10.1093/oso/9780198960287.001.0001

Printed and bound by
CPI Group (UK) Ltd, Croydon, CR0 4YY

Foreword

International development co-operation plays a vital role in promoting social, economic, and political progress and wellbeing in developing countries. However, our world has time and again witnessed that fragility, conflict, and violence present severe international development challenges. Challenges that can severely handicap global efforts to end extreme poverty, foster stability, and help countries plan and build functional institutions. By today's estimates about 1.5 billion people live in fragile and conflict-affected states—states which are being further burdened with climate change, pandemics, and food insecurity. The fragility landscape is becoming increasingly complex year on year.

Despite increased attention, much more needs to be done to understand mechanisms through which aid works and the conditions under which it has been most and least effective. A key question is how to maximize the effectiveness of aid in highly complex situations.

This book offers fresh, in-depth understandings of the effectiveness of development cooperation in fragile contexts, and where challenges regarding the effectiveness of development cooperation are most pronounced. The empirical chapters combine quantitative macro analysis of cross-country data with detailed country case studies to take stock of past research on the topic, investigate the impact of foreign aid in fragile state contexts, and explore whether and how aid delivered in accordance with the principles of effective development cooperation works in these settings. Cross-national studies provide a broader picture of the topic, while country case studies allow us to identify specific ways in which development cooperation operates. More reflective chapters discuss the feasibility of the effectiveness agenda and provide important insights on how the effectiveness principles could be improved and better put into practice.

The collection offers important new contributions to a large body of policy-relevant scholarship on the aid–development nexus, as well as to rapidly evolving research and policy debates on building strong and inclusive state institutions. It explores this topic with a particular emphasis on local ownership in the process of building resilience and legitimacy, especially in contexts where who speaks legitimately for the 'local' can be murky.

My sincere thanks go to the book's editors for their joint expertise in guiding the research work, and to the chapter authors for sharing their knowledge and understanding of such a multi-layered and nuanced research landscape.

Kunal Sen
Director, UNU-WIDER
Helsinki, December 2024

Acknowledgements

This volume emerged from our work serving as academic leads for the International Research Conference on the Effectiveness of Development Cooperation (November 2022), co-hosted by UNU-WIDER and the European Commission (DG INTPA), under its capacity of leading the work of the GPEDC Action Area 1.1 on Demonstrating the Impact of Effectiveness. We are grateful to all of the participants for their contributions and active engagement.

We thank our colleagues in the European Commission for the invitation to collaborate in the conference and gratefully acknowledge the financial support for this work. Special thanks go to Christina Etzell, Aida Fernandez, Earnán O'Cléirigh, and Arve Ofstad. Finn Tarp kindly shared expert advice and input. We are grateful for the support of Dominik Etienne and Jutta Stenholm at UNU-WIDER on the programme side; Leeni Varis on communications; and Nadia Rubtsova and her team for conference organization.

Findings from this conference were subsequently presented and discussed in a spotlight session hosted by the Centre for Policy Dialogue (Dhaka) at the 2022 Effective Development Co-operation Summit held in Geneva. We are grateful to our colleagues at CPD for the invitation to participate and for strong collaboration, in particular Debapriya Bhattacharya, Towfiqul Islam Khan, and Najeeba Mohammed Altaf. A special thanks also to Adan Corral Cossio at the OECD for guidance and support in sharing of our findings.

Additional support for the work of this volume has been provided by UNU-WIDER as part of the project, The State and Statebuilding in the Global South: International and Local Interactions, under its 2019–23 work programme. We gratefully acknowledge the financial contributions provided in support of this programme by the core donors of the governments of Finland and Sweden. Warm thanks also to the project team at UNU-WIDER—in particular, Iina Kuuttila, Tim Shipp, and Janis Vehmaan-Kreula.

Our many thanks to Lorraine Telfer-Taivainen for her expert editorial guidance and management of the publications process until submission—in the week of her retirement no less—and to Siméon Rapin for guiding the project skillfully after submission. We thank Oxford University Press, and especially Adam Swallow for their support of this volume.

Finally, this volume would not have been possible without the expert contributions of the chapter authors. Our warm thanks for their collaboration and active engagement throughout the editorial process.

The views expressed in this volume are those of the authors. The conclusions we draw in the introductory chapter reflect our views as editors and are not necessarily those of individual contributors.

Rachel M. Gisselquist, Helsinki
Patricia Justino, Helsinki
Andrea Vaccaro, Oxford
August 2024

Contents

List of Figures

List of Figures

List of Tables

List of Abbreviations

AIDS	acquired immune deficiency syndrome
AMISOM	African Mission to Somalia
ANSF	Afghanistan National Security Forces
ARTF	Afghan Reconstruction Trust Fund
BBC	British Broadcasting Corporation
CDCs	Community Development Councils
CDD	community-driven development
CDR	Community-Driven Reconstruction
CIFP	Country Indicators for Foreign Policy
COVID	Corona Virus Disease
CPP	Cambodian People's Party
CRS	Creditor Reporter System
CSO	civil society organization
DAC	Development Assistance Committee
DESA	Department of Economic and Social Affairs
DG INTPA	Directorate-General for International Partnerships
DHS	Demographic and Health Surveys
FCAS	Fragile and Conflict-Affected Situations
FCDO	Foreign, Commonwealth & Development Office
FCVs	fragile, conflict, or violence-affected states
FGM/C	female genital mutilation/cutting
FGS	Federal Government of Somalia
FMS	Federal Member States
GBV	gender-based violence
GNI	gross national income
GPEDC	Global Partnership for Effective Development Co-operation
HGS	home-grown solutions
HIPC	heavily indebted poor countries
HIV	Human immunodeficiency viruses
HPF	Health Pooled Fund
IDA	International Development Association
IDOS	Institute of Development and Sustainability
IDP	International Development Program
IGAD	Inter-Governmental Authority on Development
INCAF	International Network on Conflict and Fragility
JADF	Joint Action Development Forum
LANGO	Law on Associations and Non-Governmental Organizations
LMIC	Low- or Middle-Income Country

MICS	Multiple Indicator Cluster Surveys
MINUSMA	United Nations Multidimensional Integrated Stabilization Mission in Mali
MoWA	Ministry of Women's Affairs
MRRD	Ministry of Rural Rehabilitation and Development
MTV	Music Television
NAC	National Audit Chambers
NATO	North Atlantic Treaty Organization
NEC	National Elections Commission
NGO	Non-governmental organization
NNC	National Consultative Council
NSP	National Solidarity Program
ODA	official development assistance
OECD	Organization for Economic Co-operation Development
PFM	public financial management
RBM	results-based management
RCT	randomized control trial
SALW	small arms and light weapons
SDG	Sustainable Development Goals
SNA	Somali National Alliance
SWIFT	Society for Worldwide Interbank Financial Telecommunications
TFG	Transitional Federal Government
UCDP	Uppsala Conflict Data Program
UIC	United Islamic Courts
UK	United Kingdom
UNDP	United Nations Development Programme
UNESCO	United Nations Educational, Scientific and Cultural Organization
UNICEF	United Nations International Children's Emergency Fund
UNODC	United Nations Office on Drugs and Crime
UNSOM	United Nations Assistance Mission in Somalia
UNU-WIDER	United Nations University World Institute for Development Economics Research
US	United States
USAID	United States Agency for International Development
VSLAs	village savings and loans associations
WDR	World Development Report
WGI	Worldwide Governance Indicators
WHO	World Health Organization

Notes on Contributors

Najeeba Mohammed Altaf is a research associate at CPD, Dhaka. Her research work centres on international development, SDG accountability, youth, and education in Bangladesh. She graduated with a master's in business administration from IBA, University of Dhaka, Bangladesh.

Debapriya Bhattacharya, PhD, is a distinguished fellow at CPD, Dhaka, and Convenor of the Citizen's Platform for SDGs, Bangladesh. He is also the Chair of two global initiatives: LDC Monitor, and Southern Voice. He is engaged in high-level policy designing and advising for the national government and various bilateral and international development agencies at home and abroad. He has published extensively on trade, investment, and finance-related issues of the least developed countries (LDCs) and Sustainable Development Goals.

David Carment holds a PhD from McGill University and is Professor of International Affairs, Norman Paterson School of International Affairs, Carleton University, Ottawa. He has led the Country Indicators for Policy project (www.carleton.ca/cifp) for more than 20 years. He has held fellowships at the Hoover Institution, the Belfer Center, the Center for Global Cooperation, and UNU-WIDER. He is the founding series editor of *Canada and International Affairs* and served as editor of *Canadian Foreign Policy Journal* for 14 years. He has published more than 60 articles and 18 books on topics ranging from fragile states and aid policy to mediation, conflict risk assessment, and Canadian foreign policy.

Mathieu Cloutier is a senior economist in the Governance Global Practice of the World Bank and the Program Manager for the Coalitions for Reform Global Program. His work and research focus on addressing issues of collective action within World Bank Operations and client countries' development programmes through the use of change management and political economy tools and methodologies.

Rachel M. Gisselquist is Professor in Governance and Development, and Director of the Governance and Social Development Resource Centre (GSDRC), University of Birmingham, UK. She is also a non-resident senior research fellow with UNU-WIDER, where she was based 2011–24. Previously, she was a Research Director at Harvard University, where she co-authored and developed the first several editions of the Ibrahim Index of African Governance, which has become a standard reference on governance. Her research examines issues of inequality, ethnic and identity politics, state-building, foreign aid, governance, and democracy, with particular attention to sub-Saharan Africa. She has authored 30+ journal articles and book chapters and is editor of over a dozen edited collections in outlets such as *World Development*, *Journal of Development Studies*, and *Journal of Ethnic and Migration Studies*. She holds a PhD in political science from MIT.

Hodan Hassan is Executive Director of Kulan Consulting, partnering with governments and organizations to support programme learning and adaptation, sociopolitical context analysis, and research. She has more than 20 years of experience in international development and public advocacy and has worked in mid and senior-level positions in the management of stabilization and development assistance programmes in fragile states.

Malin Hasselskog is an associate professor at the School of Global Studies, University of Gothenburg, Sweden. Much of her research on development and development cooperation focuses on various encounters and ensuing interplay between actors involved at local, national, and transnational arenas, largely based on qualitative methods with an ethnographic approach. She has published widely in the fields of local and international development, in particular in the areas of aid relations and shifting, and often contradictory, ideals in development thinking and practice, with a geographic focus on Rwanda and Cambodia.

Anke Hoeffler is a professor of Development Policy at the Department of Politics and Public Administration, University of Konstanz. Her research is in the areas of development and security, using mainly quantitative methods in her interdisciplinary work. Broadly, she is interested in the social causes and consequences of excess morbidity and mortality. Current research projects focus on: (i) the impact of interpersonal violence on development, in particular violence against children and women, (ii) the relationship between interpersonal and political violence, and (iii) costs of violence.

Deborah Isser is Lead Governance Specialist at the World Bank, currently focusing on the political economy of development in the Africa region. She leads operational and analytical work on fiscal governance, service delivery, and judicial reform. She has published widely on law, justice, and development and has taught courses at Georgetown and George Washington Law Schools.

Patricia Justino is a development economist who works at the interface between development economics and political science. She is a leading expert on political violence and development, and the co-founder and co-director of the Households in Conflict Network. She is currently Deputy Director at UNU-WIDER and Professorial Fellow at the Institute of Development Studies (IDS) in Brighton, UK (on leave). Professor Justino's research focuses on the relationship between political violence, institutional transformation, governance and development outcomes. She has led major research programmes funded by the European Commission, the UK Economic and Social Research Council (ESRC) and the UK Department for International Development (DFID). She is currently the director of an ESRC large grant project on the relationship between inequality, social trust, and governance outcomes. Her research has been published in leading international journals such as the *Journal of the European Economic Association*, the *Journal of Development Economics*, the *Journal of Conflict Resolution*, the *Journal of Peace Research*, and the *World Bank Economic Review*, among others. She is the lead editor of *A Micro-Level Perspective on the Dynamics of Conflict, Violence and Development* (Oxford University Press).

Towfiqul Islam Khan is a senior research fellow at CPD, Dhaka. He is a member of the SDG Task Team, Prime Minister's Office, Government of Bangladesh. Khan was a member of several technical committees of Bangladesh government agencies, including the

Bangladesh Bureau of Statistics (BBS) and the Ministry of Commerce. He has several peer-reviewed works in SAGE, Springer, and Routledge and published across several areas such as macroeconomic policies, public finance management, governance, development financing, inclusive development, and SDGs.

Jennifer Brick Murtazashvili is the Founding Director of the Center for Governance and Markets and Professor of International Development at the University of Pittsburgh. Her research utilizes tools of political economy to analyse issues of pluralism, security, and development in Afghanistan, Central Eurasia, and the developing world. She is the author of five books, including two on Afghanistan, which focus on the intersection of informal institutions, conflict, and legitimacy.

Vedaste Ndizera is a lecturer at the Department of Political Science and International Relations, University of Rwanda and a post-doc at the School of Global Studies, Gothenburg University. He holds a PhD in governance and regional integration and his research interest revolve around governance and development with a focus on the African indigenous systems and the nexus between democracy and development. He has published on the African Union, pan-Africanism, local participation, and tourism management. His current research project studies local participation within the Rwandan Homegrown Development programmes.

Joakim Öjendal is a professor at the School of Global Studies, University of Gothenburg, Sweden. He is primarily active within the fields of development studies, international relations, and water management. He has published widely in the sub-fields of democratic decentralization, the local turn of peacebuilding, and river basin management. His latest publication is as an editor for a Routledge handbook on water and development.

Gaël Raballand is Practice Manager for West Africa at the World Bank. Prior to this position, he worked for five years on Somalia based in Dar es Salaam and then Nairobi. He has published extensively on aid effectiveness in fragile and conflict-affected countries as well as on political economy aspects.

Yiagadeesen Samy is a professor of International Affairs and currently the Director of The Norman Paterson School of International Affairs (NPSIA) at Carleton University. His research interests intersect the broad areas of international and development economics and his current research focuses on domestic resource mobilization, fragile states, foreign aid, and income inequality. His most recent books are *African Economic Development* (Routledge, 2018), co-authored with Arch Ritter and Steven Langdon, and *Exiting the Fragility Trap: Rethinking Our Approach to the World's Most Fragile States* (Ohio University Press, 2019), co-authored with David Carment.

Andrea Vaccaro is a postdoctoral research fellow at the Blavatnik School of Government, University of Oxford, and an associate member of St Antony's College, University of Oxford. Previously, he was a visiting researcher at the World Institute for Development Economics Research, United Nations University (UNU-WIDER) and a postdoctoral researcher at the University of Insubria. His research interests lie at the crossroads between comparative politics and global development. Recently, he has worked on the interplay between the state, political regimes, and development, as well as international aid, COVID-19 responses, and measurement and indicators. He received his PhD from the Sapienza University of Rome.

Christoph Zürcher is a professor at the Graduate School of Public and International Affairs at the University of Ottawa. His research interests include conflict and peacebuilding, fragile states, international development cooperation, and evaluations. His research in these fields has been published in leading journals. He has collaborated with various organizations, including the German Federal Ministry for Economic Cooperation and Development, Global Affairs Canada, the Swiss Federal Department of Foreign Affairs, UNDP, the World Bank, and others, on topics related to his research.

PART I
INTRODUCTION

1

Development Cooperation under Fragility

Evidence from across the Globe

Rachel M. Gisselquist, Patricia Justino, and Andrea Vaccaro

1.1 Introduction

Understanding how aid works in fragile states and conflict-affected areas is a critical question to ensure sustainable peace and development outcomes in such contexts. It is also a central question in debates about the future of international aid. Despite mixed evidence on the effectiveness of aid in these contexts, external support for development and humanitarian needs continues to be of vital importance. Recent reports show an increase in the number of fragile and conflict-affected states, as well as a persistent concentration of extreme poverty within these countries—the latter estimated to reach 86% by 2030, according to a much cited estimate from the OECD's 2022 *States of Fragility* report. As a result, the amount of development assistance targeted to fragile contexts has been steadily on the rise but questions remain about the effectiveness of international aid in those settings.

Bringing together findings from a wide array of expert studies, this volume offers new insights into the record of aid under fragility—which is both concerning and contested—and implications for research and practice going forward. It further highlights and explores two key implications.[1] First, there is a need for more systematic unpacking of the considerable diversity across fragile contexts to better understand both past experience and lessons for future practice. One promising approach, illustrated in this introduction, is to consider variation in different dimensions of the state—for instance, authority, capacity, and legitimacy—using standard metrics. Second, the globally-endorsed 'aid effectiveness principles'—country ownership, focus on results, inclusive partnerships, and transparency and mutual accountability—are an important cornerstone of better development

[1] This volume originated from the research and policy discussions that unfolded at the International Research Conference on the Effectiveness of Development Cooperation, co-hosted by UNU-WIDER and the European Commission (DG INTPA), under its capacity of leading the work of the GPEDC Action Area 1.1 on Demonstrating the Impact of Effectiveness. Findings from this conference were subsequently presented and discussed in a spotlight session hosted by the Centre for Policy Dialogue (Dhaka) at the 2022 Effective Development Co-operation Summit held in Geneva. These discussions have greatly informed our work as editors, but the views expressed in this volume, and in each chapter herein, are those of its authors only.

Rachel M. Gisselquist, Patricia Justino, and Andrea Vaccaro, *Development Cooperation under Fragility.*
In: *Fragile Aid.* Edited by: Rachel M. Gisselquist et al., Oxford University Press. © UNU-WIDER (2025).
DOI: 10.1093/oso/9780198960287.003.0001

cooperation, but there are fundamental challenges to their application in fragile contexts which require continued consideration. Country ownership—seen by many as the most important of the principles—is inherently challenging in numerous fragile contexts. While there are no easy answers for international actors operating in such environments, research and practice identify key pitfalls and promising directions for future work.

This chapter serves as both introduction and conclusion to this book. It begins by situating the volume within research and policy discussion on aid effectiveness and fragility, and proceeds to providing an overview of the chapters that follow. Building on this discussion, the chapter then offers new empirical insights into the relationship between aid and diverse fragile contexts, taking into account the multi-dimensional character of the state in terms of authority, capacity, and legitimacy. This analysis reflects briefly on the empirical relationships among authority, capacity, and legitimacy across fragile states, and shows how both aid activities and indicators of adherence to the aid effectiveness principles may vary with these dimensions. The analysis focuses in particular on the challenge of the ownership principle, given its central importance in fragile contexts.

1.2 Institutional Quality, Aid Effectiveness, and the State

Fragility is typically defined as the lack of ability or willingness of states to fulfil their governance responsibilities towards their citizens, usually due to weak institutional capacity. Since at least 9/11, international aid targeted towards fragile countries has had the implicit or explicit aim of improving the quality of institutions of governance (Justino 2019; Gisselquist 2015, 2021). Evidence on whether aid improves institutional quality in fragile countries has, however, been at best mixed, which has raised new questions about the effectiveness of aid in such contexts.

Emphasis on institutional quality as a factor in aid effectiveness is often traced to a series of research studies on the relationship between economic growth and aid published in the early 2000s. In their influential study, Burnside and Dollar (2000) found that the effectiveness of international aid depends on the quality of institutions and economic policies in recipient countries, thus suggesting that aid could be made more effective by conditioning its disbursements on improvements in the policy environment (Burnside and Dollar 2004). Similarly, Collier and Dollar (2001, 2002) and Collier and Dehn (2001) argued that the relationship between international aid and economic growth depends on the quality of the recipient country's institutional environment, while Collier and Hoeffler (2002) showed that international aid and a sound policy environment are mutually supportive in mitigating the risk of civil conflict—arguably a key factor in how economic growth is promoted in aid-recipient countries.

Subsequent research pointed to a more circumscribed relationship. Easterly et al. (2004) for instance found that Burnside and Dollar's (2000) results held only in specific periods and samples of countries, while Jia and Williamson (2019) reran Burnside and Dollar's original analysis with a more extensive sample and a broader set of indicators and found no clear evidence that aid effectiveness depends on the quality of institutions in recipient countries. Carment et al.'s (2008) analysis suggested that the positive impact of aid on economic growth was stronger in countries with fragile institutions. Other studies questioned the links between aid and economic performance altogether—finding weak links between a better policy environment and aid effectiveness (e.g., Rajan and Subramanian 2008). A substantial body of work challenged these findings, showing aid has an aggregate positive impact on economic performance and other key outcomes, regardless of institutional quality—see Hansen and Tarp (2001); Dalgaard et al. (2004); Juselius et al. (2014); Arndt et al. (2015).

A related literature explores the reverse relationship—the impact of aid on institutions. Knack (2001: 310) for instance found that 'higher aid levels erode the quality of governance, as measured by indices of bureaucratic quality, corruption, and the rule of law'.[2] More recent research challenged the so-called 'aid-institutions paradox', highlighting that while aid sometimes has negatively influenced institutions, its overall impact across countries is often positive. Jones and Tarp (2016) found generally a positive impact of aid on institutional quality, with the magnitude of the relationship being contingent on the type and volatility of aid. Askarov and Doucouliagos (2015), focusing on a sample of transition economies, showed that aid has no effect on governance quality but positively affects democratic institutions. Niño-Zarazúa et al. (2020) presented evidence of the positive impact of democracy aid around the world. Ariotti, Dietrich, and Wright (2021) found that aid aimed at promoting judicial reforms is particularly successful in countries with weak state administrative capacity.

Another body of work has analysed the impact of aid on peacebuilding, with notably mixed results (Findley 2018). For instance, Nielsen et al. (2011) and Nunn and Qian (2014) showed that aid is inversely related to the duration and intensity of civil conflict but not its onset. Adam and Tsarsitalidou (2022) found that aid reduces protests but increases more violent forms of domestic conflict, while Mousseau (2021) showed that aid increases the likelihood of the onset of ethnic war, as excluded groups are likely to be more motivated to fight the dominant group over the 'prize' of aid. In terms of aid targeted to the promotion of democratic institutions specifically (i.e., democracy aid), Savun and Tirone (2011) for instance found that democratizing countries receiving little democracy aid are

[2] See also Bräutigram and Knack (2004), Moss et al. (2006), Rajan and Subramanian (2007), and Young and Sheehan (2014).

more prone to civil conflict than those receiving larger volumes of democracy aid.[3] Braithwaite and Licht (2020) instead argue that democracy aid may be related to an increased risk of violent civil conflict particularly in contexts where civil society organizations are weak.

Notwithstanding this ongoing scholarly debate, the global policy discourse seems to have internalized the idea that building stronger, more resilient institutions is of utmost importance for successful international aid. This commitment is reflected in the Sustainable Development Goals, especially Goal 16. Countries that have remained stuck in fragility and recurrent conflicts are the ones where more effective international aid is most needed as the gap between peaceful and fragile countries grows (OECD 2022). However, some evidence suggests that aid may at times undermine statebuilding efforts (Englebert and Tull 2008; Eriksen 2017), especially in fragile countries (Zürcher 2017; Findley 2018).

Key questions remain on how development cooperation can be made more effective in fragile settings going forward, and how development actors may be able to best overcome the challenges generated by weak state institutions.

1.3 The Effectiveness Principles

Practitioner responses to the above questions often emphasize the importance of the 'effectiveness principles' set forth between 2003 and 2011 in four high-level forums coordinated by the OECD, which created the GPEDC (a multi-stakeholder platform bringing together governments, bilateral and multilateral organizations, and representatives from civil society, the private sector, parliaments, local governments, and trade unions) and the New Deal for Engagement in Fragile States in Busan.[4]

The effectiveness principles include country ownership, focus on results, inclusive partnerships, and transparency and mutual accountability. These principles represent a globally agreed framework to guide development cooperation. The GPEDC supports the implementation of the principles, promotes mutual accountability, and works to sustain political momentum for more effective cooperation and partnerships. Since its inception, the GPEDC has emphasized the importance of considering fragility. The outcome document of the 2022 Effective Development Co-operation Summit states, for instance, that 'country resilience must be

[3] Democracy aid may include, for instance, assistance for the strengthening of free and fair elections, media freedom, human rights, key state institutions such as parliaments, and support for civil society. Savun and Tirone (2011) measure it using OECD-DAC data as aid as intended for 'Government and Civil Society'.

[4] While the outcome document of the first high-level forum in Rome (in 2003) did not mention fragility, subsequent forums in Paris (2005), Accra (2008), and Busan (2011) put it more firmly at centre stage.

supported to address multiple and interconnected development challenges and fragility, cognizant of country-specific development challenges and vulnerabilities' (GPEDC 2022: 2).

Despite concerns about waning enthusiasm for the effectiveness agenda in the 2010s, the principles remain an important reference point for development practice—see Gulrajani (2022); Calleja and Cichocka (2022)—and were reaffirmed once more in the 2022 Summit. They are broadly seen to reflect shared global commitments to self-governance and public institutions that are inclusive, effective, transparent, and locally accountable, commitments reflected also in SDG 16 and SDG 17.

As discussed throughout this volume, it is precisely this reflection of shared global commitments that makes the effectiveness principles valuable guideposts for development cooperation (Gisselquist et al. 2023). Evidence is, however, mixed on the precise ways in which the effectiveness principles may be reflected in more effective aid. On the one hand, a substantial literature on specific aid projects and programmes—including some of our own work—suggests that ownership, partnerships, transparency, and accountability tend to contribute to better outcomes at the project and programme level. On the other hand, as we show in Gisselquist et al. (2023), the cross-country evidence for such a claim is not strong; we cannot show, using available data, that better adherence to the principles at the country level has contributed to more effective aid and better development outcomes overall. This absence of evidence does not mean that such a relationship does not exist—it might be just difficult to capture with currently available data due to its limitations and inherent challenges in the measurement of the principles. However, evidence suggests that we should adjust the way in which we understand and apply the effectiveness principles. This is a central question guiding this volume.

1.4 This Volume

Collectively, the chapters in this volume offer a rich set of expert perspectives on aid under fragility, focusing on case studies as varied as Afghanistan, Cambodia, Mali, Rwanda, Somalia, and South Sudan. These are some of the most fragile countries today and have also received significant amounts of international assistance. The analyses of these cases and how they reflect the main concerns of this volume are deliberately diverse, both in their arguments, as well as in their methods and disciplinary grounding. Some chapters draw on focused consideration of single cases, others on cross-country analysis. Some use quantitative methods, others qualitative and mixed approaches. Collectively they point to some common themes and, importantly, to the contested nature of the evidence base in this area.

The next section of this volume, Part II, includes three reflections by leading scholars on the global record of aid effectiveness in fragile and conflict-affected contexts, alongside implications for ways forward.

Chapter 2 by Christoph Zürcher, and Chapter 3 by David Carment and Yiagadeesen Samy, respectively provide syntheses drawn from major research programmes of findings on aid effectiveness in fragile and conflict-affected contexts. Zürcher's chapter paints a particularly sobering picture, based on systematic reviews on the impact of aid in three highly fragile states—Afghanistan, Mali, and South Sudan. The chapter concludes that 'aid did not improve governmental capacity, did not lead to better governance, and did not provide more stability' in these contexts. The evidence suggests, Zürcher argues, that instead of continuing to struggle with large but ineffective, and sometimes even detrimental statebuilding projects, better ways forward in such contexts would prioritize 'do no harm', and local, small-scale interventions to improve social outcomes like health and education, where aid has had more positive impact.

David Carment and Yiagadeesen Samy's analysis is more cautiously positive about the role for aid in fragile contexts. Building on data from their long-standing Country Indicators for Foreign Policy (CIFP) project, Carment and Samy's analysis considers three dimensions of fragility—authority, capacity, and legitimacy—which we will return to later in this chapter. They observe that countries trapped in fragility tend to be marked by legitimacy problems. Identifying improvements in state legitimacy is thus key to improving aid effectiveness. A stronger focus on legitimacy, they suggest, might also provide insight into why interventions aimed at strengthening state capacity have been often ineffective in the past. Looking ahead, they further reflect on how global shocks—such as the COVID-19 pandemic and the wars in Ukraine and Gaza—have influenced and will continue to shape aid and fragility.

The third chapter in Part II, Chapter 4 by Anke Hoeffler, shifts gears, identifying and exploring from a global perspective on an issue relevant to aid, fragility, and conflict that has thus far received little attention from development practitioners and academics: human violence beyond armed conflict. While the international development community recognizes that violence is detrimental for achieving progress, Hoeffler argues, its focus has been on collective violence, overlooking self-directed and interpersonal violence, even if both are major problems in fragile countries. Development actors have understood violence too narrowly, she argues, and more international aid should be targeted to address forms of violence beyond armed conflict. In so doing, she speaks also to the effectiveness principles, in particular the principle of 'focus on results', and how these can be broadened to consider the nexus between violence and fragility in a more comprehensive way.

In Part III, the volume turns to the particular challenge of ownership and the social contract in aid in fragile contexts. It has been argued that ownership is the most important among the aid effectiveness principles, and that 'the other principles can be seen as both premises for and results of the wider ownership agenda' (Lie 2019: 1111).[5]

Chapter 5 by Debapriya Bhattacharya, Towfiqul Islam Khan, and Najeeba Mohammed Altaf frames the discussion with focused consideration of ownership within the context of the effectiveness principles. Building on case studies in six aid-recipient countries, they show how ownership is typically understood as national ownership by recipient country governments, which can pose challenges for instance in countries where the state enjoys weak popular support and does not have the capacity to implement country-owned policies. In such contexts, a small elite may reap the rewards of country-owned aid which never reaches the broader population. Extending from this analysis, they advocate for a paradigm shift from 'country ownership' to 'collective ownership' as indispensable for more effective aid. This new approach to ownership entails ensuring meaningful participation of key stakeholders—including recipient country governments, aid providers, and non-state actors such as the private sector, civil society, and NGOs—at every stage of the development cooperation process.

Chapter 6 by Jennifer Brick Murtazashivili, and Chapter 7 by Gael Raballand, Mathieu Cloutier, Hodan Hassan, and Deborah Isser, respectively zoom in on issues of ownership and social contract in two key countries, Afghanistan and Somalia. In reflecting on international development efforts in Afghanistan after the fall of the Taliban regime in the early 2000s, Murtazashvili paints a sobering picture, highlighting key failures. While purporting to implement 'community-led' programming and driven by over-attention to measurable results, she argues, the development community in fact adopted centralized, donor-driven approaches, out of sync with customary systems of local governance and mirroring past, unpopular efforts to centralize power from local communities to the central state. Improving aid effectiveness in a country like Afghanistan, the chapter implies, requires approaches that are more truly locally owned and politically informed, and that incorporate more nuanced, broader consideration of aid impact and effectiveness.

Raballand et al.'s chapter brings in the concept of the social contract to discuss the impact of the weak social contract between the Somali state and its citizens on aid effectiveness. A stronger social contract in Somalia between the state and citizens requires improving the quality of the bargaining process between the two sides. Key initiatives ought to include increasing political accountability and transparency, concentrating public service delivery in core areas like security and education, and strengthening the state's regulatory activities. Like Murtazashvili's chapter, this analysis points to the importance of better understanding the

[5] The centrality of ownership also finds support in our empirical analysis of the cross-country data, as discussed further below.

local political context to increase the effectiveness of aid. However, it also suggests that local ownership may be problematic for statebuilding if it undermines the legitimacy of the central state.

Along related lines, the final Chapter 8 by Malin Hasselskog, Vedaste Ndizera, and Joakim Öjendal, draws on research in Rwanda and Cambodia—two countries generally understood to have 'strong' country ownership of aid—to explore the tension between country ownership and local participation. While the conventional view suggests country ownership and local participation are mutually reinforcing, Hasselskog et al. find this is not necessarily the case. Drawing on qualitative content analysis of primary interviews of local officials, civil society organization (CSO) representatives, and members of the local community in the two countries, the chapter shows how national governments in aid-recipient countries may not take into account the priorities and preferences of the citizens that are ultimately affected by government policies. The authors note that strong country ownership does not automatically lead to local participation, suggesting, in line with some other chapters of this volume, that the ownership principle may require adjustments to ensure its fruits can be reaped. This might require in turn better consideration of the local political context and the politics of ownership.

1.5 Aid across Diverse Fragile Contexts: Empirical Patterns

As the chapters in this volume illustrate, fragile contexts are diverse. This complicates broad assessments of the record of aid under fragility, as well as how to draw and apply lessons from past global experience. For instance, Zürcher's chapter spotlights synthesis of evidence on three 'highly fragile' countries, Afghanistan, Mali, and South Sudan. As Zürcher suggests, it may well be that the record of aid in these contexts is significantly different to that in more 'moderately' fragile environments and that the sobering implications of his findings for aid policy may only apply in some contexts.

Multiple contextual factors are likely to be relevant to aid activities. However, as the literature on the aid–institutions nexus suggests, the quality of domestic state institutions and policy environments might be especially relevant. In this section, we offer a simple empirical exercise to illustrate how diverse experiences of fragility across different dimensions of domestic institutional quality may affect our understanding of how the effectiveness principles operate in different contexts. For the purpose of this analysis, we measure fragility across three dimensions: state authority, capacity, and legitimacy—see also Carment et al. (2008); Call (2011); Grävingholt et al. (2015); Gisselquist and Vaccaro (2022).

We define authority as the extent of the state's monopoly of violence. Capacity is understood in terms of the state's provision of basic services. Legitimacy is defined as the degree of acceptance of the state's rule by the society (Grävingholt et al. 2015). We acknowledge that these are not the only dimensions of the state that may influence aid outcomes (for a fuller review of measures of the state, see Vaccaro 2023). For instance, the OECD (2022) emphasizes a combination of economic, environmental, human, political, security, and societal fragilities, while Rice and Patrick (2008)—in Brookings Institution's Index of State Weakness—classify weak states according to their performance in economic, political, security, and social welfare. We hope nonetheless our more institutional approach provides a useful illustration of how institutional characteristics of fragile states may influence aid experience and effectiveness (see also Hoeffler and Justino 2023).

1.5.1 Measuring Dimensions of State Fragility, Aid Flows, and the Principles of Aid Effectiveness

In measuring authority, capacity, and legitimacy, we use the German Institute of Development and Sustainability's (IDOS) Constellations of Fragility dataset (Ziaja, Grävingholt and Kreibaum 2019).[6] The core indices of the IDOS dataset aggregate multiple sub-indicators. Authority is measured using data on battle deaths and homicides, as well as expert perceptions on monopoly of violence. Capacity is measured using data on child mortality, school enrolment, and drinking water, as well as expert perceptions on administrative capacity. Legitimacy is measured with a combination of data on asylums, expert perceptions on press freedom, and a composite measure of political repression.

This underlying data effectively proxies our three dimensions of state fragility. Battle-related casualties and homicides reflect a weak monopoly of violence by the state because the state should be able to protect its citizens from both internal and external security threats. High levels of child mortality, low school enrolment, and access to water arguably reflect a dysfunctional state administration and the inability of the state to deliver basic public services. The variables used to proxy for legitimacy reflect the degree of repression of the state and the extent to which it may violate the physical integrity rights of its citizens. It is assumed that high levels of repression are unlikely to reflect widespread consent for the rule of the state (see also Ziaja et al. 2019).

We use both aggregate and sectoral data to account for aid flows. In considering aggregate aid, we follow several previous studies (e.g. Bräutigam and Knack 2004) and measure aid dependence using official development assistance (ODA) as a share of gross national income (GNI), ODA as a percentage of government expenditures, and ODA per capita. Figures are drawn from the World Bank's World

[6] These readily available data have also been used in several recent studies; for example, Gisselquist and Vaccaro (2022); Leutert, Plantan, and Strange (2022).

Development Indicators dataset. We also measure aid flows at the sectoral level, because aggregation can mask important differences between aid sectors (Zürcher 2017: 508). We focus on four sectors—education, health, government and civil society, and humanitarian aid—as these are some of the most significant in fragile countries. Sectoral aid data is based on official figures from OECD's Creditor Reporting System.

To consider the principles of aid effectiveness, we rely on the most recent publicly available version (2017) of the GPEDC's own indicators on the implementation of the principles. As we show in Gisselquist et al. (2023), these indicators have significant limitations, but remain to date the most complete source of information on the implementation of the effectiveness principles. GPEDC's dataset offers more than 20 indicators and sub-indicators of effectiveness and we focus here on a selected number of indicators. We use the continuous indicator with the most observations for each of the four principles: (1) the use of country-owned systems, (2) the presence of national results frameworks, (3) CSO enabling environment, and (4) aid recorded in the national budget. These indicators reflect respectively, country ownership, focus on results, inclusive partnerships, and transparency and mutual accountability. As ownership emerges as an exceptionally important principle, we also examine an ordinal measure of ownership on the quality of public financial management (PFM) systems.

1.5.2 The Multidimensionality of Fragility

Across countries, the three dimensions of state fragility are positively associated with each other but do not always go hand-in-hand, as the chapters in this volume suggest. Highly fragile states, like those analysed in Zürcher's chapter, tend to be weak in every dimension, while in other countries there is notable variation. Raballand et al.'s chapter suggests, for instance, that capacity and legitimacy may improve together if better provision of public services increases support for the state's rule. By contrast, Murtazashvili's chapter on Afghanistan and Hasselskog et al.'s chapter on Cambodia and Rwanda suggest that improving state capacity does not necessarily nurture legitimacy—especially at the local level. As Carment and Samy discuss, greater legitimacy could translate into more effective authority. But, as Hoeffler's discussion reminds us, a high-authority state also can undermine legitimacy by using its monopoly of violence for excessive repression or by being unwilling to protect its citizens.

Scatter plots of the interrelationships among state authority, capacity, and legitimacy are empirically suggestive of these mixed patterns (Figure 1.1). The three dimensions are positively correlated with one other, but the correlations are not particularly strong. Associations between capacity and authority (*r*: 0.30) as well as capacity and legitimacy (*r*: 0.26) are stronger than between authority and

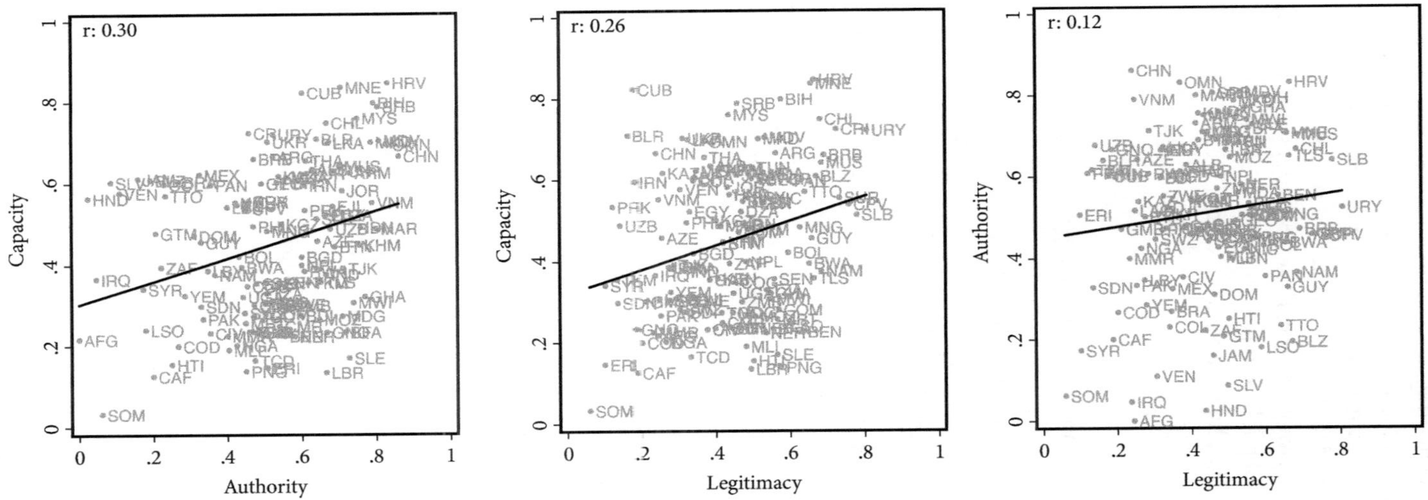

Figure 1.1 Interrelationships among the three core dimensions of state fragility

Note: Mean values per country (between 2010 and 2015). Includes only aid recipient countries (between 2010 and 2020).
Source: authors' illustration.

legitimacy (*r*: 0.12). Highly fragile countries, like Afghanistan, Central African Republic, and Somalia tend to be weak across all dimensions. Many other countries display disparities across dimensions. For example, Sierra Leone has high authority but is unable to deliver essential public services (i.e., low capacity). Honduras cannot effectively protect the security of its citizens (i.e., low authority), but offers a moderate level of public services. In East Timor, the state enjoys relatively wide popular support (i.e., high legitimacy), even if it is a weak provider of basic public services.

1.5.3 Variation in Aid Flows across Fragile Contexts

Table 1.1 presents data on three indicators of aggregate aid (average values of ODA per GNI, aid per capita, and ODA per government expenditure) across countries, alongside authority, capacity, and legitimacy measures.[7] One result that stands out is that fragile countries with low capacity appear to be more aid dependent across all three indicators than those with low authority or legitimacy. Low-authority countries receive more aid per capita than low-legitimacy countries, but the disparity is small for ODA/GNI and ODA/government expenditure. Average values suggest that aid flows are more sensitive to the degree of capacity than either authority or legitimacy, as suggested by scatter plots between ODA/GNI and the core dimensions of state fragility (Figure 1.2). Correlations are inverse regardless of the dimension—meaning that more fragile countries tend to be

Table 1.1 Aid dependence (2010–20) and level of state fragility (2010–15)

	Authority	Capacity	Legitimacy
Low fragility (≥ 0.5)			
ODA/GNI	4.37 (69)	1.76 (52)	4.55 (43)
Aid/capita	65.20 (70)	64.84 (53)	95.42 (43)
ODA (% of government expense)	18.49 (50)	7.49 (42)	18.54 (32)
High fragility (< 0.5)			
ODA/GNI	4.40 (54)	6.31 (71)	4.30 (80)
Aid/capita	63.81 (54)	64.40 (71)	48.23 (81)
ODA (% of government expense)	20.91 (38)	30.53 (46)	20.10 (56)

Note: Entries represent means (2010–20) across countries. No. of observations in parentheses. Somalia's figures on ODA (% of government expense) have been left out due to extreme values. Level of fragility is computed as a mean across years (2010–15) for a given country. Lower fragility means higher authority, capacity, and legitimacy.
Source: authors' calculations.

[7] We also considered aid flows alongside changes in fragility (see Table 1.2).

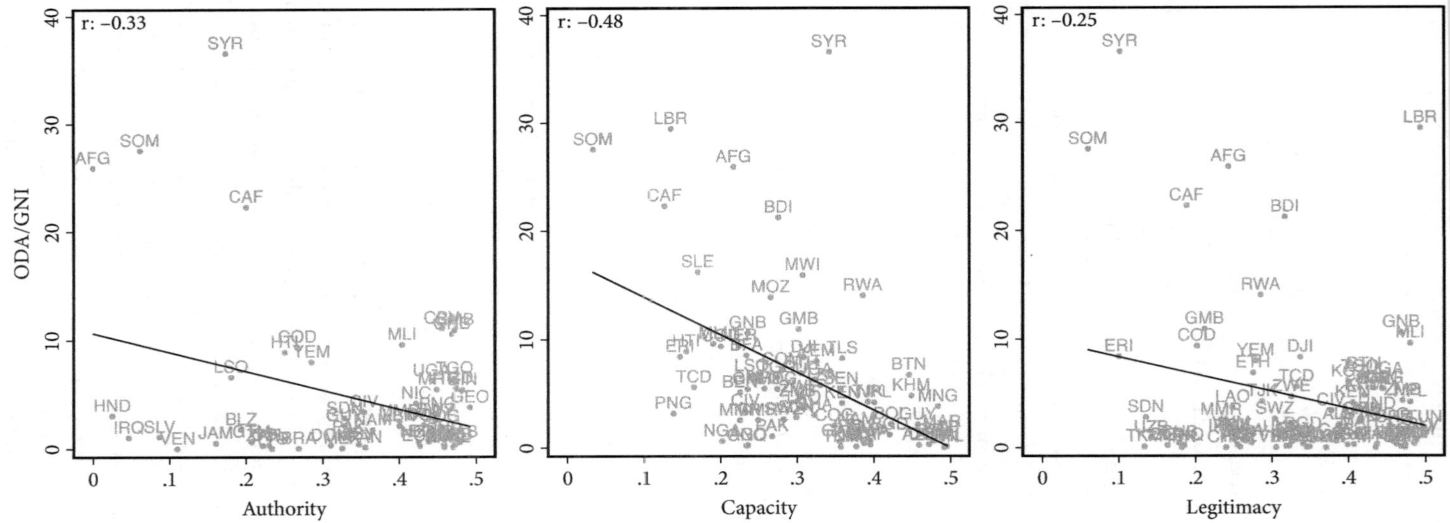

Figure 1.2 The relationship between aid dependence and state fragility

Note: Mean values per country (2010–15 for authority, capacity, and legitimacy; 2010–20 for ODA/GNI). Only fragile countries: authority includes countries where authority < 0.5; capacity includes countries where capacity < 0.5; legitimacy includes countries where legitimacy < 0.5.
Source: authors' illustration.

Table 1.2 Aid dependence (2010–20) and change in state fragility (2010–15)

	Authority	Capacity	Legitimacy
Decrease in fragility (positive Δ)			
ODA/GNI	2.96 (28)	5.32 (62)	3.69 (36)
Aid/capita	52.11 (28)	59.31 (62)	43.30 (36)
ODA (% of government expense)	14.01 (22)	26.48 (42)	16.22 (27)
No decrease in fragility (negative or no Δ)			
ODA/GNI	5.96 (26)	13.12 (9)	4.80 (44)
Aid/capita	76.41 (26)	99.46 (9)	52.17 (45)
ODA (% of government expense)	30.39 (16)	73.01 (4)	23.72 (29)

Note: Entries represent means (2010–20) across countries. No. of observations in parentheses. Somalia's figures on ODA (% of government expense) have been left out due to extreme values. Level of fragility is computed as a mean across years (2010–15) for a given country. Lower fragility means higher authority, capacity, and legitimacy. Only fragile countries: authority includes countries where authority < 0.5; capacity includes countries where capacity < 0.5; legitimacy includes countries where legitimacy < 0.5.
Source: authors' calculations.

more aid dependent—but the magnitude of the association is stronger for capacity (r: −0.48), than authority (r: −0.33) and legitimacy (r: −0.25).

Legitimacy has the weakest correlation with ODA/GNI and regardless of the indicator of aggregate aid that we use, but especially in terms of per capita aid, low-legitimacy countries receive on average less aid than low-capacity or low-authority countries. This may be in part due to weak state legitimacy (and indicators of democratic governance) discouraging donor engagement (Molenaers et al. 2015; Geddes et al. 2018). Another explanation consistent with several chapters in this volume is that aid itself may impede state legitimacy by undermining existing institutions and provoking tensions in communities, as suggested by Murtazashvili's discussion, or by weakening social contracts between the state and its citizens as discussed in Raballand et al.'s chapter.

Going beyond aggregate aid, Table 1.3 summarizes selected figures in four key sectoral areas—education, health, government and civil society, and humanitarian projects (per capita and as a share of total aid). Overall, in comparison to aggregate aid, differences in sectoral aid patterns across low-authority, low-capacity, and low-legitimacy countries seem to be less clear, while there are differences across fragile and non-fragile states. As humanitarian aid is often targeted to address conflict-related issues, it is not surprising that fragile contexts (characterized by low-authority, low-capacity, and low-legitimacy) receive much more humanitarian aid per capita than non-fragile contexts (defined as those displaying high-authority, high-capacity, and high-legitimacy). In addition, in fragile countries overall across all three dimensions, support to the humanitarian sector was

Table 1.3 Sectoral aid (2010–20) and degree of fragility (2010–15)

	Authority	Capacity	Legitimacy	Authority	Capacity	Legitimacy
	Aid per capita in USD, 2010–20			*Aid as a share of total aid, 2010–20*		
Low fragility (≥ 0.5)						
Education	54.58 (70)	58.70 (53)	80.33 (43)	0.16 (70)	0.17 (53)	0.14 (43)
Health	27.14 (70)	21.46 (53)	42.49 (43)	0.06 (70)	0.04 (53)	0.07 (43)
Government & civil society	73.47 (70)	84.98 (53)	99.50 (43)	0.13 (70)	0.16 (53)	0.13 (43)
Humanitarian	25.11 (69)	27.98 (52)	36.92 (43)	0.07 (69)	0.07 (52)	0.06 (43)
High fragility (< 0.5)						
Education	42.60 (55)	42.40 (72)	33.05 (82)	0.10 (55)	0.11 (72)	0.14 (82)
Health	22.35 (55)	27.67 (72)	15.88 (82)	0.07 (55)	0.08 (72)	0.06 (82)
Government & civil society	54.62 (55)	50.59 (72)	47.17 (82)	0.13 (55)	0.11 (72)	0.13 (82)
Humanitarian	68.60 (55)	56.26 (72)	48.37 (81)	0.15 (55)	0.13 (72)	0.13 (81)

Note: Figures refer to average cumulative aid received from DAC donors between 2010 and 2020. No. of observations in parentheses. Aid per capita has been computed by dividing the cumulative value with average total population between 2010 and 2020. Lower fragility means higher authority, capacity, and legitimacy.
Source: authors' calculations.

larger than support to any of the other three sectors. Challenges of insecurity and instability are likely to be most prevalent in countries with weak authority, and it is in these contexts that we indeed observe the highest levels of humanitarian aid per capita.

Aid per capita in health, education, and government and civil society, was on average also lower in low-fragility countries than in high-fragility countries across all dimensions—with the exception of health aid, which was higher per capita in low-capacity countries. A variety of factors may contribute to these patterns, including for instance levels of economic development. Interestingly, in high-fragility countries, aid per capita allocated to government and civil society exceeds aid per capita allocated to health or education. In light of Zürcher's findings that health and education projects are more effective than capacity-building projects in high-fragility contexts, these numbers raise some concerns.

The dimensions of the state appear to be more relevant when considering changes in state fragility (during 2010–15) in relation to sectoral aid. Positive changes in authority and capacity are associated with a smaller share of humanitarian aid, but a larger share of education and health aid (Figure 1.3). It may be that improvements in these areas signal an improved security situation, and thus, a shift in the allocation of aid from humanitarian, conflict-related interventions to core sectors of social policy. Changes in legitimacy do not seem to be associated with the share of aid allocated to the examined sectors.

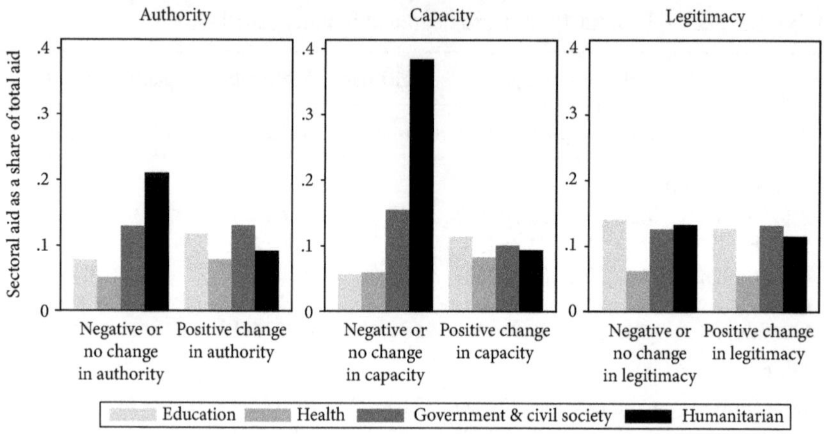

Figure 1.3 Aid in selected sectors by changes in authority, capacity, and legitimacy

Note: Changes in authority, capacity, and legitimacy from 2010 to 2015. Sectoral aid as a share of total aid between 2010 and 2020. Only fragile countries: authority includes countries where authority < 0.5; capacity includes countries where capacity < 0.5; legitimacy includes countries where legitimacy < 0.5.
Source: authors' illustration.

1.5.4 State Fragility, the Effectiveness Principles, and Ownership

Past academic research has paid scant attention to how fragile countries have adhered to the GPEDC's effectiveness principles.[8]

Consistent with our expectations, the data suggest that adherence to the effectiveness principles is challenging in many fragile states—whether they are low-authority, low-capacity, or low-legitimacy (Figure 1.4). In particular, the average level of country ownership—measured by the proportion of aid managed via country systems—is low across fragile countries. Generally, adherence to the effectiveness principles does not depend on the degree of fragility, as illustrated by the weak magnitude of nearly all correlations. There are, however, some exceptions.

First, even if the degree of authority, capacity, and legitimacy does not seem to matter much for the extent to which a country uses national results frameworks—a key indicator of the focus on results principle—numerous fragile countries perform well in terms of this indicator. It is the only indicator among the four effectiveness principles indicators where all fragile countries score above one-third of the scale. Second, the two strongest relationships, overall, are between the indicator of the ownership principle—the use of country systems—and both capacity and authority. The use of country systems is quite strongly and positively correlated with capacity (r: 0.48), and more weakly, negatively correlated with authority

[8] In our earlier study on the effectiveness principles and development outcomes (Gisselquist et al. 2023), we examined the GPEDC's data in detail, but did not consider fragile contexts specifically.

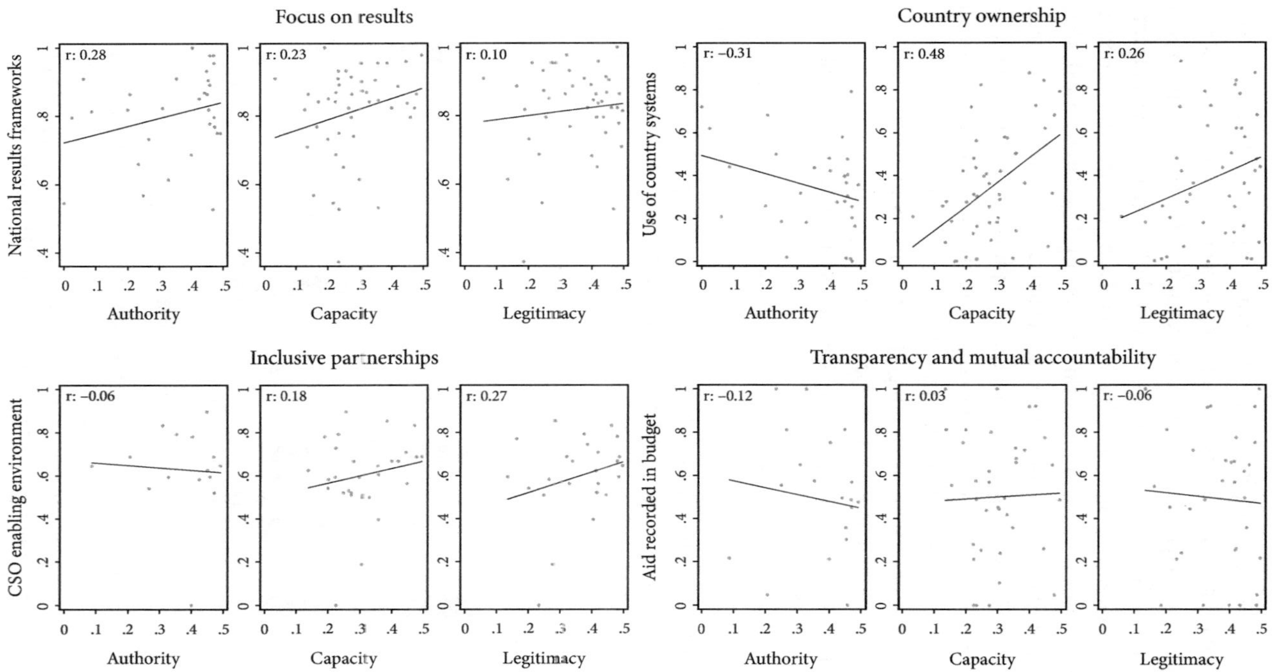

Figure 1.4 State fragility and aid effectiveness principles

Note: Average level of authority/capacity/legitimacy between 2010 and 2015. Data on aid effectiveness principles refers to 2017. Only fragile countries: authority includes countries where authority < 0.5; capacity includes countries where capacity < 0.5; legitimacy includes countries where legitimacy < 0.5.
Source: authors' illustration.

(*r*: −0.31). Its correlation with state legitimacy is comparatively weakest (*r*: 0.26). Thus, higher capacity is connected to more ownership, and higher authority to less ownership, albeit the latter relationship is weaker.

It is not surprising to find an indicator of the ownership principle to be of particular significance in the correlations. As Bhattacharya et al. argue, adherence to the other principles may require ownership, and capacity emerges as an important prerequisite for successful country ownership. Similarly, Hasselskog et al. note that country ownership is a sign of state capacity as formulating national development priorities requires political will and institutional capacity. In contrast, weak state authority can undermine country ownership, as evidenced by Murtazashvili's case study on Afghanistan, because a country that cannot uphold its monopoly on violence is likely to face challenges in setting its own priorities and strategies, as well as translating them into action. These chapters also provide insight into why ownership and state legitimacy might not often go hand-in-hand, by illustrating how national ownership can be in tension with local ownership and collective participation, potentially eroding the acceptance of the state's rule in the eyes of citizens and other non-state actors.

Additional descriptive analyses highlight further the ownership challenge in fragile countries and empirical relationships between ownership and authority, capacity, and legitimacy. Figure 1.5 considers a second key (ordinal) indicator of ownership, which classifies countries into four categories based on their progress in the quality of PFM systems: negative progress, some progress, significant

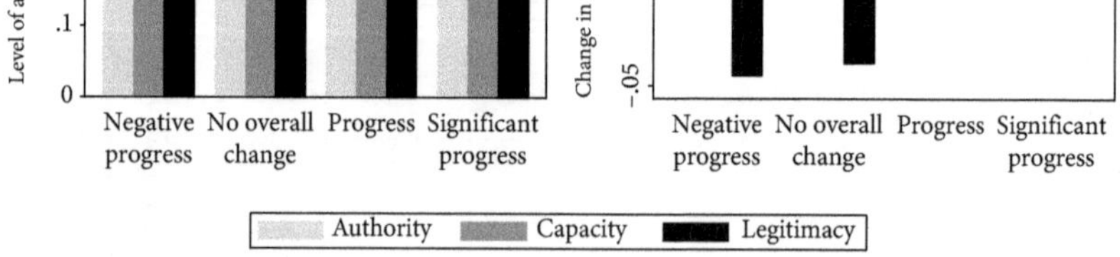

Figure 1.5 State fragility, changes in state fragility, and progress in PFM systems quality

Note: Left panel: average level of authority/capacity/legitimacy between 2010 and 2015. Right panel: changes in authority, capacity, and legitimacy from 2010 to 2015. Progress in PFM systems quality refers to 2017. Only fragile countries: authority includes countries where authority < 0.5; capacity includes countries where capacity < 0.5; legitimacy includes countries where legitimacy < 0.5.
Source: authors' illustration.

progress, or no changes at all. We find that fragile countries that have made 'significant progress' in improving the quality of PFM systems have on average higher capacity than countries that have not. Those that have made 'negative progress' in the quality of PFM systems tend to have on average weakest authority. And progress in PFM systems' quality tends to go hand in hand with changes in legitimacy: on average, legitimacy has most decreased in countries that have made 'negative progress' and most increased in countries that have made 'significant progress'.[9]

1.6 Conclusion

Despite challenges, the imperative of external support for development and humanitarian needs persists. This volume brings together findings from a diverse set of expert analyses to discuss the concerning and contested record of aid under fragility, and key implications for research and practice going forward. Collectively, the studies illustrate the contested, but overall concerning, record of aid's impact under fragility. They also point to several key implications for future research and practice.

The first is the need for more systematic unpacking of the considerable diversity across fragile contexts, to better understand both past experiences and draw valuable lessons from them for future practice. Context matters, as we illustrate in this introduction and as emphasized in various chapters in this volume.

A second key implication concerns the aid effectiveness principles, which are at once an important touchpoint for development cooperation, and particularly challenging to meet in fragile contexts. Country ownership is widely viewed as the most important of the principles and the strongest challenge in fragile contexts, especially those marked by weak legitimacy and capacity, as the analysis presented in this volume highlights.

The chapters in this volume point towards some promising areas of engagement to improve the delivery of international aid in fragile contexts and strengthen the implementation of the effectiveness principles.

The first is the need to consider ownership more broadly. As Bhattacharya et al. (Chapter 5) argue, and the analysis above indicates, in contexts where the state and government have low legitimacy, a paradigm shift from 'country' ownership to 'collective' ownership may be indispensable. Collective ownership would involve non-state actors and aid providers, alongside recipient country governments.

[9] We further consider changes in state fragility for 2010–15 and the four effectiveness principles. Again, most correlations are weak, but we find slightly stronger links between changes in capacity and authority and CSO enabling environment—an indicator of inclusive partnerships.

The second area of improvement is the strengthening of local ownership. As Raballand et al.'s analysis suggests, in some fragile contexts, legitimacy may be higher at the local level than at the national level. Thus, a bottom-up approach, in which ownership is understood as more at the local level may be more successful. However, as Murtazashvili cautions, some bottom-up interventions may mask top-down interests and caution must be taken in how to define local ownership.

Third, it is important that governments and the international community alike acknowledge the tensions that exist (or will arise) between different actors. As Hasselskog et al.'s chapter emphasizes, country ownership and local participation do not necessarily go together. Raballand et al. further suggest that promoting bottom-up, local ownership also may be problematic for statebuilding if it undermines the legitimacy of the central state. Bhattacharya et al. show, in addition, that there are multiple national stakeholders and establishing collective ownership involves managing a process of negotiation and discussion among these diverse actors, including government agencies, local governments, CSOs, private sector actors, and local communities. Acknowledging and managing these tensions are important steps in ensuring more effective aid outcomes in fragile contexts.

Finally, there is an urgent need to design and support innovative interventions that strengthen ownership. Raballand et al.'s chapter and the empirical analysis above show that ownership may be fostered through activities that strengthen the social contract between citizens and the state, including support for increasing political accountability and transparency, and improved service delivery.

Although some influential studies have recently called for increasing development efforts only in those countries where political elites are truly committed to development, this volume sees a broader role for development cooperation—even where national ownership may be weak. Even in the absence of a strong national development bargain among elites, international assistance can make a difference and can help in cultivating that political will towards development. Engaging in this way, however, requires inter alia stronger local knowledge and engagement with local political, societal, and economic priorities. Rather than *less* international aid, weak states and conflict-affected countries need *better* international aid, guided by locally owned priorities and needs.

References

Adam, A., and S. Tsarsitalidou (2022). 'The Effect of International Development Association's (IDA) Aid on Conflict. A Fuzzy Regression Discontinuity Approach'. *European Journal of Political Economy*, 74: 1–17.

Ariotti, M., S. Dietrich, and J. Wright (2021). 'Foreign Aid and Judicial Autonomy'. *Review of International Organizations*, 17: 691–715.

Arndt, C., S. Jones, and F. Tarp (2015). 'Assessing Foreign Aid's Long-Run Contribution to Growth and Development'. *World Development*, 69: 6–18.

Askarov, Z., and H. Doucouliagos (2015). 'Aid and Institutions in Transition Economies'. *European Journal of Political Economy*, 38: 55–70.

Braithwaite, J. M., and A. A. Licht (2020). 'The Effect of Civil Society Organizations and Democratization Aid on Civil War Onset'. *Journal of Conflict Resolution*, 64(6): 1095–1120.

Bräutigam, D. A., and S. Knack (2004). 'Foreign Aid, Institutions, and Governance in Sub-Saharan Africa'. *Economic Development and Cultural Change*, 52(2): 255–85.

Burnside, C., and D. Dollar (2000). 'Aid, Policies, and Growth'. *The American Economic Review*, 90(4): 847–68.

Burnside, C., and D. Dollar (2004). 'Aid, Policies, and Growth: Revisiting the Evidence'. *World Bank Policy Research Working Papers* 3251.

Call, C. T. (2011). 'Beyond the "Failed State": Toward Conceptual Alternatives'. *European Journal of International Relations*, 17(2): 303–26.

Calleja, R., and B. Cichocka (2022). 'Good for Now but Not Forever: Officials' Perspectives on the Relevance of the Effectiveness Agenda and the Need for Change'. *WIDER Working Papers* 140/2022.

Carment, D., Y. Samy, and S. Prest (2008). 'State Fragility and Implications for Aid Allocation: An Empirical Analysis'. *Conflict Management and Peace Science*, 25(4): 349–73.

Collier, P., and J. Dehn (2001). 'Aid, Shocks, and Growth'. *World Bank Policy Research Working Papers* 2688.

Collier, P., and D. Dollar (2001). 'Can the World Cut Poverty in Half? How Policy Reform and Effective Aid Can Meet International Development Goals'. *World Development*, 29(11): 1787–802.

Collier, P., and D. Dollar (2002). 'Aid Allocation and Poverty Reduction'. *European Economic Review*, 46(8): 1475–500.

Collier, P., and A. Hoeffler (2002). 'Aid, Policy and Peace: Reducing the Risks of Civil Conflict'. *Defence and Peace Economics*, 13(6): 435–50.

Dalgaard, C. J., H. Hansen, and F. Tarp (2004). 'On the Empirics of Foreign Aid and Growth'. *Economic Journal*, 114: F191–F216.

Easterly, W., R. Levine, and D. Roodman (2004). 'Aid, Policies, and Growth: Comment'. *The American Economic Review*, 94(3): 774–80.

Englebert, P., and D. M. Tull (2008). 'Postconflict Reconstruction in Africa: Flawed Ideas about Failed States'. *International Security*, 32(4): 106–39.

Eriksen, S. S. (2017). 'State Effects and the Effects of State Building: Institution Building and the Formation of State-Centred Societies'. *Third World Quarterly*, 38(4): 771–86.

Findley, M. G (2018). 'Does Foreign Aid Build Peace?'. *Annual Review of Political Science*, 21: 359–84.

Geddes, B., J. Wright, and E. Frantz (2018). *How Dictatorships Work*. Cambridge: Cambridge University Press.

Gisselquist, R. M (2015). 'Varieties of Fragility: Implications for Aid'. *Third World Quarterly*, 36(7): 1269–80.

Gisselquist, R. M (2021). 'Foreign Aid and Peacebuilding'. In O. P. Richmond and G. Visoka, editors, *The Oxford Handbook of Peacebuilding, Statebuilding, and Peace Formation*. New York: Oxford University Press: 532–48.

Gisselquist, R. M., P. Justino, and A. Vaccaro (2023). 'Do the Principles of Effective Development Co-operation Improve Development Outcomes? The Case for Clearer Definitions and Measurement'. *Development Policy Review*, doi: 10.1111/dpr.12731.

Gisselquist, R. M., and A. Vaccaro (2022). 'COVID-19 and the State: Exploring a Puzzling Relationship in the Early Stages of the Pandemic'. *Journal of International Development*, doi: 10.1002/jid.3702.

GPEDC (2022). 2022 *Effective Development Co-operation Summit Declaration.* Final unedited version. https://www.effectivecooperation.org/sites/default/files/2022-12/Final%20Outcome%20Document.pdf.

Grävingholt, J., S. Ziaja, and M. Kreibaum (2015). 'Disaggregating State Fragility: A Method to Establish a Multidimensional Empirical Typology'. *Third World Quarterly*, 36(7): 1281–98.

Gulrajani, N. (2022). 'Development Narratives in a Post-Aid Era: Reflections on Implications for the Global Effectiveness Agenda'. *WIDER Working Papers* 149/2022.

Hansen, H., and F. Tarp (2001). 'Aid and Growth Regressions'. *African Development Review*, 64(2001): 547–70.

Hoeffler, A., and P. Justino (2023). 'Aid and Fragile States'. *WIDER Working Papers* 2023/83.

Jia, S., and C. R. Williamson (2019). 'Aid, Policies, and Growth: Why So Much Confusion?'. *Contemporary Economic Policy*, 37(4): 577–99.

Jones, S. and F. Tarp (2016). 'Does Foreign Aid Harm Political Institutions?'. *Journal of Development Economics*, 118: 266–81.

Juselius, K., N. F. Møller, and F. Tarp (2014). 'The Long-Run Impact of Foreign Aid in 36 African Countries: Insights from Multivariate Time Series Analysis'. *Oxford Bulletin of Economics and Statistics* 76(2): 153–84.

Justino, P. (2019). 'Governance Interventions in Conflict-Affected Countries'. *Journal of Development Studies*, 55(7): 1364–78.

Knack, S. (2001). 'Aid Dependence and the Quality of Governance: Cross-Country Empirical Tests'. *Southern Economic Journal*, 68(2): 310–29.

Leutert, W., E. Plantan, and A. Strange (2022). 'Puzzling Partnerships: Overseas Infrastructure Development by Chinese State-Owned Enterprises and Humanitarian Organizations'. *Studies in Comparative International Development.* doi: 10.1007/s12116-022-09368-7.

Lie, J. H. S. (2019). 'Local Ownership as Global Governance'. *European Journal of Development Research*, 31(4): 1107–25.

Molenaers, N., S. Dellepiane, and J. Faust (2015). 'Political Conditionality and Foreign Aid'. *World Development* 75: 2–12.

Mousseau, D. Y. (2021). 'Does Foreign Development Aid Trigger Ethnic War in Developing States?'. *Armed Forces and Society*, 47(4): 750–69.

Moss, T. J., G. Pettersson, and N. van de Walle (2006). 'An Aid-Institutions Paradox? A Review Essay on Aid Dependency and State Building in Sub-Saharan Africa'. *CGD Working Paper 74.* Washington, DC and London: Center for Global Development.

Nielsen, R. A., M. G. Findley, Z. S. Davis, T. Candland, and D. L. Nielson (2011). 'Foreign Aid Shocks as a Cause of Violent Armed Conflict'. *American Journal of Political Science*, 55(2): 219–32.

Niño-Zarazúa, M., R. M. Gisselquist, A. Horigoshi, M. Samarin, and K. Sen (2020). *Effects of Swedish and International Democracy Aid.* Stockholm: Expert Group for Aid Studies (EBA). EBA Report 2020:07.

Nunn, N., and N. Qian (2014). 'U.S. Food Aid and Civil Conflict'. *American Economic Review*, 104(6): 1630–66.

OECD (2022). *States of Fragility 2022.* Paris: OECD Publishing.

Rajan, R., and A. Subramanian (2007). 'Does Aid Affect Governance?'. *American Economic Review*, 97(2):322–27.

Rajan, R., and A. Subramanian (2008). 'Aid and Growth: What Does the Cross-Country Evidence Really Show?'. *Review of Economics and Statistics*, 90(4):643–65.

Rice, S., and S. Patrick (2008). Index of State Weakness in the Developing World. Washington, DC: Brookings Institution.

Savun, B., and D. C. Tirone (2011). 'Foreign Aid, Democratization, and Civil Conflict: How Does Democracy Aid Affect Civil Conflict?'. *American Journal of Political Science*, 55(2): 233–46.

Vaccaro, A. (2023). 'Measures of State Capacity: So Similar, yet so Different'. *Quality & Quantity*, 57(3): 2281–302.

Young, A. T., and K. M. Sheehan (2014). 'Foreign Aid, Institutional Quality, and Growth'. *European Journal of Political Economy*, 36: 195–208.

Ziaja, S., J. Grävingholt, and M. Kreibaum (2019). 'Constellations of Fragility: An Empirical Typology of States'. *Studies in Comparative International Development*, 54(2): 299–321.

Zürcher, C. (2017). 'What Do We (Not) Know About Development Aid and Violence? A Systematic Review'. *World Development*, 98: 506–22.

PART II

WAYS FORWARD IN WEAK STATES AND CONFLICT SITUATIONS

2

What Aid Works (or Not) in Highly Fragile States? Evidence from Afghanistan, Mali, and South Sudan, 2008–21

Christoph Zürcher

2.1 Introduction

Fragile and conflict-affected states cause great harm to their own population.[1] They require and deserve help, and a significant part of global ODA (official development assistance) therefore goes to fragile states. In 2022, 48.8% of total ODA from Development Assistance Committee (DAC) countries was allocated to fragile contexts.[2] At the same time, most observers agree that making aid effective in fragile states is extremely challenging.

For donors, this is an ethical dilemma that is difficult to navigate. In accordance with the foundational reason for giving development aid, it should be allocated to where the needs are greatest. Helping the populations of highly fragile states, therefore, is the right thing to do. Yet, if aid is indeed not effective in such a context, then aid would better be allocated to contexts where it can be effective, so that the overall utility of aid is maximized. In other words, it is more ethical to allocate aid to contexts where it can be effective, than allocating aid to a context where aid is ineffective, even if needs may be greater. What is needed to better navigate this dilemma is solid and nuanced evidence about the effectiveness of aid in highly fragile states. Solid, because we need evidence that is more robust than anecdotal insights or scattered evidence from single evaluations. Nuanced, because there is a need to go beyond the overgeneralized dichotomy of 'effective vs ineffective', by documenting the effectiveness (of lack thereof) of aid across different sectors.

One way to provide such evidence is by conducting systematic reviews at the country level. A systematic review is a well-established research method

[1] This chapter is a revised and updated version of Zürcher (2022). The original data comes from Zürcher et al. (2022).

[2] Source: INCAF Facts and Figures Series: ODA final data and trends for 2022 in relation to fragile and conflict-related contexts. Available at: https://one.oecd.org/document/DCD/DAC/INCAF(2024)1/en/pdf (accessed 6 July 2024).

Christoph Zürcher, *What Aid Works (or Not) in Highly Fragile States? Evidence from Afghanistan, Mali, and South Sudan, 2008–21*. In: *Fragile Aid*. Edited by: Rachel M. Gisselquist et al., Oxford University Press. © UNU-WIDER (2025).
DOI: 10.1093/oso/9780198960287.003.0002

used to summarize the results of all available studies (in this case, mostly evaluation reports) on a particular topic in a structured and comprehensive manner. Systematic reviews are considered high-quality evidence because of their rigorous methodology. They are widely used in evidence-based practice, to inform policy and decision-making. Different from traditional literature reviews, systematic reviews seek to identify all existing evidence on a given question. A systematic review is based on a redefined protocol that outlines the criteria for including studies in order to reduce bias and ensure that all included studies meet a predefined threshold for methodological quality.

This chapter presents the results of three country-level systematic reviews of the effectiveness of ODA in Afghanistan, South Sudan, and Mali between 2008 and 2021, conducted by the author of this chapter. These systematic reviews address the following question: How effective is ODA (by sector) in these three highly fragile countries? The three systematic reviews are convergent mixed-method reviews that include both statistical/experimental and qualitative project evaluations in the final synthesis. All project evaluations had to meet a pre-defined threshold of methodological quality. Country and programme level evaluations were included by default and were not assessed for methodological quality. A total of 322 evaluations were included in the three systematic reviews. Readers are invited to consult the systematic reviews[3] and/or the methods report[4] for more details.

Table 2.1 shows how these studies are distributed among the three countries and among ten aid sectors: women's rights; health; rural development and climate change; rule of law; stabilization; education; sustainable economic development; nutrition; humanitarian assistance; and good governance.

The remainder of this chapter is structured as follows. The second section provides an overview of the country contexts of Afghanistan, South Sudan, and Mali. The third section presents the main findings from the systematic reviews on aid effectiveness across various aid sectors. The fourth section examines the reasons why aid is often ineffective where it is needed most, namely in enhancing governmental capacity, stability, and good governance. The fifth and final section discusses the implications of these findings for donors.

[3] Christoph Zürcher, with P. Labelle, L. Borges, K. Hoare, M.A. Javid, K. Kavanagh, S. Sarna, and E. Woolner (November 2022), 'Impact of Aid in Highly Fragile States: A Synthesis of Three Systematic Reviews of Aid to Afghanistan, Mali and South Sudan, 2008–2021', The Hague: IOB. Available at: https://english.iob-evaluatie.nl/publications/sub-studies/2022/11/10/synthesis-of-systematic-reviews-in-afghanistan-mali-and-south-sudan (accessed 17 November 2022).

[4] Christoph Zuercher (principal investigator) and Patrick Labelle (research librarian) (2022), 'Systematic Review of Evaluation Reports Effects of Development Aid to South Sudan and Mali, 2008–2021'. Available at https://english.iob-evaluatie.nl/binaries/iob-evaluatie-eng/documenten/sub-studies/2022/11/10/systematic-reviews-south-sudan/Method+report+-+Effects+of+Development+Aid+to+South+Sudan+and+Mali.pdf (accessed 6 July 2024).

Table 2.1 Evidence base

	Afghanistan (2008–18)		Mali (2008–20)		South Sudan (2008–20)			
	Included studies, total	(Of which 'statistical/ experimental)	Included studies, total	(Of which 'statistical/ experimental)	Included studies, total	(Of which 'statistical/ experimental)	Total per sector	(Of which 'statistical/ experimental)
Country-level programme evaluations	15		18		12		45	
Women's rights	14	2	9	4	4		27	6
Health and nutrition	21	9	35	27	13	7	69	43
Rural development, climate	5		26	8	7	2	38	10
Rule of law	2				1		3	0
Stabilization	12	11	4		12	1	28	12
Education	14	3	5	3	3		22	6
Sustainable economic development	29	2			3	1	32	3
Humanitarian assistance, refugees, migration*			3	1	7	2	10	3

Continued

Table 2.1 *Continued*

	Afghanistan (2008–18)		Mali (2008–20)		South Sudan (2008–20)			
	Included studies, total	**(Of which 'statistical/ experimental)**	**Included studies, total**	**(Of which 'statistical/ experimental)**	**Included studies, total**	**(Of which 'statistical/ experimental)**	**Total per sector**	**(Of which 'statistical/ experimental)**
Good governance	18		4		8		30	0
Afghanistan Reconstruction Trust Fund**	11						11	0
Other	7						7	0
Total (per country)	148	27	104	43	70	13	322	83
Total studies						322		
(Of which rigorous)						83		

Notes
*evaluations on humanitarian assistance, refugees, and migration were not part of the search for the Afghanistan review.
**applies only to Afghanistan.
Source: author's compilation from systemic reviews and Zürcher et al. (2022).

2.2 Country Contexts

Afghanistan, Mali, and South Sudan are among the most fragile and underdeveloped countries in the world. In 2021, they ranked 16th, 9th, and 3rd on the Fragile States Index, and 169th, 184th, and 185th (out of 189) on the Human Development Index.[5] Between 2008 and 2020, the international community provided US$70.75 billion in ODA to these three countries.

All three countries suffer from the typical symptoms of fragility, such as low economic growth, widespread poverty, low life expectancy, high population growth especially in rural areas, low education levels, internal migration, and so on. In addition, all three counties suffer from violence that exacerbates the developmental problems. Afghanistan has experienced four decades of war. After the victory of the Taliban in August 2021 violence ebbed, but the country is far from a stable place. Mali is caught in intertwined conflicts, with secessionist Tuareg and Islamist rebellions in the north and inter-ethnic violence in the centre of the country. South Sudan plunged into an inter-ethnic civil war only three years after it gained its independence. By 2018 the most intense fighting was over, but violence remains endemic.

As in all highly fragile states, real political power in these three countries resides not with formal political institutions but rather in networks of patronage which transcend the formal political institutions. This creates a political economy where elites have little incentive to strengthen formal state institutions. Instead, they need to nurture the patronage networks which are the basis for their authority and their political and often physical survival. Rent-seeking, widespread institutionalized corruption, and intense competition between rival networks are the typical symptoms of such a political economy of fragile statehood. One important implication of this political economy is that elites are not interested in political reforms which would endanger this mode of governing. Donors therefore often find that their partners show no political will to implement policies which might lead to more accountability, more robust formal institutions, or democratic procedures.

Despite many commonalities stemming from the fact that all three countries belong to the group of extremely fragile states, there are some differences in how these states became fragile and how the international community reacted.

Afghanistan, more than any other country, exemplifies the shattered dreams of externally led state-building. After nearly two decades of massive international civil and military engagement, Afghanistan today remains one of the poorest countries in the world and is again ruled by the Taliban. In the early days of the international engagement, optimism was high. The Afghan population welcomed

[5] The Fragile States Index is accessible at https://fragilestatesindex.org/data. Higher ranks mean higher levels of fragility. The HDI is accessible at https://hdr.undp.org/en/data. Lower ranks mean a lower development score.

the international engagement and its promise of stability and development. The Taliban appeared to have been defeated, and there were some quick gains enabled by their ousting and the improvements in everyday security. Starting from a very low level, access to basic health services and education improved, roads and other transport infrastructure were rehabilitated, some development aid started to reach rural regions, and the nascent government in Kabul received generous support. However, there were already clear signs that the donors' vision of a stable, democratic, and self-sustainable Afghanistan might be out of reach. The constant stream of external funding had built a burgeoning rentier state with high levels of corruption, entrenched patronage networks, and little capacity or will for reforms. Despite massive investments in government capacities, the Afghan state remained weak.

Just as troublesome was the fact that the Afghan government was not able to earn legitimacy among its population. The new government, despite the massive support from donors, could not build a social contract with the citizens. Instead, the Afghan population increasingly saw the government as ineffective and corrupt. Similarly, the reputation of international donors suffered. Without tangible progress in poverty alleviation and security, the Afghan government and its foreign backers were losing the battle for the hearts and minds of the Afghan people.

While ODA peaked in 2011 at nearly US$6 billion, it was still at US$3.68 billion on average for the years 2012–18.[6] The vision of a self-sustainable and democratic Afghanistan was reiterated at a series of large pledging conferences. Regarding the overall aid portfolio, there were surprisingly few adjustments. Notably, the share of aid for 'government and civil society' between 2008 and 2020 remained very high, with an average of 42%, and 43% in 2020, even though it was clear to most observers that aid in this sector was not effective. At the same time, funding for humanitarian aid and rural development remained low, at 6.1% and 10.2% of total ODA respectively for the period 2008–20. These numbers suggest that donors continued to treat Afghanistan as a 'normal' developing country (unlike South Sudan, where spending for 'government and society' shrank to 6%), despite the lack of progress in fields such as state capacity and good governance.

By 2018, it became evident that the United States wanted a fast exit option. Talks between the United States and the Taliban led to the peace agreement in Doha of 29 February 2020. This agreement was negotiated between the United States and the Taliban only, leaving out the government of Afghanistan as well as the wider international community. Following the signing of the agreement, the United States announced the withdrawal of the remaining US

[6] ODA numbers here and in the following sections are from the Creditor Reporter System (CRS), Development Assistance Committee (DAC), Organisation for Economic Co-operation and Development (OECD): https://stats.oecd.org/Index.aspx?DataSetCode=crs1 (accessed 2 November 2022).

troops by September 2021. The Taliban, seizing the opportunity, increased its military pressure on the Afghan security forces. After capturing many major cities, often without a fight, the Taliban gained control of Kabul in August 2021.

Landlocked Mali faces a multitude of development challenges, including high population growth rates and an undiversified economy dependent on subsistence agriculture. Mali also experiences recurring natural hazards such as droughts, irregular rains, and floods. In addition, there is endemic violence and insecurity in the north and the central regions. Northern Mali is also a drug trafficking hub for cocaine from Latin America to Europe. The competition over lucrative smuggling routes fuels political instability and further complicates the search for peace.

Prior to 2012, Mali was a 'donor darling', with foreign governments keen to provide support for the democratic transitions that began in the 1990s. A toxic brew of drought, insurgencies, and a military coup ended the positive trajectory as well as the optimistic outlook of donors. By 2012, Tuareg and Islamist secessionist rebellions in the north had destabilized the country. The Tuareg rebellion crystallized around heavily armed Tuaregs who had fought in the Libyan civil war and returned to Mali after NATO's intervention in Libya.

In reaction to the ineffective response of the government to the new threats, the military overthrew the democratically elected President Touré. Unable to restore its authority in the rebel-held areas, the Malian government requested international support. French forces intervened to stabilize the northern regions, followed by the UN Multidimensional Integrated Stabilization Mission in Mali (MINUSMA), established in 2013 with a broad mandate to support security and stabilization.

Unrest gripped not only the north. In 2013, violence also erupted in central Mali. The conflict was fought mainly between agricultural and pastoral communities, fuelled by competition for land and water and exacerbated by climate change.

In June 2015, a peace agreement was brokered between the government and an alliance of various rebel groups. However, the implementation of this agreement proved to be extremely difficult. Constitutional reforms which were promised under the peace agreement remained on hold, and the peace process lacked popular support.

In August 2020, and then again in May 2021, two more military coups d'état took place. The international community condemned these, and tension between the government of Mali and Western countries rose to new heights.

In hindsight, the escalation of the conflict in northern Mali and the breakdown of the democratic order in 2012 was a watershed moment for the country and for its relations with donors. During the decade prior to 2012, Mali had been treated by the donor community as a positive example of democratic governance. Over 2002–11, annual ODA steadily increased from US$610.35 million to US$1.14 billion. A substantial part of the aid was channelled through the government in the form of budget support, which was credited with a positive effect on public finances, education, and health outcomes. Donor engagement in Mali changed in reaction to the rupture of 2012. While ODA still consistently grew, budget support was drastically reduced and a larger share was channelled through multilateral organizations and NGOs. Humanitarian assistance dramatically increased.

It is also noteworthy that in reaction to the breakdown of the democratic order, donors invested more aid in sectors such as government and elections, because they assumed that increasing aid to these sectors would help the return to democracy. Despite an overall investment of US$5.245 billion in ODA since 2013, Mali today is less secure, less democratic, and more fragile than it was before the breakdown of the democratic order in 2012.

South Sudan came into existence in 2011. It was born as an extremely fragile state, and it has remained so ever since. Between 2011 and 2020, South Sudan received US$11.43 billion in ODA. South Sudan had been fighting for autonomy from the north since 1983. The violent struggle for independence from the north went hand in hand with violence between political factions and ethnic groups within the south. In 2005, South Sudan signed a peace agreement with the government in Khartoum that called for a transition period of six years, after which the final status of South Sudan would be determined by a popular referendum. Donors rushed to provide support. It was assumed that such support would help to make the fragile peace permanent, and to prevent South Sudan from pushing for independence. However, in January 2011, 99% of the South Sudanese population voted for independence in a referendum. Donors continued to provide financial and political support for the newborn country.

Despite high hopes and big efforts, the peace did not hold. In 2013, a civil war along ethnic lines broke out. Between 2013 and 2018, the war had displaced four million South Sudanese (out of a population of 11 million). An estimated 400,000 people were killed, the economy collapsed, and food shortage was widespread. South Sudan had become a major humanitarian disaster.

Between independence in 2011 and the resurgence of war in 2013, donors provided massive levels of aid for state-building. ODA almost tripled between 2011 and 2013, from US$351 million to US$1,083 million. Donors, however, grew increasingly frustrated with the lack of political will on the side of the South Sudanese government to engage in the state-building project.

The outbreak of the civil war in 2013 marked the beginning of a new phase in donor engagement in South Sudan. Donors now predominantly engaged in emergency assistance, food security, and local-level peacebuilding, hoping to prevent a humanitarian catastrophe and to contribute to stability and eventually peace. Support for government institutions was scaled down but ODA was still climbing, from US$1,083 million in 2013 to US$1,751 million in 2017, the year when ODA peaked. While aid for state-building shrank, humanitarian aid dramatically increased.

2.3 Aid Effectiveness in Highly Fragile States

This section summarizes the main findings of the three systematic reviews. A total of 322 evaluation reports were included and analysed (148 on Afghanistan, 104 on Mali, and 70 on South Sudan). The evaluations included in the original reviews were grouped into 10 sectors (see Table 2.1). In this chapter, for the sake of clarity and manageability, the presentation of findings is divided into four areas:

- The first is what might be called 'support for core government functions'. This includes stabilization interventions, capacity building for the government, and good governance interventions. These interventions are at the heart of Western state-building, as they directly aim to build states that are stable, have sufficient capacity, and are governed by the rule of law and democratic procedures.
- The second area focuses on assistance to improve health and education outcomes. These are basic services that are lacking in highly fragile states, and most donors allocate a substantial part of their aid to such basic services.
- The third area focuses on interventions to improve livelihoods and economic opportunities, another essential component of aid portfolios for fragile states.
- The fourth area focuses on the effectiveness of interventions aimed at women's empowerment and gender equality—an area of growing concern for all donors.

2.3.1 Aid for Core State Functions: Stabilization, Capacity for the Government, and Good Governance

Weak state capacities are what makes a state fragile in the first place. Not surprisingly, (re-)building capacity across all levels of government is an essential part of donor engagement in most fragile states. The overall aim of these interventions is to enable government actors to act more effectively. Some interventions directly target government capacity, for example by providing technical assistance to ministries and by offering training to the public servants working in these ministries. More often, capacity building is one important component of larger programmes. The systematic reviews summarized evaluation reports on programmes that directly sought to improve government capacities as well as all references to government capacities at the central, regional, and district level that were referenced in the included evaluation reports.[7]

[7] In order to capture all references to capacity building for government institutions across the 322 included evaluation reports, a qualitative data analysis software (ATLAS.ti) was used to identify and code these references.

Unfortunately, the evidence strongly suggests that capacity building for government institutions in fragile states rarely works. For Afghanistan, capacity-building measures were mostly not successful in enhancing the overall capacity of the state. In the few instances where progress was made, it remained confined to small silos, not translating into more overall state capacity. Often, capacity improvements were rather technical in nature and borrowed from the so-called 'second civil service', consisting of well-paid Afghan returnees or international consultants. There is no clear case of a successful capacity-building programme in the Afghanistan sample, but there are quite a few examples of rather ineffective capacity-building programmes. For example, donors mostly agreed that the massive Afghan Reconstruction Trust Fund (ARTF) had no impact on better governance, nor did it contribute to better capacity in the Afghan government beyond some narrow and technical functionalities. Likewise, programmes for decentralization and capacity-building for the subnational administration were not successful at building more capacity for the local administration or providing incentives for a meaningful decentralization process.

In Mali, the results are similarly disappointing. There is no evidence that capacity-building at the level of central governance was effective. While capacity-building for the central government was usually not effective, there were some pockets of success. It appears that the capacity of the government for administering technical and apolitical fields, such as health, education, and rural development may have been somewhat improved.

Regarding South Sudan, there is broad consensus in the evaluation reports that capacity-building measures for the government were not effective. Donors overestimated both existing state capacity and the government's political will for reforms. As a result, programming for capacity-building was overambitious, unsustainable, and ineffective. The hope that the government would become a partner in service delivery was never realized. Least effective were capacity-building measures in 'politicized' fields which offer opportunities for lucrative corruption, and which are therefore vital for maintaining the rentier and patronage state. For example, Norway's support for the natural resource sector did not lead to more accountability and transparency, since there was no political will for it. Support for the legislature and the judicial sector appear to have had little effect either, since there is no sign of improvement in this sector. While it was possible to provide skills to individuals, this did not translate into more-effective and more-accepted political institutions.

To compensate for the lack of government capacities, donors created parallel systems for service delivery, which helped to provide outputs, but these results were not sustainable and did not address the underlying issues of the lack of state capacity. Like in Mali, some positive results were found in the health sector, where donor support did help to increase individual and institutional capacity, leading to better treatment of malaria, diarrhoea, and pneumonia and to better healthcare provision for mothers and children.

In sum, the available evidence clearly suggests that capacity-building for governments in very fragile states is ineffective, especially when it is applied to fields which can affect political processes in general and the patronage and rent-seeking economy in particular. The obstacles are smaller in strictly technical fields, which are not overly politicized, where there is less opportunity for rent-seeking, and when the subnational rather than the national level is targeted.

The reasons for these disappointing results vary but are mostly linked to the difficult context: there was little demand from the government for such programmes, the permanent competition for power among various networks hampered cooperation within and among institutions, and the frequent changes of key personnel made institutional learning difficult. Most importantly, capacity-building was not effective when there was no political will to have capacity built, which was often the case in politicized fields such as, for example, decentralization, which the central government opposed.

A second component of what we have called 'core state functions' is good governance. This is a broad sector, including public sector and regulatory policy reform, democracy promotion, election support, anti-corruption programmes, and rule of law, among other things. Promoting good governance is seen not only as a normatively desirable goal but also as a prerequisite for stable, self-sustainable, and violence-free statehood. Donors rarely give up on their vision of bringing good governance to fragile and conflict-affected states. One of the few exceptions is South Sudan after 2014, when donors admitted that the South Sudanese government was unwilling to work towards better governance. As a result, donors largely gave up on working with the government for better governance and instead increased humanitarian and emergency aid which bypassed government channels. By contrast, in Afghanistan and Mali donors continued to invest in good governance projects.

For Afghanistan, there is no evidence that interventions aiming to improve governance were effective. Regarding democracy promotion, the available evidence suggests that development assistance could provide the technical capacities needed for conducting elections; however, projects aimed at democratic awareness or democratic participation had little effect. Initiatives aiming to reform public administration and to create better regulatory frameworks for private sector development and for the agriculture sector were also not effective. Likewise, evaluations of rule of law programmes suggest that interventions were not successful because they were overly ambitious, were not based on the political-economic realities on the ground, and were ideologically framed by an unrealistic theory of change.

In Mali, the included evaluations cover a range of interventions in various fields, such as management of public resources, fiscal decentralization, political decentralization, rehabilitation of governmental infrastructure, capacity-building for government officials and civil society, strengthening the relationship between citizens and public authorities, and establishing spaces for public debate. There is no example of an effective intervention in any of these fields in our sample. One field where donors saw some success was in election support. Support from the UN Development Programme (UNDP) for elections in 2013 and 2016 was seen as mainly effective in the sense that this technical help enabled the government to conduct elections. But it must also be noted that conducting elections did not result in improved democracy, since Mali's democracy has been in steady decline since 2008.

Not surprisingly, good governance initiatives in South Sudan were also not effective. After South Sudan gained independence, donors invested in good governance projects by supporting institutions such as the National Legislative Assembly, the Anti-Corruption Commission, the National Audit Chambers (NAC), and the National Elections Commission (NEC). Also supported were reforms in public financial management and budget strengthening. Still other interventions aimed at support for the rule of law, for community policing, for the free media, and for civil society organizations. However, donors generally overestimated South Sudan's state capacity and its political will to improve governance, leading to over-ambitious and ineffective programmes. By 2014, a consensus among donors had emerged that governance projects had not been effective, that ownership by the government for such projects remained low, and that South Sudan lacked not only the capacity but also the political will to become a committed partner for good governance.

In sum, interventions in the field of good governance were not effective in Afghanistan, Mali, and South Sudan. Factors which hampered such programmes were entrenched patronage-based practices within the government, a lack of buy-in from the government, donor-driven top-down project design with little regard for the core institutional requirements and the demands of the partner institutions, and the lack of political will of the government.

A third important component of functional statehood is stability. So called stabilization interventions have become an important aspect of aid portfolios for fragile states. Stabilization is a somewhat vague term, and the many theoretical definitions that are used by different donors can be confusing. It is more pragmatic, then, to look at what donors actually do under the label of stabilization. Twenty-eight evaluations of stabilization interventions were included (see Table 2.1). These interventions aimed to:

- Quickly restore basic services to the population in fields such as education, water, sanitation, transportation, and health services, in the hope that this will encourage them to work with the government and to loosen ties with insurgents.

- Provide economic opportunities, for example by providing training, investing in job creation, or providing access to credits in order to encourage people to work with the government rather than with the insurgents.
- Strengthen the mediation and conflict resolution capacity of communities and political actors.
- Support political institutions and processes which are seen as contributing to stability such as DDR programmes, support for truth and reconciliation processes, or support for transforming rebel groups into political parties.
- Support for civil society actors who are seen as counteracting unresponsive, corrupt, and thus destabilizing governments

Afghanistan provides the largest evidence base for stabilization interventions. The available evaluations (n = 12) suggest that these interventions did not win the hearts and minds of the population, did not reduce violence, did not increase trust between groups, and did not increase the legitimacy of the government, all of which are good indicators of stabilization. On the contrary, some of these interventions actually exacerbated inter-group tensions and attracted violence.

The evidence from Mali and South Sudan corroborates the findings from Afghanistan. In South Sudan, interventions in stabilization were not effective and could not prevent a resurgence in violence. After the outbreak of the civil war in 2014, donors helped to create spaces for dialogue in society and supported the various peace negotiations between the warring parties. Donors also supported conflict management and peacebuilding processes at the local level, including dispute resolution, peace meetings, livelihood programmes, and local-level justice support. There is no evidence that such interventions led to less violence, more intergroup trust or more support for the government.

Findings from Mali are similar. At the national level, donors provided support for the Truth, Justice, and Reconciliation Commission (CVJR), for political communication via mass media in support of peace, for political and fiscal decentralization, and for cantonment in the framework of the DDR processes. At the local level, donors supported income-generating activities for the private sector, capacity-building in conflict resolution, and restoring access to basic services. The available evidence does not suggest that interventions in any of these fields contributed to greater stability.

In sum, the existing evidence from these three countries strongly suggests that aid is not a good tool for making very unstable regions less unstable. This ties in with mounting evidence from academic studies (Iyengar Plumb et al. 2017; Zürcher 2017, 2020; Findley 2018; SIGAR 2018; Sexton and Zürcher 2024). Aid might even increase violence, when injected into highly insecure regions where violence is a reality and insurgents still retain some capacity. It is beyond the scope of this chapter to review the explanations for this in detail. The short version is this: at the national level, aid is not a strong-enough lever to fix the many woes that plague governments in fragile states, such as lack of capacity, predatory elites, and a lack of a political settlement among rival fractions. And at the micro level, aid is not a strong-enough incentive to convince local strong men and the local population that they should side with the government and oppose insurgents (Sexton and Zürcher 2024).

2.3.2 Aid for Basic Services: Health and Education

As we have seen, aid for core state functions (capacity, stability, and good governance) in fragile states appears to be not effective. What about interventions for improving services in health and education? For Afghanistan, the available studies point to massive improvement in many health indicators, especially child and maternal mortality. The reports reviewed suggest that successful interventions took place in midwifery training, antenatal care visits, deliveries attended by health workers, conditional cash transfers for women and community health workers, and improved family planning. For Mali, the evaluation reports agree that there were some positive outcomes, especially regarding maternal, newborn, and child health, access to health for women, and mobilizing resources for the fight against HIV/AIDS. Budget support, which was widely used until 2012, is credited with the improved capacity of the healthcare system and better access to healthcare. For South Sudan, the available evaluations also report some positive outcomes, again especially in maternal, newborn, and child health. Notably, the massive Health Pooled Fund (HPF) was credited with significant results in improving health services.

A similar picture emerges for education. For all three countries, the available evaluation reports agree that substantial progress has been made regarding better access to primary education for boys and girls. Effectiveness appears to be higher in Afghanistan and Mali, and lower in South Sudan, which may reflect the fact that state capacities in South Sudan were even lower than in the other two countries.

In sum, interventions in the health sector as well as in education were mostly effective in all three countries. It is noteworthy that governments in Mali and Afghanistan both saw health and education as a priority, and that buy-in for this sector was relatively high. That said, the sustainability of the achieved results relies on continued funding from donors. Results are therefore often not sustainable without external support.

2.3.3 Aid for Livelihoods and Economic Opportunities

The strengthening of livelihoods and the creation of economic opportunities is another important objective of donors in fragile contexts, and donors use a wide variety of interventions in this field. At the macro level, donors support projects in the fields of macroeconomic policies and financial management, support for the private sector, or investments in sectors such as telecommunications, transportation, and energy. On the local level, there are interventions in rural development and resilience, including small infrastructure for irrigation, roads, energy, access to credits and savings, and a wide array of community-driven development approaches.

Interestingly, the bulk of the available evidence from our three countries refers to more localized interventions in rural development. Information on macro-level economic interventions is rather scarce for all three countries.

In Afghanistan, programmes supporting economic development, macroeconomic policies, and financial management capacities achieved some progress in the early stages of reconstruction after 2004. For example, there was initial growth in telecommunications, transport, and construction, but results were not sustainable, nor was it realistic to expect sustainable economic growth, given the insecure environment and the shrinking aid flows after 2013. Interventions aimed at promoting the private sector were rarely effective.

Regarding rural development, the evidence suggests that the interventions, often implemented through newly created community-level organizations, helped to build a large amount of small infrastructure such as roads, irrigation, and access to energy. This contributed to improved livelihoods and strengthened coping mechanisms, but it has not led to sustainable economic growth that translated into jobs or income opportunities.

For Mali and South Sudan, we only have evidence on interventions in rural development. In Mali, rural development was an important aspect of donors' aid portfolios. After 2012, most interventions focused on food security, coping mechanisms, and resilience. Results appeared to have been satisfactory, and interventions such as rural credits, cash and in-kind transfers, saving associations, introduction of new crops, and irrigation projects were all effective to some extent. It is also noteworthy that the cooperation between donors and the government in the sector of rural development was satisfactory, and that capacity-building and training for government officials at the subnational level in technical fields relating to rural development were effective. In South Sudan, projects on rural development, including those related to food security, livelihoods, water and sanitation, and small infrastructure, proved to be reasonably effective at improving coping strategies and resilience.

Overall, macro-level interventions (for which we only have evidence from Afghanistan) were not effective in promoting sustainable economic growth. At the local and rural level, interventions in all three countries were reasonably effective in building resilience and improving coping strategies among beneficiaries. However, there is little evidence that rural development interventions aimed at increasing productivity beyond subsistence agriculture were successful.

Small-scale resilience projects were reasonably successful. More complex projects, such as value chains or agribusiness innovations, were much less effective.

2.3.4 Aid for Women's Empowerment and Gender Equality

Interventions for women's empowerment and gender equality have been a mainstay in aid portfolios and gained even more importance with some donors, for example Canada and Germany, embracing feminist development policies.

Interventions in this field differ in scope and ambition. At one end of the spectrum are interventions designed to improve the economic situation of women and their access to services. At the other end are interventions which explicitly aim at transforming gender relations, leading to a more gender-equal society.

The gender dimension was especially prominent in development cooperation in Afghanistan. In the political narrative of many donors, helping Afghan women and girls was portrayed as both an important objective and a legitimizing factor for international engagement.

The end of Taliban rule in 2002 and the rehabilitation of infrastructure in health and education meant that access to health and education markedly improved for women. These successes, however, were a result of changing political context, and not a result of ODA. In fact, aid interventions that directly targeted gender inequality were not effective. For example, despite sustained support, donors reported that the capacity of the Ministry of Women's Affairs (MoWA) remained weak. Donors also noted that both the capacity and the political will of the Afghan government and political elites for gender equality programming remained very limited, as prevailing cultural norms made progress difficult. There were, however, pockets of modest success. Examples include rural literacy for women, increased access to health and education, and better livelihoods in women-specific activities within agriculture, such as mushroom farming and kitchen gardening. In sum, small, modest projects embedded in traditional structures helped to increase access to health and education and modestly improved livelihoods for women. By contrast, larger, more ambitious projects aimed directly at changing gender norms and relations had no discernible impact. This finding is in line with the result from a recent systematic review on women's empowerment (Lwamba et al. 2022).

Results are similar for Mali and South Sudan. In Mali, the political and cultural context made it difficult to make tangible progress on women's rights and gender equality. Donors pushed for new laws on gender quotas in parliament, better protection of victims of gender-based violence (GBV), and better representation of women in formal and informal institutions dealing with issues of peace but it remains unclear whether such legal changes contributed to improved gender equality through actual implementation. At the local level, however, projects aimed at tangible benefits for women were often effective. For example, village savings and loans associations (VSLAs) helped improve women's economic status. Interventions aimed at better educational outcomes for girls led to concrete results. Finally, reports noted that removing health user fees increased access to healthcare for women.

South Sudan is the most challenging context, and projects in this field were mostly not effective. Some small pockets of success can be found in projects in the education sectors. Targeted interventions helped increase female enrolment and retention. Also worth mentioning is the fact that some positive results regarding women's economic empowerment were achieved in aid sectors such as rural development or emergency aid. While community-level projects aimed at enhancing women's social or political empowerment produced few tangible outcomes, projects with an economic component, specifically targeting women's economic situation, fared better, since they had broader acceptance and reach.

In sum, interventions that aimed to improve gender equality were not very effective. Donors were sometimes successful in pushing for institutional reforms. However, such institutional changes often did not translate into action, as laws were not implemented or ministries were not capacitated. As a result, there was little real change in gender relations. More effective were smaller, local interventions providing tangible benefits for women, for example in fields such as literacy for rural women, increased access to health and education, support for livelihood projects in women-specific activities within agriculture, better access to microcredits and saving associations for women, or better retention rates for girls in basic education.

We can now summarize the main results from the systematic reviews on aid effectiveness in three highly fragile states. Not surprisingly, aid proved to be somewhat effective in improving the provision of basic services, such as health and basic education, and in fields such as livelihoods and resilience in rural areas. Importantly, women in rural areas also benefited from such livelihood programmes. Support for small infrastructure improved food security. Interventions resulted in more skills in farming or income-generating activities, leading to more resilience. These gains were mainly achieved 'in the heads' of people, in the form of skills, knowledge, and practices. Occasionally, interventions also led to increased technical capacities in subnational government structures regarding agriculture practices, but overall, institutional gains were rare. However, rural development programmes did not lead to sustainable economic growth that translated into jobs or income opportunities.

Programmes supporting macroeconomic development, macroeconomic policies, financial management, and support for the private sector were mostly not effective and generally did not contribute to sustainable economic growth.

Also not effective were interventions aiming at gender equality. However, some results were obtained in improving the situation of rural women. Examples include rural literacy, increased access to health and education, and better livelihoods in women-specific activities within agriculture, such as mushroom farming and kitchen gardening. Also, VSLAs helped to improve women's economic status, and interventions aimed at better educational outcomes for girls were often effective. In general, gender projects with an economic component, specifically targeting women's economic situation, fared better than norm-changing, awareness-raising interventions, since they had broader acceptance among women and men and provided tangible and immediate benefits.

Finally, interventions aimed at the core of state fragility—improving stability, (re)building state capacity and nudging the country towards more rule of law and democratic practices—have not been effective. Donors were very rarely able to improve state capacity. Small pockets of success were limited to very technical, non-political areas at the sub-national level, such as education, rural development, and health. Good governance interventions were also ineffective. Despite substantial aid flows, these countries did not become more democratic, less corrupt, or better governed. Nor did so-called stabilization measures lead to greater stability, as reflected in less violence, less mistrust between groups, or more legitimacy for the government.

2.4 Why Aid Is Mostly Not Effective in Fragile States

These findings are perhaps not too surprising and are consistent with a solid body of scholarship suggesting that aid to improve governance structures in fragile states is less effective than aid to improve access to basic services (e.g., Kaplan 2008; Zürcher 2012; Gisselquist 2014; Caselli and Presbitero 2021). Yet, they are still disappointing. For many aid professionals, these results are a blow to what is perceived as an important goal of aid, namely to help fragile countries become less fragile and more like the 'Denmarks' of the world. Over the past year, the author of this chapter has presented the findings of these three systematic reviews to a wide range of development professionals from bilateral and multilateral organizations, and many have expressed their unwillingness to accept these results, even given that these systematic reviews represent our best current knowledge on aid effectiveness in highly fragile states. I understand this reaction, but I don't think it's helpful. I will come back to it at the end of this chapter.

But why is aid not effective where it is most needed? The reasons are many, but four interrelated factors emerge from the evaluation reports: first, the particular political economy of fragile states; second, a lack of government capacity; third, endemic violence; and fourth, over-ambitious interventions.

As noted above, in highly fragile states, political power is not vested in formal political institutions, but rather in patronage networks that transcend formal political institutions. Rent-seeking, widespread institutionalized corruption, and intense competition between rival networks are the typical symptoms of such a political economy of fragile statehood. An important implication is that elites in such a system are not interested in political reforms that would threaten a mode of governance that is the sole source of authority. As a result, there is a distinct lack of political will to truly embrace reforms that could lead to greater accountability, more robust formal institutions, and more democratic procedures. Consequently, the effectiveness of aid programmes in areas such as good governance, decentralization, anti-corruption, and the like is particularly low.

This situation is undoubtedly exacerbated by a lack of capacity. Many evaluation reports stress that government structures lack the capacity to use aid productively. Unfortunately, many donors have consistently overestimated state capacity, especially in Afghanistan, and have designed programmes based on largely imagined absorptive and administrative capacities. Unfortunately, as we have seen, capacity building rarely works in such contexts, leading to a vicious circle from which few fragile countries can escape. Moreover, elites in such contexts tend to be highly fragmented, with intense and often violent competition between different networks. Foreign donors are therefore rarely able to establish reliable partnerships with government officials, as turnover is high and government officials are often preoccupied with internal power struggles.

The third factor explaining the lack of effectiveness is insecurity and violence. A constant theme in the evaluation reports is that the lack of basic security is a pervasive problem that affects every aspect of development cooperation. The reports highlight how difficult it is to implement and monitor development projects when sites are inaccessible or when development workers are at risk of being targeted by insurgents. Many reports describe how a lack of security has led to delays and cost overruns. Insecurity has also required aid agencies to adopt security measures that have increased implementation costs. As we have seen, the antidote to this, so-called stabilization measures, is not effective. It is beyond the scope of this chapter to discuss why this is the case. But the short answer is that ending violence requires complex domestic political processes that cannot be influenced by outsiders handing out gifts of better irrigation, offering meeting places, providing conflict resolution training and the like. These tools are simply no match for the powerful forces that tear these societies apart.

Finally, a recurring theme in the evaluation reports is that donors have often designed overly ambitious projects based not on the political-economic realities on the ground, but on overly optimistic assumptions and ideologically charged theories of change.

2.5 Discussion and Implications

The evidence collected through these three systematic reviews paints a clear picture: Aid did not improve governmental capacity, did not lead to better governance, and did not provide more stability. In short, development aid was not a suitable tool for addressing the core problems that plagued Afghanistan, South Sudan, and Mali. This finding is not entirely surprising. There is a solid academic literature that argues that external actors rarely succeed in strengthening institutions in fragile states (Ottaway 2002; Englebert and Tull 2008; Barnett and Zürcher 2009; Chowdhury 2018; Bliesemann De Guevara 2010; de Waal 2015), that fragile states are often trapped in fragility (Collier 2008; Pritchett et al. 2013; Carment and Yiagadeesen 2019), and that aid faces many challenges in fragile states (Gisselquist 2014).

The presented evidence stems from a sample of three highly fragile states. We therefore have to be cautious when generalizing results. That said, there is no reason to believe that aid effectiveness is higher in the approximately two dozen countries (see footnote 8) that are at the same or lower level of fragility as Mali and share characteristics such as very weak state capacities, open or latent violence, predatory elites, high levels of corruption, and governance systems based on patronage. In sum, donors should assume that these results hold for this specific group of highly fragile countries and adopt their policies accordingly.

Another possible limitation concerns time. Many aid practitioners, confronted with these sobering results, argue that it takes time for aid to produce results and especially so when it comes to aid for such difficult fields as governance. With regard to Afghanistan, the official position of many donors has indeed been that the transformation simply needs more time, which is why donors have continued with the same aid approach right up to the collapse of the Afghan republic in summer 2021. The assumption that 'more of the same' will, over time, lead to better results is not plausible. As we have seen, the main impediments to aid effectiveness are endemic violence, factionalized elites, corruption, patronage, and a political economy not conducive to reforms. There are challenges that cannot be overcome with aid alone. Furthermore, the systematic reviews cover a 13-year period, which is reasonably long. If aid were effective in the longer term, we would have found some evidence of it over this time.

So, what should donors do when faced with this evidence? I strongly believe that aid allocation should be guided by practical ethics. As mentioned in the introduction to this chapter, this means that aid allocation should be guided by utilitarianism, that is, the most ethical and therefore optimal allocation of aid is when the utility of aid is maximized. In practice, of course, it is very complicated and perhaps impossible to determine which aid allocation has the highest overall utility. However, it is easy to see that it is wrong to allocate aid where it is not effective at all. Shifting aid from sectors such as good governance, capacity, and stabilization, where aid does no good, to sectors such as livelihoods, resilience, health, and education, where aid can do good, is therefore an important step towards more effective, and more ethical, aid allocation in the most fragile states.

In 2021, the world allocated US$2260 million to 18 countries which were at similar fragility levels or lower than Mali.[8] As a very rough estimate, let us assume that 25% of these funds were spent on sectors where aid has a very low probability of being effective.[9] This implies that the world allocates, every year, US$565 millions of ODA, knowing that this aid will have no impact at all. A lot of good could be done with this money if it were spent more effectively.

A new approach to aiding the most fragile states requires a new modesty. Rather than allocating aid to normatively desirable but unrealistic goals, donors should allocate aid to where it can be most effective. This could include restoring basic services, improving access to health and education, and strengthening livelihoods and resilience. Furthermore, the reviewed evaluation reports suggest that smaller projects performed better than larger, more-complex projects. Also, projects aimed at direct results were often reasonably effective, such as those building small infrastructure; providing services such as access to water, electricity, and education; or improving livelihoods. By contrast, more complex and ambitious programmes often assume unrealistic partner capacity, ignore the context, spend too much money too fast, and are thus neither effective nor efficient.

The aid community should therefore adopt a new paradigm when dealing with highly fragile states: 'big visions out, small tangible local gains in'. This may be a bitter pill to swallow. Most aid practitioners are driven by a genuine desire to be 'transformational'—to use aid as a lever to change societies so that structural barriers to development are removed and the country has the opportunity to move towards the 'Denmarks' of this world. For many, embracing this new and modest paradigm may feel like abandoning the desire to be transformational and leaving the populations of the most fragile states without help.

[8] Net official development assistance, from OECD Development Assistance Committee donors. Source: UN Statistics Division, via Our World in Data. There is no commonly accepted measure for fragility. Here we use World Governance Indicator data. We compute the first principal component (normalized) of four dimensions: Government effectiveness, control of corruption, rule of law, and political violence as our measure for fragility. Countries that were at similar fragility levels or lower than Mali in 2021 are Afghanistan; Burundi; Central African Republic; Chad; Democratic Rep. of Congo; Dominican Republic; Eritrea; Haiti; Iraq; Korea; Libya; Mali; Myanmar; Somalia; South Sudan; Sudan; Syria; Venezuela; Yemen.

[9] The assumption of 25% is based on the fact that in Afghanistan, Mali, and South Sudan between 2008 and 2020, on average 25% of all ODA was classified as 'Government and Society' by the OECD DAC classification. The 'ineffective' aid sectors which we have discussed in this chapter belong to 'Government and Society'.

I disagree with such a sentiment. I believe it is a worthwhile goal in itself to help the populations of highly fragile states get access to health, basic education, and livelihoods. Furthermore, poverty, lack of education, and lack of access to basic service all are strongly associated with violent conflict, weak governance capacity, and other forms of fragility. So improving those sectors might generate second order effects and help prepare the foundation for exiting fragility at a later stage.

However, ODA alone is clearly not the tool that will make such a transformation more likely. We know too little about the causal factors that enable a country to exit fragility, but it is safe to say that at its core, the enabling factors for such exits are closely tied to complex domestic political processes. In essence, highly fragile states have a chance of exiting fragility when there is political settlement. A political settlement can be broadly defined as 'a series of tacit and more explicit agreements, usually among elites, about the distribution of power and resources and the nature of the linkages between state and society. Crucially, the "rules of the game" that underpin political settlements incorporate both formal and informal institutions and arrangements' (Pospisil and Rocha Menocal 2017: 553; also Gray 2019). A similar concept is the 'development bargain' introduced by Dercon (2022), which refers to an agreement among a country's elites to commit to economic growth and development over maintaining their own power and privileges via maintaining predatory patronage networks. The concept underscores the importance of elite consensus in driving national development outcomes. It is unclear to what extent—if at all—external actors can influence such domestic political processes. However, it seems very unlikely that ODA is an effective tool to this end. Other instruments from different toolboxes such as foreign policy and diplomacy may be more effective. Accepting that development aid is not the right tool to shape complex domestic processes in highly fragile countries liberates development aid from a task which it cannot do. This creates opportunities to use development aid where it can be helpful.

Not all highly fragile states are stuck in fragility forever. While many are, some escape. Once a highly fragile state has embarked on a path of transformation, there may be a window of opportunity to support this process with an intelligent mix of ODA. The assumption here is that at a certain level of state capacity, 'transformational' ODA can be used effectively. What does not work in Mali may work in Malawi; what does not work in Guinea may work in The Gambia. In the three systematic reviews mentioned in this chapter, we saw that aid effectiveness in South Sudan—the most fragile of the three—was very low across all sectors. In Mali—the least fragile of the three—effectiveness appears to have been slightly higher, especially before the breakdown of democratic order in 2012.

Of course, the idea that aid is best given to countries that have the institutional capacity to use it well has been around for decades. But so far we lack a convincing way of measuring the level of state capacity required for transformational aid to be effective. One entirely feasible and quick way to identify that threshold would be to conduct more country-level systematic reviews, where the countries included should have different levels of fragility. By systematically varying the level of fragility, we could learn whether and how aid effectiveness in different sectors is correlated with initial fragility. In this chapter we have presented evidence from three countries, all with very low levels of state capacities. Scholars need to produce similar evidence from a much larger sample of countries, where state capacities vary. By analysing the differences in aid effectiveness, especially in what we have called core government functions sectors, we can then infer which levels of state capacity allow aid to be effective. Armed with this knowledge, donors can then design aid portfolios that are appropriate for the given context.

References

Barnett, M., and C. Zürcher (2009). 'The Peacebuilder's Contract: How External Statebuilding Reinforces Weak Statehood'. In R. Paris and T. D. Sisk, editors, *The Dilemmas of Statebuilding: Confronting the Contradictions of Postwar Peace Operations.* London and New York: Routledge: 37–66.

Bliesemann de Guevara, B. (2010). 'Introduction: The Limits of Statebuilding and the Analysis of State-Formation'. *Journal of Intervention and Statebuilding*, 4(2): 111–28. https://doi.org/10.1080/17502970903533652.

Carment, D., and S. Yiagadeesen (2019). *Exiting the Fragility Trap: Rethinking Our Approach to the World's Most Fragile States.* Athens: Ohio University Press. https://doi.org/10.2307/j.ctv224tvcv.

Caselli, F., and A. Presbitero (2021). 'Aid Effectiveness in Fragile States'. In: Chami R., Espinoza R., and Montiel P. J., editors, *Macroeconomic Policy in Fragile States.* Oxford: Oxford University Press: 493–520.

Chowdhury, A. (2018). *The Myth of International Order: Why Weak States Persist and Alternatives to the State Fade Away.* Oxford: Oxford University Press. https://doi.org/10.1093/oso/9780190686710.001.0001.

Collier, P. (2008). *The Bottom Billion: Why the Poorest Countries Are Failing and What Can Be Done about It.* Oxford: Oxford University Press.

De Waal, A. (2015). *The Real Politics of the Horn of Africa: Money, War and the Business of Power.* Cambridge: Polity Press.

Dercon, S. (2022). *Gambling on Development: Why Some Countries Win and Others Lose.* London: Hurst.

Englebert, P., and D. M. Tull (2008). 'Postconflict Reconstruction in Africa: Flawed Ideas about Failed States'. *International Security*, 32(4): 106–39. https://doi.org/10.1162/isec.2008.32.4.106.

Findley, M. G. (2018). 'Does Foreign Aid Build Peace?'. *Annual Review of Political Science*, 21: 359–84. Available at: www.annualreviews.org/doi/full/10.1146/annurev-polisci-041916-015516 (accessed 2 November 2022).

Gisselquist, R. M. (2014). 'Aid and Institution-Building in Fragile States: What Do We Know? What Can Comparative Analysis Add?'. *The ANNALS of the American Academy of Political and Social Science*, 656(1): 6–21. https://doi.org/10.1177/0002716214546991.

Gray, H. (2019). 'Understanding and Deploying the Political Settlement Framework in Africa'. *Oxford Research Encyclopedia of Politics*. https://doi.org/10.1093/acrefore/9780190228637.001.0001/acrefore-9780190228637-e-888.

Iyengar Plumb, R., J. N. Shapiro, and S. Hegarty (2017). *Lessons Learned from Stabilization Initiatives in Afghanistan: A Systematic Review of Existing Research*. Santa Monica, CA: RAND Corporation. Available at: www.rand.org/pubs/working_papers/WR1191.html (accessed 2 November 2022).

Kaplan, S. D. (2008). *Fixing Fragile States: A New Paradigm for Development*. Bloomsbury Publishing USA.

Lwamba, E., S. Shisler, W. Ridlehoover, M. Kupfer, N. Tshabalala, P. Nduku, L. Langer, S. Grant, A. Sonnenfeld, D. Anda, and J. Eyers (2022). 'Strengthening Women's Empowerment and Gender Equality in Fragile Contexts towards Peaceful and Inclusive Societies: A Systematic Review and Meta-analysis'. *Campbell Systematic Reviews*, 18(1): 1214.

Noyes, J., A. Booth, M. Cargo, K. Flemming, A. Harden, J. Harris, R. Garside, K. Hannes, T. Pantoja, and J. Thomas (2022). 'Qualitative Evidence'. In J. P. T. Higgins, J. Thomas, J. Chandler, M. Cumpston, T. Li, M. J. Page, and V.a. Welch, editors, *Cochrane Handbook for Systematic Reviews of Interventions*, version 6.3 (updated February 2022). London: Cochrane. Available at: https://training.cochrane.org/handbook/current/chapter-21 (accessed 2 November 2022).

Ottaway, M. (2002). 'Rebuilding State Institutions in Collapsed States'. *Development and Change*, 33(5): 1001–23. https://doi.org/10.1111/1467-7660.t01-1-00258.

Pospisil, J., and A. Rocha Menocal (2017). 'Why Political Settlements Matter: Navigating Inclusion in Processes of Institutional Transformation'. *Journal of International Development*, 29(5): 551–8.

Pritchett, L., M. Woolcock, and M. Andrews (2013). 'Looking Like a State: Techniques of Persistent Failure in State Capability for Implementation'. *The Journal of Development Studies*, 49(1): 1–18. https://doi.org/10.1080/00220388.2012.709614.

Sexton, R., and Zürcher, C. (2024). 'Aid, Attitudes, and Insurgency: Evidence from Development Projects in Northern Afghanistan'. *American Journal of Political Science*, 68(3): 1168–82.

SIGAR (Special Inspector General for Afghanistan Reconstruction) (2018). *Stabilization: Lessons from the U.S. Experience in Afghanistan*. Available at: www.sigar.mil/interactive-reports/stabilization/index.html (accessed 2 November 2022).

Zürcher, C. (2012). 'Conflict, State Fragility and Aid Effectiveness: Insights from Afghanistan'. *Conflict, Security & Development*, 12(5): 461–80. https://doi.org/10.1080/14678802.2012.744180.

Zürcher, C. (2017). 'What Do We (Not) Know about Development Aid and Violence? A Systematic Review'. *World Development*, 98: 506–22. https://doi.org/10.1016/j.worlddev.2017.05.013.

Zürcher, C. (2020). 'The Impact of Development Aid on Organised Violence'. 3IE Working Paper 37. New Delhi: International Initiative for Impact Evaluation (3IE). Available at: https://www.3ieimpact.org/sites/default/files/2020-08/WP37-Systematic-Review-Aid-Violence.pdf (accessed 2 November 2022).

Zürcher, C. (2022). 'Evidence on Aid (in) Effectiveness in Highly Fragile States: A Synthesis of Three Systematic Reviews of Aid to Afghanistan, Mali, and South Sudan, 2008–21'. WIDER Working Paper 2022/160. Helsinki: UNU-WIDER.

Zürcher, C., P. Labelle, L. Borges, K. Hoare, M. A. Javid, K. Kavanagh, S. Sarna, and E. Woolner (2022). 'Impact of Aid in Highly Fragile States: A Synthesis of Three Systematic Reviews of Aid to Afghanistan, Mali and South Sudan 2008–2021'. The Hague: IOB. Available at: https://english.iob-evaluatie.nl/publications/sub-studies/2022/11/10/synthesis-of-systematic-reviews-in-afghanistan-mali-and-south-sudan (accessed 17 November 2022).

3

Fragile States in an Era of Geopolitical Rivalry, Pandemic, and War

Insights from the Country Indicators for Foreign Policy

David Carment and Yiagadeesen Samy

3.1 Introduction

The objective of this chapter is to focus on fragility research findings to examine what works or does not work in development aid and development cooperation in fragile and conflict-affected contexts. In our analysis, we draw on our research findings from prior reports, working papers, and publications based on research led by Carment using the Country Indicators for Foreign Policy project methodology (CIFP)—see for example Carment and Samy (2019a, 2019b, 2023a, 2023b) and Carment et al. (2006, 2009, 2020).

We examine questions of aid effectiveness in the context of states trapped in fragility in the first part of the chapter. We then consider the impact of COVID-19 and implications for aid effectiveness in fragile states. We conclude by briefly examining how the wars in Ukraine and Palestine are impacting fragile states and the long-term prospects for aid effectiveness in an era of geopolitical rivalry and great power competition.

As the development challenges facing fragile states have become better understood, the World Bank Group's terminology has evolved over the years: from Low Income Countries Under Stress from 2006 to 2009, to the Fragile States List in 2010, to the Harmonized list of Fragile Situations from 2011 to 2015, and currently the List of Fragile and Conflict-Affected Situations (FCAS or FCS). These changes reflect the need to move beyond low incomes and problems related to governance and weak institutions, to those of conflict, violence, and instability, and more importantly to recognize the various types of circumstances facing fragile states.

Similarly, the Organisation for Economic Co-operation and Development (OECD), which has been compiling lists of countries considered fragile since 2008 has increasingly recognized the multidimensional idea of fragility advanced by CIFP (see the CIFP project initiated on behalf of the Canadian government described in Carment et al. 2006). In a recent States of Fragility 2020 report,

David Carment and Yiagadeesen Samy, *Fragile States in an Era of Geopolitical Rivalry, Pandemic, and War*.
In: *Fragile Aid*. Edited by: Rachel M. Gisselquist et al., Oxford University Press.© UNU-WIDER (2025).
DOI: 10.1093/oso/9780198960287.003.0003

the OECD (2020) identified 57 fragile contexts (including 13 extremely fragile contexts), while the World Bank Group lists 39 countries in fragile and conflict-affected situations in fiscal year 2023. The World Bank Group listed 37 countries as fragile in 2020 and thus a much smaller number than OECD (2020). Despite these differences, there is a consensus that a group of countries labelled as fragile, including a few that have been trapped in fragility for decades, have been continually vulnerable over time despite receiving significant amounts of development assistance.

3.2 Overview of Trends and Data

After a brief period of declining fragility at the turn of the century, fragile states became more prominent as their precarious situation worsens in a post-COVID-19 world beset by war and violence. Conflicts in Ukraine, Palestine, Haiti, and Sudan are all having serious impacts globally but they are not the only ones. In the last decade or so, we have seen an increase in armed conflicts and violence around the world with unprecedented increases over the last three years. Recent data from the Uppsala Conflict Data Program (UCDP) saw an upsurge in organized violence by 46% in 2021 due to conflicts in Afghanistan, Ethiopia, and Yemen (Davies et al. 2022). By 2023, the number of conflicts involving states totalled 59, the highest number ever since the data collection's starting point in 1946 (UCDP 2024).

The COVID-19 pandemic exacerbated fragile states' performance in several important ways by further weakening their capacity for response and prevention and by delinking their economies from global financial, trade, and aid flows. Prior to the COVID-19 pandemic, more than three-quarters of the world's extremely poor were already living in fragile and conflict-affected contexts.

The global pandemic also had the effect of causing millions of people living in fragile contexts to fall into extreme poverty. Although poverty has declined in a few fragile states, many are not on track to meet the global target of eradicating poverty and it is expected that poverty will become increasingly concentrated in these fragile states by 2030 (Carment and Samy 2019a, 2019b, 2023a, 2023b). Aid or official development assistance (ODA) is the second largest source of external finance for fragile countries (OECD 2020) after remittance flows (and often the first when examined country by country). Unlike other countries where investment flows are more predominant, fragile countries depend much more on external official financing and do not mobilize enough resources domestically to create a strong fiscal pact and build legitimacy. So, unlike other developing countries where poverty has declined significantly and the need for foreign aid has declined relative to other resource flows, fragile states continue to be characterized by the persistence of poverty and a high dependency on foreign aid.

The needs for both humanitarian[1] and development assistance are pressing and real in fragile contexts. Nowhere was this clearer than in the case of Afghanistan—a country trapped in fragility—where net ODA as a percentage of that country's gross national income was more than 20% in recent years (World Development Indicators, World Bank) before the return of the Taliban. With its foreign assets frozen and cuts in aid spending from major donors that are reluctant to recognize the legitimacy of the new regime, the country was, in the immediate aftermath of US withdrawal, unable to provide basic services to its population. Only now is Afghanistan slowly emerging from a severe economic and humanitarian crisis (Carment and Belo 2021b).

ODA to fragile countries has steadily increased in the past few years as both bilateral and multilateral agencies have reallocated aid away from stable to fragile countries. Drawing on data from 2020, Desai shows that Development Assistance Committee (DAC) member countries gave more than US$60 billion, or 63% of their net country allocable ODA to fragile contexts in 2018. However, by 2023 the percentage of overall aid flowing to eligible countries dropped in proportion to the amount of aid flowing to Ukraine. For example, bilateral net ODA to Ukraine from all DAC countries rose to US$20 billion, a 9% increase in real terms over 2022. At the same time aid to other conflict affected countries, including Palestine Haiti, Sudan, Syria, and Yemen, has not risen to the same extent though the need is just as great (Kiernan et al. 2024).

If we start from the premise that development is a homegrown process that cannot be controlled from outside, can foreign aid be effective in fragile states where, by definition, governance is lacking? Can aid buy reforms and improve governance in fragile contexts or could it even cause unintended harm?

Since the seminal contribution by Burnside and Dollar (2000) and those of other macro aid effectiveness studies which showed that the impact of aid on growth was conditional on the quality of policies and institutions, the effectiveness of aid in fragile states has been questioned. McGillivray (2006) and McGillivray and Feeny (2008) find that aid to fragile states was volatile, with both aid darlings and aid orphans. This speaks to both the volatility and unpredictability of aid flows, which have been shown to reduce aid effectiveness (Bulir and Hamann 2008). McGillivray and Feeny (2008) argue that aid works in the sense that it is associated with growth in fragile states, even if, as one would expect, the impact of aid on growth is higher in non-fragile countries.

McGillivray and Feeny (2008) also find that fragile states face more difficulties in absorbing amounts of aid received when compared to non-fragile countries and that there are diminishing returns to aid. The issue of absorptive capacity seems

[1] The rise in the frequency and severity of natural disasters due to climate change is already having a disproportionate impact in fragile states; a case in point is the recent floods in Pakistan. More frequent and severe natural disasters are partly responsible for the steady increase in humanitarian assistance per capita and as a percentage of total aid (Milante and Lilja 2022).

to be less of an issue in post-conflict settings (Collier and Hoeffler 2004), suggesting that more aid can be allocated after the end of conflicts. However, such an approach will only work if there are good policies in place.

Another issue that has been examined with respect to aid effectiveness generally is that of donor proliferation and aid fragmentation, given the emergence in recent years of new actors—such as non-DAC donors, private philanthropic foundations, and global funds—in addition to traditional bilateral and multilateral donors. For example, Kimura et al. (2012) find that aid concentration (proliferation) has a positive (negative) impact on economic growth while Han and Koenig-Archibugi (2015) uncover a U-shaped relationship between health aid donors and child survival. While these studies do not consider fragile states specifically, there is no a priori reason to assume that donor proliferation and aid fragmentation would not be relevant in such contexts. There have also been ongoing debates in the literature about the choice of aid modalities (e.g., technical assistance, project vs programme or budget support, multi-donor trust funds), whether bilateral vs multilateral aid should be prioritized, and how these choices impact aid effectiveness, with no clear consensus emerging (Bandstein 2007; Heinzel and Reinsberg 2024).

Going back to macro aid effectiveness studies, while the Burnside and Dollar (2000) results have been found to be less robust than expected, the fact that progress in fragile states has been lacking when compared to the amounts of aid spent in them has raised serious doubts about the latter's effectiveness in fragile contexts. Beyond aid effectiveness studies, there has also been much focus on aid practices and good principles of aid delivery, whether through the 2005 Paris Declaration, the 2007 Principles for Good International Engagement in Fragile States and Situations, and the G7+ New Deal on Fragile States. On paper and in theory, these principles make sense for the most part; their applications, however, have been more difficult; see for example, Samy and Aksli (2015) about the Paris Principles and Hearn (2016) about the New Deal. Chauvet and Collier's (2008) study on failing states shows how difficult reform really is. They found the average duration of a failing state is a lengthy 54 years because external financing for resource exports and foreign aid tend to encourage rents and thereby retard reforms. In essence the idea that state fragility is solely a transitory phenomenon associated with, for example, a post-conflict peace process or a massive infusion of economic aid is empirically untrue (Ziaja et al. 2019). Indeed, research on fragile, closed, and unstable states (Tikuisis and Carment 2017) shows that they move both forward and backward in terms of their development so that stability and openness are never secure.

In regard to understanding why some states remain deeply fragile and resistant to reform, research initiated by the CIFP project has shown that monocausal explanations are inadequate (Carment et al. 2006, 2009; Carment and Samy 2019a, 2019b, 2023a). Those fragile states whose stagnation is so tenacious despite generous aid programmes and substantial and costly interventions are considered to be stuck in a fragility trap. Focusing on one factor such as economic development or political development is rarely sufficient; not all trapped states experience large-scale violence, and neither is conflict intensity constant within a given trapped state. Indeed, using the CIFP ALC framework, Carment and Samy (2019a) show that states trapped in fragility (see Table 3.1) face challenges related mostly to legitimacy and authority, as opposed to capacity (Figure 3.1).

Authority is defined as the extent to which a state possesses the ability to enact binding legislation over its population, to exercise coercive force over its sovereign territory, to provide core public goods, and to provide a stable and secure environment to its citizens and communities. Legitimacy refers to the extent to which a particular state commands public loyalty to the governing regime and generates domestic support for that government's legislation and policy. Such support must be created through a voluntary and reciprocal arrangement of effective governance and citizenship founded upon broadly accepted principles of government selection and succession that is recognized both locally and internationally. Capacity considers the extent to which a state can mobilize and employ resources towards productive ends. States that are lacking in capacity are generally unable to provide services to their citizens and cannot respond effectively to sudden shocks such as natural disasters, epidemics, food shortages, or refugee flows (Carment et al. 2006, 2009).

In the Country Indicators for Foreign Policy's recent list of fragility trapped countries (Table 3.1), we see that Chad ranks the highest. Sudan, Somalia, the

Table 3.1 Fragility trap countries, 1980–2019

Country	Fragility score (2019)	Ranking (2019)
Afghanistan	7.01	7
Burundi	6.84	19
Chad	7.23	1
Dem. Rep. of Congo	7.15	8
Ethiopia	6.49	24
Pakistan	6.70	17
Somalia	7.55	3
South Sudan	7.59	5
Sudan	7.18	2
Uganda	6.46	13
Yemen	7.28	6

Note: Sudan and South Sudan were considered together for earlier years.
Source: authors' compilation from CIFP data (Carment et al. 2020).

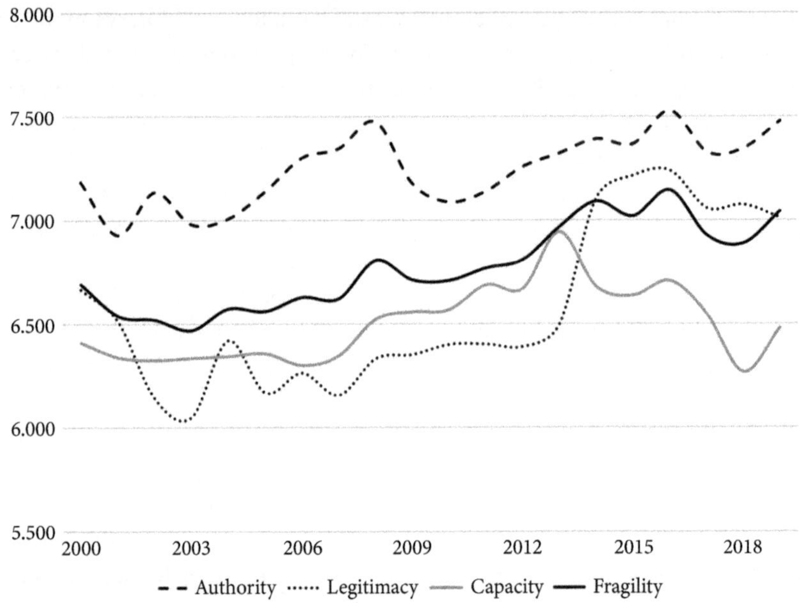

Figure 3.1 Fragility and ALC, trapped states, 2000–19

Source: authors' compilation from CIFP data (Carment et al. 2020).

Central African Republic, and South Sudan make up the top five. Ranks five to ten are occupied, in order, by Yemen, Afghanistan, the Democratic Republic of the Congo, West Bank and Gaza (Palestine), and Eritrea.

A year-over-year comparison with previous rankings from the project (not included here) shows that Somalia, Chad, the Central African Republic, Afghanistan, Sudan, and South Sudan rank consistently among the top poor performers and usually almost always within the top five for several years and in some cases decades. These are the countries that we would typically characterize as being trapped in fragility (Carment and Samy 2019a).

The majority of the trapped states are located in sub-Saharan Africa, a finding that is consistent with our historical data.[2] The rest are in the Middle East and North Africa, namely Syria, Yemen, and the West Bank and Gaza (Palestine), and in Central and South Asia, namely Afghanistan and Pakistan.

When we examine the average performance over 40 years of data with a focus on these trapped states only, their performance on authority is worse, on average, followed by legitimacy and then capacity. In fact, despite an improvement in capacity and a slight improvement in legitimacy in recent years, average authority scores have deteriorated and contributed to a deterioration in fragility scores.

[2] See https://carleton.ca/cifp/.

Average legitimacy scores have also been consistently worse than capacity scores for the trapped states since 2014 (Figure 3.1). Higher scores in each category are associated with higher fragility (Carment and Samy, 2019a, Carment et al. 2009).

3.3 Is Legitimacy the Key?

To assess the relationship between authority and legitimacy with state fragility, we mapped 24 relevant indicators measuring how the trapped states identified above perform along these two dimensions using data up to and including 2020. We end up with 15 indicators that reflect authority structures (such as conflict and violence, government effectiveness, level of corruption, and rule of law) and nine that are related to legitimacy (such as service delivery, effective institutions, inclusive decision-making, freedom of the press, and human rights); details on this methodology can be found in Carment et al. (2006, 2009) and Carment and Samy (2019a).

The best performing trapped country on Transparency International's Corruption Perceptions Index for is Ethiopia with a score of 39 over 100. All the others score less than 30 and are at the bottom of the rankings. Using the measure of rule of law[3] from the Worldwide Governance Indicators (WGI) of the World Bank, seven of the 11 trapped states saw a deterioration in their performance from 2015 to 2020. In the case of legitimacy (examined here through voice and accountability and regime type), the voice and accountability[4] measure from the WGI deteriorated in five of the 11 trapped states during the period 2015–20, with a clear improvement in only three of the remaining six. The 2022 *Freedom in the World* report by Freedom House rates all the trapped states as 'not free' except for Pakistan which is rated as 'partly free'. Overall, trapped states do not have full control over their borders, territories, and peoples, and they are characterized by ungoverned spaces. They cannot guarantee a secure environment for their citizens. Their governing regimes cannot command public loyalty, neither can they build domestic support for their legislative agendas.

Weak legitimacy conjures up ideas of limited societal consent and participation in systems of good governance and effective leadership. For example, states where the ruling regime lacks broad, voluntary domestic support suffer from a lack of legitimacy and poor institutional design. Indeed, elites may be incentivized to undermine institutional design for their own purposes

[3] The rule of law measure estimates the perception of how much agents trust and respect rules of society such as quality of contract enforcement, property rights, the police, and the courts, and those related to crime and violence.

[4] The voice and accountability measure estimates the perception of how much citizens can participate in selecting their government and freedom of expression, freedom of association, and a free media.

(Carment and Samy 2019a). In such instances, political interference, rent seeking, elite capture, and lobbying are the key culprits in propagating extreme fragility (Asongu and Kodila-Tedika 2013).

Pritchett et al. (2010) and Andrews et al. (2017) argue that fragile states adopt 'isomorphic mimicry' to maintain international legitimacy despite structural dysfunctionality. Isomorphic mimicry allows trapped states to exist while creating the illusion of implementing effective developmental policies. Similar studies have identified mechanisms through which trapped states artificially 'prop up' their institutions, so that the institution looks and feels like an ideal model; however, the actual functionality and resilience is left lacking (Pritchett et al. 2013). Closely related to 'isomorphic mimicry' is the idea of 'premature load bearing', wherein newly formed state institutions are expected to achieve much more than is possible in a short period of time (Pritchett et al. 2010).

Legitimacy is further weakened when development agencies rely on results-based management (RBM) approaches to decide where and how much aid to allocate. That is, recipient states adapt to the expectations placed on them. Bermeo (2016) shows that fragile state reversals and 'regressive' trends in governance are partly due to the fact that governance abuses by regimes have become subtler over time and are more difficult to monitor through an RBM approach. For example, outright military coups have become less common and those coups which do occur are framed in the context of an effort to restore or improve democracy. Coups in Burkina Faso, Guinea, Mali, Mauritania, and Gambia, all of which were led by US trained officers, are considered to be efforts to restore stability and good governance to the country (The Intercept 2022). Such adaptive strategies allow elites to 'buy time' to enable reforms to work, to mask non-accomplishment, or actively resist or deflect internal and external pressures for improvement.

Simply put, it is dangerous to conflate institutional form with institutional function (Baliamoune-Lutz and McGillivray 2008). Further, implementing development policy that does not consider the specific incentive structures that help provide order can be ineffective or further exacerbate core structural problems. For example, Ethiopia's ongoing civil war, one of the bloodiest in recent history, is driven in part by America's security first agenda, which has favoured military aid over good governance (Carment et al. 2019a).

When state repression leads to disengagement from formal institutions, societal compliance with the law tends to decline. This decrease in compliance stems from the perceived loss of legitimacy of state institutions by significant segments of the population. As a result, the idea of establishing legitimate political orders, as expressed in SDG16, may become more rhetorical than practical, failing to drive economic development. Governments often justify their authority through ideology or external threats rather than meaningful governance improvements. Without effective enforcement mechanisms or a clear understanding of how legitimacy leads to positive outcomes, enhancing governance remains challenging; see Carment and Samy (2023b).

North et al. (2007) argue that external interventions often fail in fragile states because they promote institutions and procedures modelled after developed nations. Political development can stagnate or regress when elite interests undermine inclusivity. Contrary to the assumption that institutional structures inherited from colonial powers are discarded, Carment and Samy (2019a) suggest that elite incapacity and unwillingness to reform are the real issues.

Fatton (1995) posits that elites create structures to maintain popular support for the status quo. He distinguishes between local, regional, and national elites, noting that while these groups may converge on national projects like independence, their cohesion fragments over time due to economic interests and ethnic loyalties. This fragmentation leads to patron–client relationships and personal rule, where patron authority determines system stability (Jackson and Rosberg 1982).

In fragility analysis, under-governed spaces emerge when disadvantaged groups disengage from national institutions, the economy, and politics. This disengagement often results from a failure to protect minority groups' autonomy, leading to their underservice and political disengagement. Coerced participation is as delegitimizing as de-participation, reflecting an unhealthy state–society relationship. Under-governed spaces obstruct national identity formation, intensify regional and ethnic differences, and hinder economic development. They also reinforce the power of elites who benefit from maintaining these spaces.

Hybrid regimes, common in fragile states, reflect the relationship between governed and under-governed spaces. These regimes maintain a facade of democracy without the risks of free political competition (Ottaway 2003). Marshall and Cole (2014) argue that hybrid regimes are inherently unstable and vulnerable to political instability, such as armed conflict or regime changes, due to the lack of commitment to democratic principles by elites and the public. Bratton (2007) found that while people may support the idea of democracy, they often lack knowledge of its institutional components (Carment and Samy 2023b).

Governments perceived as illegitimate must expend more resources on repression and coercion, weakening their effectiveness. In contrast, legitimate governments can rely on voluntary compliance from citizens, reducing the costs of surveillance and punishment (Levi et al. 2009). Horizontal inequalities, where certain groups are excluded from political and economic benefits, can harm state legitimacy. Efforts to reform these inequalities can be stymied by a lack of legitimacy (Stewart and Brown 2009). Additionally, states heavily dependent on foreign aid, particularly in sub-Saharan Africa, often prioritize international legitimacy over domestic sources, leading to weaker institutions and services (Moss et al. 2006). This disproportionate reliance on international support undermines elite legitimacy.

Overall, the interplay between legitimacy, elite interests, and governance structures significantly impacts the stability and development of fragile states. Addressing these issues requires a nuanced understanding of local contexts and the dynamics between state and society.

3.3.1 Illustrative Case Studies: Mali, Afghanistan, Haiti

Mali's increase in international development assistance, particularly since its transition to a hybrid form of democracy, has paradoxically led to negative outcomes. Despite increased aid, Mali remains aid-dependent and underperforms in development (Bergamaschi, 2014). The reason lies in how the elites manipulate aid distribution for personal gain. Elites, acting as brokers for aid, form political alliances with NGOs, benefiting from the aid flow (Carment and Samy 2019a; Carment and Samy 2023b).

Instead of establishing and adhering to democratic institutional performance measures, politicians in Mali create patronage networks, seeking control over zones to distribute resources. This system of elite bargaining, rather than public demand-driven policy, undermines genuine democratic governance. Only groups with significant power are co-opted into the patronage system, perpetuating a cycle of elite dominance and marginalization of weaker groups. The ongoing conflict in Mali's North exemplifies the harmful effects of this elite bargaining, where clans rebel for control over administrative zones to secure rents.

Mali's rent economy provides a veneer of democratic reform for international donors while allowing local politicians to skim funds through partnerships with development NGOs. This system diverts resources from key societal sectors, undermining the potential for genuine democratic institutions and public accountability (Bergamaschi, 2014). The elites remain accountable primarily to external donors rather than the Malian people (see in particular Carment and Samy 2023b).

Afghanistan's situation offers a sobering parallel. Despite over US$2 trillion spent by the USA, the intervention failed to achieve long-term stability or significant progress towards SDG 16 targets. Donor priorities conflicted with local needs, particularly regarding gender equality, and poorly managed projects led to widespread mistrust. The Special Inspector General for Afghanistan Reconstruction reported in 2018 that stabilization efforts largely failed, with aid efforts fuelling corruption rather than development (Carment et al. 2019a, Carment and Belo 2021b).

The coalition's focus on short-term military objectives over long-term development and human rights skewed Afghanistan's development. Massive military expenditures overshadowed minimal investment in local infrastructure. The approach favoured conflict-ridden provinces over peaceful ones, exacerbating regional inequalities. The inability to establish a legitimate governance structure across the entire territory left Afghanistan more fragile after foreign troops' withdrawal (Carment and Belo 2021b).

Afghanistan's hybrid system, characterized by a weak central government and pervasive corruption, failed to provide effective governance. The failure to account for Afghanistan's political, cultural, and ethnic complexities led to policies that often-promoted inter-ethnic rivalries. The inadequate coordination among international donors and reliance on security-focused aid contributed to the country's enduring fragility (Carment and Belo 2021b).

Haiti's current fragility is deeply rooted in its colonial past, foreign aid dependence, and ongoing external interference. These historical factors have led to a legacy of weak governance and political instability. Today, Haiti lacks elected leaders and functional democratic institutions, with governance practices that further delegitimize the state. The absence of stable governance is a primary contributor to Haiti's fragility, exacerbated by high unemployment rates, urban–rural inequalities, and minimal government expenditure on public services, all of which deepen public distrust (Cotton et al. 2023).

Haiti suffers from hollowed-out and captured democratic institutions, characterized by violence against citizens, lack of essential services, and widespread corruption. The parliament, judiciary, and executive are viewed as slow, harmful, and ineffective, leading to a legitimacy crisis that is unlikely to change as long as Haiti's economic development remain stagnant (Cotton et al. 2023).

Driven by aid dependence, institutional weakness, corruption, and obstacles to development and service delivery, Haiti's capacity to govern and provide services effectively has been compromised since at least the 2010 earthquake. The majority of the economy is controlled by a small elite group, with the government failing to maintain service delivery functions for the whole society.

Haiti's economy remains undiversified and heavily reliant on foreign aid and remittances. This inequality is compounded by the government's inability to provide essential services, such as electricity, and the country's high exposure to natural disasters with little infrastructure preparedness. Climate change is expected to increase the frequency and intensity of extreme weather events, further exacerbating these challenges.

Haiti's extreme environmental degradation, especially deforestation, is a direct result of pervasive poverty. Rural Haitians often turn to local forests for cooking fuel due to the lack of reliable and affordable alternatives. The degradation of the environment leads to chronic soil erosion, loss of rural livelihoods, and further delegitimization of the government.

This has led to a deepening poverty spiral, delegitimization of the government, and perverse incentives created by rent distributions and aid flows. Weak private property rights and poor contract enforcement exacerbate these issues, allowing money to unduly influence policy due to the government's weakness (Cotton et al. 2023).

The experiences of Mali, Afghanistan, and Haiti highlight the importance of legitimacy in aid interventions. Trapped states often fail to provide public goods and effective service delivery, even with improved capacity. Legitimacy must encompass both process and outputs, including better service delivery, human development, and civil society space. Aid interventions should consider indigenous political and economic structures, address under-governed territories, and ensure equitable resource distribution. Donors must be aware of the potential for aid to distort incentives and exacerbate fragility. Effective aid should promote sustainable fiscal systems and a genuine fiscal pact between people and governments (Carment and Samy 2023a).

Addressing the challenges of elite manipulation and aid dependence in fragile states like Mali, Afghanistan, and Haiti requires a nuanced understanding of local dynamics and a focus on legitimacy. Sustainable development and stability hinge on the ability of states to deliver public goods, foster inclusive governance, and build genuine accountability to their citizens. Aid interventions must be carefully designed to support these goals without reinforcing elite dominance or perpetuating dependency.

3.4 COVID-19

If trapped states perform poorly on authority and legitimacy measures as demonstrated above, capacity, especially in regard to poverty, is also problematic. Before the COVID-19 outbreak in 2019, which was subsequently declared a global pandemic by the World Health Organization (WHO) in March 2020, the situation faced by fragile states was already worrisome for a number of reasons. First, several recent studies and reports had indicated that the geography of poverty was changing in such a way that extreme poverty would become more concentrated in places characterized by fragility and conflict in the next few years (Gertz and Kharas 2018; Foresight Africa 2019). Second, evidence gathered in the last few years (see, for example, ODI 2018) has shown that very few fragile and conflict-affected states (FCAS) were on track to meet their SDGs such as hunger (SDG 2), universal access to sanitation (SDG 6), and secondary school completion (SDG 4). Finally, as noted above, conflict and violence, inequalities, refugees, and forced displacement—have also been on the rise in fragile contexts in recent years (Affricot 2021).

As a result of the pandemic, most countries, whether fragile or not, were moving into a recession by 2020. That trend was further worsened by the Ukraine–Russia war (Carment and Belo 2021b). Estimates on the impact of COVID-19 from the

World Bank indicate that COVID-19 increased extreme poverty in the world, as measured by the international poverty line of US$2.15, from 8.9% in 2019 to 9.7% in 2020 (Sumner and Ortiz-Juarez 2020). According to the World Bank an estimated 23 million more people were living in extreme poverty in 2022, compared to 2019 (World Bank 2024).

According to data from the OECD's States of Fragility platform, due to their relative isolation from the rest of the world, the number of cases and deaths in fragile contexts remained relatively low when compared to other non-fragile developing contexts. For example, confirmed cases and confirmed deaths from COVID-19 in fragile contexts were respectively 8% and 7% of total cases and total deaths globally in 2020. However, many of these calculations masked deep-seated problems in accurately reporting cases and accurately measuring fatality rates due to COVID-19. Therefore, efforts to reduce the risk of exposure have not necessarily prevented countries from weakening even further.

Consider the case of Lebanon, which made headlines as a result of a massive explosion of ammonium nitrate on 4 August 2020 at the port of Beirut that killed nearly 200 people, causing billions in damages and leaving an estimated 300,000 people homeless. Lebanon was not among the top 40 fragile countries in our ranking and was in fact in 53rd position. However, even before COVID-19, its situation had deteriorated as a result of a dysfunctional government and poor economy. The explosion contributed to the collapse of the government in August 2020 despite measures to contain COVID-19 that included protocols for social distancing, reduced mobility, and border controls, as well as restrictions such as curfews on refugees.[5] Low oil and gas demand worldwide due to COVID-19 has delayed offshore oil and gas exploration, and Lebanon's economy continues to face high levels of debt and unemployment rates exacerbated by the pandemic. As a mostly service-oriented economy heavily dependent on tourism, COVID-19 has led to massive unemployment and a scarcity of foreign currency (which normally comes from tourism, foreign aid, and remittances).

The country does not have a solid industrial base and depends heavily on imports for food and other basic necessities such as medicine and fuel which are paid from foreign exchange that has now become scarce.

Over the next several years, COVID-19's impact combined with the fallout from the Ukraine and Gaza crises will make it more likely that worst-case scenarios will be more easily realized for those countries emerging from sustained humanitarian emergencies. The economies of most fragile states are not expected to recover until late 2024 (Bosquet 2022). Indirect impacts include lower demand for commodity exports and reduced mobility for aid programming in urban centres. For example, the Global Health Security Index score for South Sudan was 21.7 in 2019. This gives South Sudan an extremely low ranking of 180 out of 195 countries. Notably,

[5] See CIFP (2020a); see also Carment and Samy (2023a introduction).

South Sudan scored lowest within the category of having a sufficient and robust health system compared to the other categories that were analysed. Fifty-six per cent of people do not have access to primary health care services and over half of the health facilities in the country are not operational.[6]

There have been wide variations in COVID-19 cases and deaths that exist even within the group of countries considered as fragile. For example, COVID-19 deaths per million were 36 in the case of Afghanistan and 28.4 in the case of Pakistan, compared to 0.08 in Burundi and 2.85 in neighbouring Democratic Republic of the Congo as of 2020. Sudan, Afghanistan, West Bank and Gaza, Cameroon, Nigeria, and Pakistan were all experiencing sizeable outbreaks of COVID-19 as of 2020 (CIFP 2020b).

However, by 2023 estimates showed that deaths rates per 100,000 in fragile states were lower than on average than the more advanced economies. Indeed, for fragile countries, there is only a weak correlation between fragility, on the one hand, and cases or deaths, on the other. Many fragile states imposed restrictions and lockdowns and it would appear that the number of cases and deaths across countries reflect the unique circumstances that they each face (Stowell et al. 2022). For example, the very high number of cases in the West Bank and Gaza was the result of the blockade that it has been facing since 2007 (Moss and Majadle 2020). For others, it was a combination of various factors, which include the degree of connectivity with the rest of the world, the extent of testing, and the accuracy of properly reporting cases and deaths.

Yet, indirect and long-term impacts remain. For example, according to Decerf et al. (2024), the estimates of well-being include a loss of almost three weeks of life, an additional two and half weeks spent in poverty in 2020 and 2021, and the possibility of an additional month of life in poverty in the future due to school closures. In many fragile states, the pandemic made it clear that healthcare systems have a very limited capacity to provide adequate care for individuals in future outbreaks. Most fragile states have few medical personnel per capita, weak or non-existent infrastructure, long-term chronic underfunding, limited numbers of hospital beds, and limited ventilators.

The increase in war-related deaths since the pandemic must also be noted. In several trapped states, such as Afghanistan, Somalia, Sudan, Palestine, Yemen, and Syria, longstanding violent conflict has directly destroyed hospitals, caused medical personnel to flee the country, and generally further weakened healthcare capacity (often funded by, and dependent on, foreign aid) in these states. In many instances, fragile states lack the capacity to implement containment and contact-tracing measures. For example, Chad, was specifically noted as not having enough

[6] See CIFP (2020b).

testing kits and was also experiencing staff shortages after many of those conducting tests fell ill. Instead of testing, aggressive and economically damaging shutdown policies are one of the only recourses for some states seeking to limit the spread of COVID-19.

Ongoing healthcare challenges such as cholera, HIV, tuberculosis, malaria, and other diseases remain unmet. In Yemen, the largest modern cholera epidemic ever recorded was impacting the population concurrently with COVID-19. This led many to not seek treatment for cholera as the pandemic unfolded.

Another highly visible example of the disruptive impact of COVID-19 on other health challenges were the interruption and suspension of vaccination campaigns. Disruptions were caused by a number of factors, with one specific example being chronic staff shortages. The international personnel critical to many vaccination campaigns were forced to leave as shutdown policies and travel restrictions were implemented. For example, at least 30 measles vaccination campaigns had been cancelled or are at risk of being cancelled as of July 2020.

The UN's Framework for the Immediate Socio-Economic Response to the COVID-19 Crisis notes that the COVID-19 pandemic was far more than a health crisis: it increased poverty and inequalities at 'a global scale' (United Nations 2020). According to the World Bank, by 2030, an estimated 59% of the world's extreme poor will live in countries impacted by fragility and violence (World Bank 2024).

Another direct example of COVID-19's economic impact was mass job losses. In 2020, the International Labour Organization estimated that 1.6 billion workers in the informal economy—that is nearly half of the global workforce are in 'immediate danger of having their livelihoods destroyed' (Inman 2020) Given the relatively larger importance of informal economic sectors in fragile states, these job losses are likely to be felt even more strongly. Additionally, women often make up a greater proportion of the workforce in certain informal sectors and are more significantly impacted.

Other crucial economic impact areas include reduced economic activity damaging states' tax bases, remittance flows that were severely curtailed by job losses abroad, potential reductions in foreign aid in the future, and worsening food insecurity. Food insecurity is of particular concern in the context of COVID-19 as containment policies are likely to be less effective among the chronically hungry and the consequences of imposing such policies far more severe. Those who are food insecure and live in countries affected by prolonged conflict are one of the populations experiencing the greatest degree of socio-economic marginalization during this crisis.

The social impacts of COVID-19 have been troubling and widespread. Domestic violence is widely reported to have risen significantly globally during the pandemic, and it is believed that this trend has increased even more as the fallout of the Ukraine–Russia war takes hold (Onsongo 2021). In the most fragile education systems, the interruption of the school year appears to have had a disproportionately negative, and potentially long-term impact on the most vulnerable pupils. The most vulnerable students were impacted by conditions at home, such as lacking adequate internet or a safe workspace, which negatively impact their ability to continue learning remotely (The Economist 2022).

Whether longer-term political changes occur with COVID-19 as a primary cause of increasing fragility is unclear. It is clear that some armed groups have taken advantage of the uncertain environment created by the pandemic and as the case of Lebanon discussed earlier shows, COVID-19 may itself cause civil unrest as socio-economic conditions in fragile states deteriorate further. For example, militant groups such as Al-Shabaab have attempted to use the pandemic to their benefit. Al-Shabaab based some propaganda around COVID-19, claiming that it was spread 'by the crusader forces who have invaded the country and the disbelieving countries that support them' (BBC News 2020).

In contrast, there is also evidence that leaders of fragile states have used the pandemic to exert increasing control over their political and social environment. According to Hilhorst and Mena: the leaders of fragile states that experienced social conflict at the advent of the pandemic, instrumentalized COVID 19 to strengthen their control and agendas. 'Responsibility was assumed for lockdowns, but this was not accompanied by care to mitigate their adverse effects' (Hilhorst and Mena 2021).

3.5 The Wars in Ukraine and Palestine

Sanctions on Russia have had a deleterious ripple effect on all parts of the post-Soviet region wherever diaspora-sending nations benefit from a robust oil export-driven Russian economy (Belo and Rodriguez 2023). It is well known that sanctions impact many ordinary people in post-Soviet republics that rely on Russia's economic wellbeing. With economic decline, Central Asian republics such as Uzbekistan, Kyrgyzstan, and Tajikistan, who depend on remittances from Russia, have experienced a deterioration in their gross domestic product since 2014. More recently there were some three million guest workers in Russia in 2021 from these Central Asian republics. Their remittances constituted close to 30% of the gross domestic product of Tajikistan, 28% for the Kyrgyz Republic, and almost 12% for Uzbekistan (Ratha et al. 2024).

After sanctions were imposed on Russia in 2022, the Ruble's fall against the dollar by 30% had an immediate effect on the value of these remittances being sent by workers to their home nations. The impact was most directly felt by the states of Central Asia, generating additional political instability in an already fragile part of the world. Remittances to Europe and Central Asia fell by 10% to US$71 billion in

2023. The decline was driven by reduced transfers from Russia to the Central Asian countries, exacerbated by a sharp (39%) depreciation of the Russian Ruble against the US dollar. Additionally, the ongoing war contributed to weaker-than-expected remittances to Ukraine and Russia. Remittance flows to Europe and Central Asia are projected to decline by 1.9% in 2024. Sending US$200 to the region (excluding Russia) cost on average 6.7% (up from 6.4% the previous year), the second-highest cost among developing-country regions (Ratha et al. 2024).

This overall decline in remittance wealth was partially offset by a large number of Russians entering these countries to escape the draft. However, without gainful employment, these Russians place a burden on local economies (Ratha et al. 2024).

The war has also inevitably raised the price of agricultural products and energy globally. For example, Russia is the world's third-largest wheat producer and is among the top three oil producers in the world. Ukraine is also a major producer of grains and cereals, and a major exporter of products such as sunflower oil, maize, and wheat. Comprehensive sanctions have disrupted Moscow's ability to export essential commodities such as wheat, oil, gas, and aluminium, as well. Prices of wheat and corn have risen to their highest levels in over a decade (Carment and Belo 2021b).

Western companies and Russian energy producers and the removal of major Russian institutions from the SWIFT payment system have raised the prospects of fuel shortages in both the short and long run. Other commodity exporters not directly affected by the conflict but eager to reap windfalls that will be generated by constrained supply are looking to renegotiate their contracts, withholding exports as a bargaining chip. Collectively, these decisions have placed an even greater constraint on the world's food and energy supply. Ultimately, developing and politically fragile states that are generally net food importers are among those most affected (Carment and Belo 2021a).

Since the end of the Cold War, the conventional wisdom driving foreign policies including the West's aid agenda was that strong economic relations and interdependence align strongly with peace (Belo and Rodriguez 2023). The West's response to Russia's invasion of Ukraine, so far, shows that, as the cost of engagement in conventional military operations increases, the economic domain becomes increasingly important for the exercise of power and overall interaction between states (Konwer 2023). The preference for economic warfare on a global scale challenges prevailing beliefs about why states go to war and how they fight wars. But as we see in the current crisis, economic actions, just short of formal war declarations, can also have broad and debilitating global effects far beyond those that are directly involved (Carment and Belo 2021a).

Beyond the impact on Central Asian states the global impact of the Russia–Ukraine war has been two-fold. First, the war's global impact comes from the fact that most nations do not support American sanctions (Narine 2022, 2023). Nor do they necessarily agree with the position the West has taken on confronting Russia with economic and proxy warfare. Mitigating the negative impacts that escalatory actions are having on the global economy and geopolitical stability now appear as important as defeating Russia (Harris-Brandts et al. 2024). The net result has been a skewing of aid towards Ukraine and a decline in aid towards other fragile states. According to the OECD, by 2022 significant increases in the amount of DAC ODA allocated to Ukraine were delivered to the detriment of other fragile states experiencing crisis (OECD-INCAF 2022), including Syria, Yemen, and Sudan, all of which have insufficient aid levels given their pressing needs.

Instead of pursuing a diplomatic path, belligerent interactions have shifted the Russia–Ukraine war from one that was subregional to one that is continental and now global. Indeed, the United States has framed this conflict as one in which all nations must choose a side, imposing secondary sanctions on countries that do not support US policy on Russia (Carment and Belo 2022). Washington and its Western allies are clearly committed to supporting Kyiv militarily. But evidence on protracted conflict shows that such skewed support that is focused on a weak country's security and military domains generates mostly negative outcomes. Thus, a second outcome of the war is the near collapse of the Washington Consensus which helped shaped trade and aid policies for more than 20 years. In its place is rising protectionism, more selective aid programmes that favour countries that support the Western security agenda, and the rise of alternative multilateral fora such as the Belt and Road Initiative and, BRICS (Carment et al. 2022).

More recently, the war between Israel and Hamas that has devastated Gaza and to a lesser extent the West Bank is generating major implications and ramifications for foreign aid to fragile states (Fantappiè and Tocci, 2023). According to most experts, Israel's attacks on Gaza, violate laws of war and constitute 'crimes against humanity'. South Africa has taken Israel to the International Court of Justice (ICJ), accusing it of committing or planning to commit 'genocide' against the Palestinians of Gaza (Mokhiber 2023; Echols 2024).

Some argue that Western silence on or, in the case of the United States, active complicity in, the war on Gaza has done enormous damage to the West's collective standing as aid providers (Narine 2023, Burchill 2024). Typically, aid policy should be front and centre in any effort to address an ongoing humanitarian crisis, let alone one involving 'war crimes' and forced displacement. Yet what we have witnessed thus far is the complete helplessness of aid programmes to meet the minimal needs of the people of Gaza. At stake is the integrity of the 'rules-based international order' amid the failure to prevent and mitigate a massive humanitarian disaster. This situation reflects a decline of Western influence overall and the ineffectiveness of aid specifically in situations where it is most needed (Marcetic 2023).

The fate and future of global contributions to collective security instruments, including the ICJ, the International Criminal Court, and the Responsibility to Protect agendas, are in doubt. More importantly, the war on Gaza forces researchers to rethink their understanding of fragility as a dynamic driven by long-standing, unresolved and deep-rooted civilizational animosities (Swan 2023). Given Israel's uncertain future as a viable political entity faced with the potential for ongoing regional wars and a weak economy heavily dependent on the United States, the idea of fragility in an era of competitive multilateralism must be recast.

Both the Ukraine–Russia war and the war on Gaza also show the importance of and the need for consensus on how to deal with thorny partition issues when fragile states are essentially the battleground for proxy geopolitical warfare (Carment et al. 2019; Carment and Belo 2022). In both instances there is only a limited possibility for unbiased international oversight of these conflicts in order to achieve a lasting settlement. Recent history has shown that by separating belligerent groups, partition can provide security and lead to a decrease in the need for interaction among groups that do not get along. But this is only possible when major powers remain aloof from these conflicts and are not engaged in competitive multilateralism and proxy war (Carment and Belo 2020, 2022).

When domestic and international violence is considered, a partition's consequences largely depend on its timing. It must be done quickly rather than dragged out and it must avoid strengthening militias and radicalized groups on both sides. Partition of a state is not the only solution to protracted war, but it is often preferable to intense ongoing fighting (Bell 2024). Unfortunately, for settlements in Ukraine and Palestine to succeed, it is not enough for the opposing sides to resolve the underlying issues. They must also meet the much more difficult challenge of mutually designing (and enforcing) credible institutionalized security guarantees (Carment and Belo 2022). Until an effort is made to confront this fundamental impasse in both wars, a coherent strategy to 'kick-start' multilateral renewal to address other shared global problems such as rising inequality, climate change, and pandemics will remain elusive.

References

Affricot, B. (2021). 'COVID-19 Derailed Humanitarian Aid. What Will it Take to Get it Back on Track?'. https://iaffairscanada.com/covid-19-derailed-humanitarian-aid-what-will-it-take-to-get-it-back-on-track/.

Andrews, M., L. Pritchett, and M. Woolcock (2017). *Building State Capability Evidence, Analysis, Action*. Oxford: Oxford University Press.

Asongu, S. A., and O. Kodila-Tedika (2013). 'State Fragility, Rent Seeking and Lobbying: Evidence from African Data'. AGDI Working Paper WP/13/019. Yaoundé: African Governance and Development Institute.

Baliamoune-Lutz, M. N., and M. McGillivray (2008). 'State Fragility: Concept and Measurement'. Research Paper 2008/44. Helsinki: UNU-WIDER.

Bandstein, S. (2007). 'What Determines the Choice of Aid Modalities?—A Framework for Assessing Incentive Structures?' Report from EBA's predecessors Organisation and Management of Aid Swedish Agency for Development Evaluation (SADEV),

No. 4. https://eba.se/en/historiska-rapporter/report-20074-what-determines-the-choice-of-aid-modalities-a-framework-for-assessing-incentive-structures/.

BBC News (2020). 'Coronavirus: Fighting al-Shabab propaganda in Somalia'. BBC News online, 2 April. Available at: https://www.bbc.com/news/world-africa-52103799 (accessed 18 January 2023).

Bell, J. (2024). 'Policy Talks Podcast Episode 71: A Path to Peace?: Analyzing the State of the Israel–Palestine Conflict and a Way Forward'. https://iaffairscanada.com/policy-talks-podcast-episode-71-a-path-to-peace-analyzing-the-state-of-the-israel-palestine-conflict-and-a-way-forward/.

Belo, D., and F. Rodríguez (2023). 'The Conflict in Ukraine and Its Global Implications'. *Canadian Foreign Policy Journal*, 29(3): 235–48. https://doi.org/10.1080/11926422.2023.2258227.

Bergamaschi, I. (2014). 'The Fall of a Donor Darling: The Role of Aid in Mali's Crisis'. *The Journal of Modern African Studies*, 52(3): 347–78. https://doi.org/10.1017/S0022278X14000251.

Bermeo, N. (2016). 'On Democratic Backsliding'. *Journal of Democracy*, 27(1): 5–19. https://doi.org/10.1353/jod.2016.0012.

Bosquet, F. (2022). 'Fragile and Conflict-Affected Economies Are Falling Further Behind'. IMF Chart of the Week. https://www.imf.org/en/Blogs/Articles/2022/01/21/fragile-and-conflict-affected-economies-are-falling-further-behind.

Bratton, M. (2007). 'Institutionalizing Democracy in Africa: Formal or Informal?'. *Journal of Democracy*, 18(3): 96–110.

Bulir, A., and A. J. Hamann (2008). 'Volatility of Development Aid: From the Frying Pan into the Fire?'. *World Development*, 36(10): 2048–66. https://doi.org/10.1016/j.worlddev.2007.02.019.

Burchill, S. (2024). 'America: A Rogue State in the Twilight of Imperial Age'. https://iaffairscanada.com/america-a-rogue-state-in-the-twilight-of-imperial-age/.

Burnside, C., and D. Dollar (2000). 'Aid, Policies, and Growth'. *American Economic Review*, 90(4): 847–68. https://doi.org/10.1257/aer.90.4.847.

Carment, D., and D. Belo (2020). 'Unilateralism and Competitive Multilateralism in Gray-zone Conflict: A Comparison of Russia and the United States'. *Wild Blue Yonder* https://www.airuniversity.af.edu/Wild-Blue-Yonder/Articles/Article-Display/Article/2292990/unilateralism-and-competitive-multilateralism-in-gray-zone-conflict-a-compariso/ (accessed 20 June 2024).

Carment, D., and D. Belo (2021a) 'The Ukraine Crisis: Is Economic Warfare the Road to Ruin?'. Institute for Peace & Diplomacy Working Paper. Available at: https://peacediplomacy.org/2022/03/14/the-ukraine-crisis-is-economic-warfare-the-road-to-ruin/ (accessed 15 December 2022).

Carment, D., and D. Belo (2021b). 'Turning the Page on Afghanistan in a Post 9-11 World'. Institute for Peace & Diplomacy Working Paper. Available at: https://peacediplomacy.org/2021/09/13/turning-the-page-on-afghanistan-in-a-post-9-11-world/ (accessed 15 December 2022).

Carment D., and D. Belo (2022). 'The Ukraine Crisis—More War or Shared Responsibility?'. Iaffairs Canada. Available at: https://iaffairscanada.com/2022/the-ukraine-crisis-more-war-or-shared-responsibility/ (accessed 18 January 2023).

Carment, D., and Y. Samy (2019a). *Exiting the Fragility Trap: Rethinking our Approach to the World's Most Fragile States*. Athens: Ohio University Press. https://doi.org/10.2307/j.ctv224tvcv.

Carment, D., and Y. Samy (2019b). 'Aid Targeting in Fragile and Conflict Affected States and Implications for Aid Effectiveness'. *Politics and Governance*, 7(2): 93–102. https://doi.org/10.17645/pag.v7i2.1852.

Carment, D., and Y. Samy (2023a). *Handbook of Fragile States*. Cheltenham, UK: Edward Elgar Publishing.

Carmen, D., and Y. Samy (2023b) 'Exiting the Fragility Trap: SDG 16 Is the Key but Attaining It Remains Elusive'. In T. Donais, A. D. Edgar, and K. Van Houten, editors, *Sustainable Development Goal 16 and the Global Governance of Violence: Critical Reflections on the Uncertain Future of Peace* (1st ed.). Routledge: 163–82. https://doi.org/10.4324/9781003291121.

Carment, D., S. El-achkar, S. Prest, and Y. Samy (2006). The 2006 Country Indicators for Foreign Policy: Opportunities and Challenges for Canada. *Canadian Foreign Policy Journal*, 13(1), 1–35. https://doi.org/10.1080/11926422.2006.9673417.

Carment, D., M. Haichin, and Y. Samy (2019). 'Failed and Fragile States: The Unfinished Agenda'. In R. Mansbach and J. McCormick, editors, *Foreign Policy Issues for America: The Trump Years*. London: Routledge: 175–88. https://doi.org/10.4324/9781351186872-13

Carment, D., L. Macdonald, and J. Paltiel (2022). *Canada and Great Power Competition: Canada among Nations 2021* (New York: Palgrave). https://link.springer.com/book/10.1007/978-3-031-04368-0.

Carment, D., K. Muñoz, and Y. Samy (2020). *Fragile and Conflict-Affected States in the Age of COVID 19: A 2020 Country Indicators for Foreign Policy Report*. Ottawa: Norman Paterson School of International Affairs, Carleton University.

Carment, D., S. Prest, and Y. Samy (2009). *Security, Development and the Fragile State: Bridging the Gap between Theory and Policy*. London: Routledge. https://doi.org/10.4324/9780203873977.

Carment, D., P. Tikuisis, R. Calleja, and M. Haichin (2019). 'Backsliding and Reversal: The J Curve Revisited'. *Democracy and Security*, 15(1): 1–24. https://doi.org/10.1080/17419166.2018.1517334.

Chauvet, L., and P. Collier (2008). 'What are the Preconditions for Turnarounds in Failing States?'. *Conflict Management and Peace Science*, 25(4): 335–48. https://doi.org/10.1080/07388940802397475

CIFP (Country Indicators for Foreign Policy) (2020a). 'Fragile States and COVID19—Lebanon Project'. Available at: https://carleton.ca/cifp/2020/fragile-states-and-covid19-lebanon-project/ (accessed 15 December 2022).

CIFP (Country Indicators for Foreign Policy) (2020b). 'Fragile States and COVID19—South Sudan Project'. Available at: https://carleton.ca/cifp/2020/fragile-states-and-covid19-south-sudan-project/ (accessed 15 December 2022).

Collier, P., and A. Hoeffler (2004). 'Aid, Policy and Growth in Post-Conflict Societies'. *European Economic Review* 48(5): 1125–45. https://doi.org/10.1016/j.euroecorev.2003.11.005.

Cotton, J., M. Hammel, and L. Noofoory (2023). *Haiti Fragility Brief*. https://carleton.ca/cifp/wp-content/uploads/Haiti-Fragility-Brief-2023.pdf.

Davies, S., T. Pettersson, and M. Oberg (2022). 'Organized Violence 1989–2021 and Drone Warfare'. *Journal of Peace Research*, 59(4). https://doi.org/10.1177/00223433221108.

Decerf, Benoit Marie A, Jed Friedman, Arthur Galego Mendes, Steven Michael Pennings, Nishant Yonzan. *Lives, Livelihoods, and Learning : A Global Perspective on the Well-Being Impacts of the COVID-19 Pandemic (English)*. Policy Research working paper; no. WPS 10728; COVID-19 (Coronavirus); RRR; PROSPERITY: Washington, D.C.: World Bank Group. http://documents.worldbank.org/curated/en/099537503202413127/IDU1f944e1ca18e2814ce0198221694a75dd5654

Echols, C. (2024). 'Bombs, Guns, Treasure: What Israel Wants, the US Gives'. https://iaffairscanada.com/bombs-guns-treasure-what-israel-wants-the-us-gives/.

Fantappiè, M., and N. Tocci (2023). 'Europe is Stuck over the Israel-Hamas War' https://iaffairscanada.com/europe-is-stuck-over-the-israel-hamas-war/.

Fatton, R. (1995). 'Africa in the Age of Democratization: The Civic Limitations of Civil Society'. *African Studies Review*, 38(2): 67–99. https://doi.org/10.2307/525318.

Foresight Africa (2019). 'Fixing Fragility: The Role of the Private Sector and Local Institutions'. In B. S. Coulibaly (ed.), *Foresight Africa: Top Priorities for the Continent in 2019*. Washington, DC: Brookings: 59–75.

Gertz, G., and H. Kharas (2018). 'Leave No Country Behind: Ending Poverty in The Toughest Places'. Global Economy and Development Working Paper 110. Washington, DC: Brookings.

Han, L., and M. Koenig-Archibugi (2015). 'Aid Fragmentation or Aid Pluralism? The Effect of Multiple Donors on Child Survival in Developing Countries, 1990–2010'. *World Development*, 76: 334–58. https://doi.org/10.1016/j.worlddev.2015.07.014.

Harris-Brandts, S., M. Nikolko, J. Sahadeo, and D. Sichinava (2024). 'Local Impacts, Global Consequences: Assessing the Mass Displacement and Migration Tied to Russia's Invasion of Ukraine'. *Canadian Foreign Policy Journal*, 30(1), 1–10. https://doi.org/10.1080/11926422.2024.2302476.

Hearn, S. (2016). *Independent Review of the New Deal for Engagement in Fragile States*. New York: Center on International Cooperation.

Heinzel, M., and Reinsberg, B. (2024). 'Trust Funds and the Sub-national Effectiveness of Development Aid: Evidence from the World Bank'. World Development, 179. https://doi.org/10.1016/j.worlddev.2024.106609.

Hilhorst, D., and Mena, R. (2021). 'When Covid-19 Meets Conflict: Politics of the Pandemic Response in Fragile and Conflict-Affected States'. *Disasters*, 45(Suppl 1): S174–S194. https://www.ncbi.nlm.nih.gov/pmc/articles/PMC8653116/.

Inman, P. (2020). 'Half of World's Workers "at Immediate Risk of Losing Livelihood Due to Coronavirus"'. *The Guardian*, 29 April 29. Available at: https://www.theguardian.com/world/2020/apr/29/half-of-worlds-workers-at-immediate-risk-of-losing-livelihood-due-to-coronavirus (accessed 18 January 2023).

Jackson, R., and C. Rosberg (1982). *Personal Rule in Black Africa*. Berkeley, CA: UC Press. https://doi.org/10.1525/9780520313071.

Kiernan, A., L. Turroques, and Y. Ahmad (2024). 'Official Development Assistance Trends in Times of Crisis', in Development Co-operation Profiles. Paris: OECD Publishing https://doi.org/10.1787/479b1a72-en.

Kimura, H., Y. Mori, and Y. Sawaa (2012). 'Aid Proliferation and Economic Growth: A Cross-Country Analysis'. *World Development*, 40(1): 1–10. https://doi.org/10.1016/j.worlddev.2011.05.010.

Konwer, S. (2023). 'The Ukraine Crisis and India: Quandaries and Implications'. *Canadian Foreign Policy Journal*, 29(3), 317–31. https://doi.org/10.1080/11926422.2023.2184842.

Levi, M., A. Sacks, and A. Tyler (2009). 'Conceptualizing Legitimacy, Measuring Legitimating Beliefs'. *American Behavioral Scientist*, 53(3): 354–75. https://doi.org/10.1177/0002764209338797.

Marcetic, B. (2023). 'US Will Take Massive Hit in Global Standing over Israel'. https://iaffairscanada.com/us-will-take-massive-hit-in-global-standing-over-israel/

Marshall, M., and B. R. Cole (2014). *Global Report 2014: Conflict, Governance, and State Fragility*. Vienna, VA: Center for Systemic Peace.

McGillivray, M. (2006). 'Aid Allocation and Fragile States'. WIDER Working Paper 2006/01. Helsinki: UNU-WIDER.

McGillivray, M., and S. Feeny (2008). 'Aid and Growth in Fragile States'. WIDER Working Paper 2008/03. Helsinki: UNU-WIDER.

Milante, G., and J. Lilja (2022). 'Chronic Crisis Financing? Fifty Years of Humanitarian Aid and Future Prospects'. SIPRI Insights on Peace and Security 2022/5. Stockholm: Stockholm International Peace Research Institute. https://doi.org/10.55163/AGAR2561.

Mokhiber, C. (2023). 'Resignation Letter from Craig Mokhiber, Director of the New York Office of the UN High Commissioner for Human Rights—28/102023'. https://iaffairscanada.com/resignation-letter-from-craig-mokhiber-director-of-the-new-york-office-of-the-un-high-commissioner-for-human-rights-28-10-2023/.

Moss, D., and G. Majadle (2020). 'Battling COVID 19 in the Occupied Palestinian Territory'. *The Lancet*, 8(9): E1127–E1128. https://doi.org/10.1016/S2214-109X(20)30237-0.

Moss, T., G. Pettersson Gelander, and N. van de Walle (2006). 'An Aid-Institutions Paradox: A Review Essay on Aid Dependency and State Building in sub-Saharan Africa'. CGD Working Paper 74. Washington, DC: Center for Global Development. https://doi.org/10.2139/ssrn.860826.

Narine, S. (2022). 'The War in Ukraine Started with Iraq'. https://iaffairscanada.com/the-war-in-ukraine-started-with-iraq/.

Narine, S. (2023). 'The Problem of a 'Rules-Based International Order': The Significance of the Non-Western World's Restrained Response to the Russia–Ukraine war'. *Canadian Foreign Policy Journal*, 29 (3), 301–16. https://doi.org/10.1080/11926422.2023.2193420.

North, D., J. J. Wallis, S. B. Webb, and B. R. Weingast (2007). 'Limited Access Orders in the Developing World: A New Approach to the Problems of Development'. World Bank Policy Research Working Paper 4359. Washington, DC: World Bank Group. https://doi.org/10.1596/1813-9450-4359.

ODI (2018). *SDG Progress: Fragility, Crisis and Leaving No One Behind*. London: Overseas Development Institute.

OECD (2020). *States of Fragility 2020*. Paris: OECD Publishing. https://doi.org/10.1787/ba7c22e7-en.

OECD-INCAF (2022). 'INCAF Facts and Figures Series: ODA Final Data and Trends for 2022 in Relation to Fragile and Conflict-Related Contexts'. https://one.oecd.org/document/DCD/DAC/INCAF(2024)1/en/pdf

Onsongo, E. (2021). 'The Gendered Impacts of COVID-19 on Economic Development in Sub-Saharan Africa'. https://iaffairscanada.com/covid-19-derailed-humanitarian-aid-what-will-it-take-to-get-it-back-on-track/.

Ottaway, M. (2003). *Democracy Challenged: The Rise of Semi-Authoritarianism*. Washington, DC: Carnegie Endowment for International Peace.

Pritchett, L., M. Woolcock, and M. Andrews (2010). 'Capability Traps? The Mechanisms of Persistent Implementation Failure'. CGD Working Paper 234. Washington, DC: Center for Global Development.

Pritchett, L., M. Woolcock, M., and M. Andrews (2013). 'Looking Like a State: Techniques of Persistent Failure in State Capability for Implementation'. *The Journal of Development Studies*, 49(1): 1–18. https://doi.org/10.1080/00220388.2012.709614.

Ratha, D., V. Chandra, E. Kim, S. Plaza, and A. Mahmood (2024). 'Remittances Slowed in 2023, Expected to Grow Faster in 2024'. World Bank, KNOMAD, Washington, DC. https://www.knomad.org/sites/default/files/publication-doc/migration-and-development-brief_40.pdf.

Samy, Y., and M. Aksli (2015). 'An Examination of Bilateral Donor Performance and Progress under the Paris Declaration on Aid Effectiveness'. *Canadian Journal of Development Studies* 36(4): 516–35. https://doi.org/10.1080/02255189.2015.1083413.

Stewart, F., and G. Brown (2009). 'Fragile States'. CRISE Working Paper 51. Oxford: CRISE.

Stowell, N., J. Immormino, A. Ortiz Salazar, Y. Zeng, and M. Arbetman-Rabinowitz (2022). 'Politics, Policy, and Pandemic Control: A Global Perspective'. *Canadian Foreign Policy Journal*, 28(1), 1–21. https://doi.org/10.1080/11926422.2021.2007966.

Sumner, A., C. Hoy, and E. Ortiz-Juarez (2020). 'Estimates of the Impact of COVID-19 on Global Poverty'. WIDER Working Paper 2020/43. Helsinki: UNU-WIDER. https://doi.org/10.35188/UNU-WIDER/2020/800-9.

Swan, E. (2023). 'An Interview with Emma Swan: Canada's Past, Present, and Future in the Middle East'. https://iaffairscanada.com/an-interview-with-emma-swan-canadas-past-present-and-future-in-the-middle-east-2/.

The Economist (2022). 'Governments Are Ignoring the Pandemic's Disastrous Effect on Education'. https://www.economist.com/leaders/2022/07/07/governments-are-ignoring-the-pandemics-disastrous-effect-on-education.

The Intercept (2022). 'U.S.-Trained Officers Have Led Numerous Coups in Africa'. The Intercept Podcast, 9 March. Available at: https://theintercept.com/2022/03/09/intercepted-podcast-africa-coup/ (accessed 15 December 2022).

Tikuisis, P., and D. Carment (2017). 'Categorization of States Beyond Strong and Weak'. *Stability: International Journal of Stability and Development.* 6(1). https://stabilityjournal.org/articles/10.5334/sta.483.

UCDP (2024). Uppsala Conflict Data Program, Department of Peace and Conflict Research, https://ucdp.uu.se/.

United Nations (2020). *A UN Framework for the Immediate Socio-economic Response to COVID-19.* Available at: https://unsdg.un.org/sites/default/files/2020-04/UN-framework-for-the-immediate-socio-economic-response-to-COVID-19.pdf (accessed 15 December 2022).

World Bank (2024). 'Pursuing Development Goals amid Fragility, Conflict, and Violence'. World Bank Results Brief. https://www.worldbank.org/en/results/2024/01/16/pursuing-development-goals-amid-fragility-conflict-and-violence?

Ziaja, S., J. Grävingholt, and M. Kreibaum (2019). 'Constellations of Fragility: An Empirical Typology of States'. *Studies in Comparative International Development*, 54(2): 299–321. https://doi.org/10.1007/s12116-019-09284-3.

4
Can Aid Reduce Violence?

Anke Hoeffler

4.1 Introduction

Development economists have long argued that armed conflict is a major impediment to development (World Bank 2011).[1] Therefore, aid is being directed towards reducing armed conflict. This chapter examines the question of how much aid is spent to reduce armed conflicts and whether this aid is effective in preventing and reducing armed conflicts. In addition to armed conflict, aid recipients also experience high rates of interpersonal violence, causing great human and economic costs (Fearon and Hoeffler 2018). However, there is little evidence to suggest that this is considered a major development problem. This chapter aims to broaden the debate on violence and development by including self-harm. It explores whether there is any evidence to suggest that aid could be effective in tackling suicide and self-harm. The chapter is structured as follows. Section 4.2 presents definitions for the key terms: aid and violence. We categorize violence into self-directed, interpersonal, and collective violence and present some global statistics. Section 4.3 addresses the question whether aid can reduce violence and summarizes the evidence. In Section 4.4 we examine the amount of aid spent on violence prevention. Based on insights from the AidData3 database, our findings suggest that relatively little aid is spent on addressing the issue of interpersonal violence, which is a highly prevalent issue in many aid-recipient countries. Additionally, almost no aid is spent on suicide prevention and mental health. The conclusions are presented in Section 4.5, including a reflection of what our findings mean for the principles of ownership and results as set out in the Busan Partnership for Effective Development Co-operation.

[1] This chapter is based on previous work with James Fearon and Patricia Justino, and I would like to thank them for their generous support. Rachel Gisselquist, Andrea Vaccaro, and participants at the International Research Conference on the Effectiveness of Development Cooperation (Brussels, 17–18 November 2022) offered helpful comments and suggestions. Flora Risse, Dušan Ristic and Maximillian Hecht provided excellent research assistance.

Anke Hoeffler, *Can Aid Reduce Violence?*. In: *Fragile Aid*. Edited by: Rachel M. Gisselquist et al., Oxford University Press. © UNU-WIDER (2025). DOI: 10.1093/oso/9780198960287.003.0004

4.2 Definitions and Data

Before we discuss the violence-reducing effect of aid, we provide definitions and some descriptive data.

4.2.1 Aid

The term *aid* is commonly used, but development agencies refer to official development assistance (ODA), and we use them interchangeably. The main objective of ODA is economic development and welfare, and military aid and anti-terrorism activities are explicitly excluded from development aid. ODA includes the provision of technical assistance, grants, and 'soft' loans, that is, loans with a below-market rate of interest. In order to qualify as ODA, the concessional or the grant element has to make up a minimum percentage of the flows (for more detail see OECD 2018). In recent years, total net annual ODA amounted to US$187 billion, of which 71% was bilateral ODA (averages for the years 2019–22). The top bilateral donors are the United States, followed by Germany, Japan, France, and the United Kingdom; their contributions make up 45% of total ODA. The European Union is the largest multilateral donor, followed by the International Development Association (IDA), which is the part of the World Bank that assists the poorest countries. Together, these two donors account for 20% of total ODA.

4.2.2 Violence

The field of public health has long highlighted the importance of violence as a health problem (WHO 1996, 2002). The World Health Organization (WHO) defines violence as 'the intentional use of physical force or power, threatened or actual, against oneself, another person, or against a group or community that either results in or has a high likelihood of resulting in injury, death, psychological harm, maldevelopment or deprivation' (WHO 1996). This is a relatively broad definition of violence, including suicide, psychological harm, threats of violence as well as actual violence, and acts that result in economic deprivation. The WHO produced a number of reports focusing on specific forms of violence, such as against women (WHO 2021), children (WHO 2020b), female genital mutilation/cutting (FGM/C) (WHO 2019), and suicide (WHO 2018). These reports present prevalence estimates and recommendations as to how to prevent, reduce, and treat violence. However, there are neither globally comparable data on violent threats nor on the consequences of violence such as psychological harm, maldevelopment, or deprivation. We agree that these are important harms but want to compare the prevalence of violence across countries and therefore rely on data on the *actual use of physical force.*

The WHO distinguishes between self-directed, interpersonal, and collective violence. The full definitions are set out in WHO (2002: 6, 185–9). The category 'self-directed violence' consists of *suicide, suicidal behaviour* (suicidal thoughts and attempted suicide), and *self-abuse* (acts of self-mutilation without conscious suicidal intention). 'Interpersonal violence' is defined as 'violence inflicted by an individual or a small group of individuals' in contrast to 'collective violence' defined as 'violence inflicted by larger groups such as states, organised political groups, militia groups and terrorist organisations ... committed to advance a particular social agenda'. While these definitions are stated in clear language, it is challenging to provide reliable estimates. We just highlight some of the numerous challenges. First, it can be difficult to distinguish between small groups of individuals, such as gangs or other criminal organizations, and organized groups with political aims (Lessing 2017, 2021). Second, WHO data are primarily based on national health statistics (vital registration data), with the addition of criminal justice data. However, many countries do not provide either data source. This is a particular problem for sub-Saharan Africa, where 44 countries provide no national data. For these countries, the data are estimated (UNODC 2019). Third, suicides are illegal in many jurisdictions, and mental health problems are still stigmatized in many societies, many suicides are then recorded as accidental deaths. On the other hand, weaknesses in the criminal justice system enable the misclassification of homicides as suicides, thus underreporting interpersonal violence and overreporting self-directed violence (see Sanghavi et al. 2009; Prinsloo et al. 2017; Osafo et al. 2020).

Since fatality data are generally regarded as more reliable than physical and sexual assault data, we focus on the WHO's deaths by cause from their global health estimates. This is also suggestive of non-fatal violence since fatal and non-fatal violence are highly correlated. WHO (2020a) data show global prevalence rates for deaths due to self-directed violence are 9.1 per 100,000 population, compared to a rate of 6.2 for interpersonal violence and 0.9 for collective violence. In absolute annual numbers, more people kill themselves (over 700,000) compared to the sum of the two other forms of violence, collective and interpersonal violence (just under 550,000).

The prevalence of violence varies greatly across countries. Comparing the different income groups shows that suicide is more prevalent in high-income countries (13 per 100,000) and least prevalent in low-income countries (6.1 per 100,000). The other forms of violence are more prevalent in low-income countries. The prevalence rate of interpersonal violence is 8.6 per 100,000 in low-income countries, while it is only 2.4 in high-income countries. Collective violence is a much more pressing problem for low-income countries—the prevalence rate is 8.1 per 100,000 compared to 0.1 in high-income countries.

Given that the lower-middle income and upper-middle income country groups contain not only a large number of countries but also very populous ones (India, China, Indonesia, Pakistan, Brazil, and Bangladesh), it is not surprising that when we consider countries by World Bank income group, both sets of middle-income countries have large absolute numbers of fatalities due to violence (see Figure 4.1). In total, about 473,000 people die due to violence in upper-middle-income countries. Of these, very few die in collective violence (1.7% of total violent deaths) while interpersonal deaths make up 48.8% and suicides 49.5%. For lower-middle-income countries, the total number of violent deaths is slightly lower (435,000), but the percentages of the different forms of violence are similar (2% collective violence, 36.2% interpersonal violence, and 61.8% suicide). The situation is very different for low-income countries. This group of countries accounts for the vast majority of collective violence worldwide—about 74.6% of all global collective violence deaths. Considering all violence categories, a total of 152,000 people die violently in low-income countries, with similar percentages

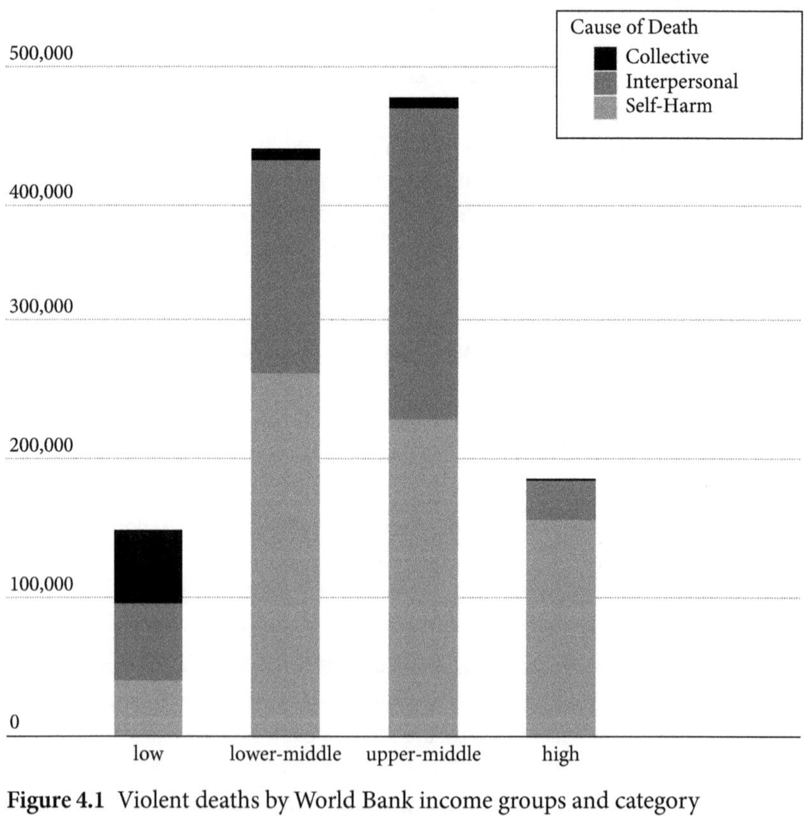

Figure 4.1 Violent deaths by World Bank income groups and category
Source: author's illustration using data from WHO (2020a).

due to the different forms of violence (35.5% collective violence, 37.7% interpersonal violence, and 26.8% suicide).

4.3 Aid and Violence Reduction: Evidence

Following the WHO categorization of the different types of violence, we provide an overview of the evidence for the impact of aid on self-directed, interpersonal, and collective violence.

4.3.1 Aid and Self-directed Violence

According to the WHO, depression is one of the leading causes of disability, and suicide is the fourth-leading cause of death among 15–29-year-olds.[2] While global public mental health is a growing area in medical and epidemiological research, it is difficult to detect the development community's engagement with this pressing health challenge. We could not identify a body of literature on the topic of aid and self-directed violence; therefore, we focus on the WHO efforts. To address the burden of mental health problems, the WHO works with partners in a number of state and efforts include the promotion of mental well-being and increased availability and access to mental health care. For this purpose, the WHO has developed scalable psychological programmes for use in settings affected by adversity, such as post-conflict societies, refugee camps, and those in the aftermath of natural disasters. The most prominent example is the family of interventions under 'Problem Management Plus (PM+)'; these programmes are short, can be delivered by trained peers, and are based on well-tested cognitive behavioural and problem-solving techniques. They do not target a specific mental disorder but are suited to treat the symptoms arising from anxiety, depression, and post-traumatic stress disorder. Emerging evidence suggests that group PM+ is feasible for the treatment of refugees (Acarturk et al. 2022), effective for treating earthquake-affected communities (Jordans et al. 2021), and in post-conflict settings (Hamdani et al. 2020). Many more PM+ research projects are pre-registered, and the evidence base will broaden over the coming years. It is likely that aid will finance much of this ongoing research effort, and it would therefore be of great interest to development economists whether these aid-financed projects can reduce (self-directed) violence.

[2] WHO factsheet on suicide, https://www.who.int/news-room/fact-sheets/detail/suicide (accessed 13 June 2023).

4.3.2 Aid and Interpersonal Violence

Interpersonal violence, which includes homicide and assault, is highly prevalent in low- and middle-income countries, and while men make up the majority of the homicide victims, much of the non-fatal violence is directed at women and children (Fearon and Hoeffler 2018). While violence reduction is highlighted as an important policy goal by international agencies (e.g., UNODC 2005, 2014; WHO 2014; Geneva Declaration, 2015; UNICEF 2017), there does not seem to be specific literature on the impact of aid on interpersonal violence. We therefore focus on violence reduction interventions that are (or could be) financed through aid with the aim to reduce (a) homicide and assault, (b) violence against women, and (c) violence against children.

Reducing Homicide and Assault through Law Enforcement

There are a number of studies using natural and policy experiments to identify a causal link between an increase in law enforcement officers and the reduction in crime (Di Tella and Schargrodsky 2004; Klick and Tabarrok 2005; Draca et al. 2011; Chalfin and McCrary 2017). Table 4.1 compares law enforcement across countries. Low and lower-middle-income countries have a much lower average number of armed force personnel, police officers, and judges per 100,000 population. The comparison across the income spectrum shows that in high-income countries there are on average 694 armed force personnel per 100,000 population compared to only 523 in low-income countries. For police forces, there are 421 police officers for 100,000 population in high-income countries while there are only 81 in low-income countries. Thus, low-income countries maintain relatively large armies in comparison to their police forces. Their armies are only 25% smaller than those in high-income countries, but their police forces are 81% smaller. Thus, low-income countries appear to undersupply security through

Table 4.1 Security and justice personnel by income group

Income category	Armed forces	Police	Judges
Low income	523	81	3
Lower-middle income	457	225	8
Upper-middle income	644	424	13
High income	694	421	20

Note: armed forces, police, and judges per 100,000 population. Income category according to the World Bank classification.
Source: author's compilation based on data from World Development Indicators (WDI) for armed forces (2000–18) and UNODC for police and judges (2003–18).

police in the international comparison. However, upper-middle income and high-income countries look very similar with respect to the armed forces and police, although high-income countries have a considerably higher number of judges (20 per 100,000) than any other region.

Given the high prevalence of interpersonal violence and the relatively low number of law enforcement officers, increasing police numbers appears an important instrument in reducing homicide and assault in LMICs. However, police forces have to be well trained and resourced to be effective. In many countries, this is currently not the case. Take the example of India, with a relatively small police force (135 police officers per 100,000 population). Officers work long shifts, and the vast majority (about 85%) have received no specific training in criminal investigation or crime-fighting skills (Gupte 2015).

Another important aspect in improving policing is to increase trust in the police. In many societies the police are not regarded as the solution but part of the problem. Citizens perceive them as incompetent, corrupt, and brutal. According to representative surveys, almost one-quarter of all African respondents trusted their police 'not at all', and on average 17.5% in each country said that 'all' police were corrupt (Afrobarometer 2020). The numbers for Latin America are comparable (Latinobarómetro 2020). Perceptions of incompetence, corruption, and abuse of power prevent victims from coming forward, making it more difficult to apprehend the perpetrators. The resulting impunity is a characteristic of many high violence societies (UNODC 2019, booklet 2).

Can trust in the police be improved? Evidence from the Indian state of Rajasthan suggests that police were more likely to register a crime after additional training of three to six days to improve scientific techniques and soft skills. The intervention also included random checks of police stations. Public satisfaction increased; however, a reduction in crime was not observed. It may be that these interventions have to be implemented at scale and that citizens need more time to experience the improvement in public service (Banerjee et al. 2021).

A number of countries apply a strategy of community policing where the focus is on the police developing relationships with community members in order to collaboratively identify and solve problems (Brogden and Nijhar 2013). Thus, community policing builds trust between the police and the community. There are recent efforts to adapt this strategy to settings outside high-income countries. The results so far are not encouraging. The new community police force in Kakuma refugee camp (Kenya) could not establish a trusting relationship with the refugee population (Brankamp 2020). A much larger trial of community policing in six low- and middle-income countries (Brazil, Columbia, Liberia, Uganda, Pakistan, and the Philippines) also failed to increase citizens' trust. The reasons for this outcome vary across the six different sites, but commitment, adherence to the programme, and lack of resources were identified as obstacles (Blair et al. 2021).

Historically, the police have been repressive in many low-income countries. Policing was used to protect the political elite rather than provide security to the public. Police forces also tend to be highly centralized, making it difficult for the population in the periphery to hold police officers accountable (Francis 2012). This suggests that police reforms can only have a major impact if they are embedded in a set of larger political reforms, aiming to strengthen democratic processes as well as providing a reform of the security services that are linked into reforms of the courts and penal system. The implementation of such major reform programmes is challenging, but there tends to be a window of opportunity in post-conflict societies. However, police reforms are often modest in comparison to military reforms, as the examples of Sierra Leone and Liberia show. Police forces remain under-resourced and unable to provide effective policing to the local populations. Officers often have no fuel and have to use their private vehicles when on duty, and there is a shortage of fingerprint kits, forensic experts, and laboratories, pathologists, forensic, and ballistic experts (Bekoe 2012; Kabia 2012).

4.3.3 Violence against Women

Evidence from victimization surveys indicates that women are at very high risk of experiencing violence. Former and current intimate partners (boyfriends, husbands) are the main perpetrators. Globally, 26% of ever-partnered women have experienced physical and/or sexual violence from their intimate partner, and 6 per cent of women over 15 years old report being sexually assaulted by a non-partner during their lifetime (WHO 2020b). Although this form of violence occurs in every society, violence against women is more prevalent in low-income countries (Devries et al. 2013; Hoeffler 2017; WHO 2021).

There are numerous programmes that empower women economically. Many micro-finance programmes and government cash-transfer programmes target women. Systematic reviews suggest that most women's economic empowerment programmes are associated with a significant reduction in intimate partner violence (Klugman et al. 2014; Buller et al. 2018; Eggers Del Campo and Steinert 2020).

There are also legal changes that have reduced violence against women and girls, such as making rape within marriage an offence, outlawing FGM/C (Engelsma et al. 2020), and increasing the minimum age at marriage (Garcia-Hombrados 2022). However, these are not changes that can be obtained through aid; de jure and de facto change can only be achieved when the gap between customary practices and formal law is small and can be bridged (Platteau and Wahhaj 2014; Acemoglu and Jackson 2017; Auriol et al. 2018).

Many men, as well as women, have internalized that violence is a normal part of a woman's life and that a husband is justified to hit his wife or demand sex (e.g., Cools and Kotsadam 2017). Various interventions, such as SASA!, aim to change these attitudes. Activists worked within Ugandan communities to raise awareness of the causes and consequences of violence against women in the home. SASA! successfully promoted the view that violence against a partner is unacceptable, and rates of intimate partner violence decreased (Abramsky et al. 2014, 2016). Messages to challenge traditional attitudes towards women can also be embedded in popular entertainment programmes, referred to as 'edutainment' in the development literature. In South Africa, the television series *Soul City*is believed to have significantly changed citizen's attitude towards domestic violence and is credited with accelerating the implementation of the Domestic Violence Act in South Africa in 1998 (Usdin et al. 2000). However, an edutainment experiment in Nigeria failed to establish a link between watching an episode of the MTV series *Shuga 3* (which included a storyline of intimate partner violence) and changing attitudes (Banerjee et al. 2019). Thus, although edutainment appears to provide a good medium to raise awareness of violence against women, so far the evidence is weak, and it is often unclear how much of the change in attitudes can be attributed to edutainment. Aid organizations sponsoring edutainment may also be faced with accusations of 'social engineering' or 'neo-imperialism'.

4.3.4 Violence against Children

Parental violence is the most frequent form of violence against children, mostly taking the form of physical punishment (Pinheiro 2006; UNICEF 2014). Many parents do not regard physical punishment as harmful but as a normal part of raising a child. For example, the African Charter on the Rights and Welfare of the Child, adopted in 1990, allows for 'domestic discipline' if it is 'consistent with the inherent dignity of the child' (Article 20 (1c)). Notwithstanding different attitudes towards physical discipline, there is overwhelming evidence that it does not only cause immediate pain and suffering, but that it has a number of adverse long-term consequences for the individual due to a disruption of social and psychological learning processes and physiological changes in brain development (see among many Nemeroff 2004; Straus et al. 2013; Webb et al. 2017; Heilmann et al. 2021). Parents who use harsh parenting methods often have unrealistic expectations of children's developmental capabilities and lack the skills to bring up their children without the use of violence. Parenting programmes have shown to be effective in reducing physical punishment (Sanders et al. 2014; Backhaus et al. 2023) and to be one of the most effective interventions to reduce anti-social behaviour and delinquency (Farrington et al. 2022).

In addition to violence in their home, children experience a lot of violence at school. Although physical punishment is banned in 136 states, it continues to be a widespread practice in settings with and without legal bans (Heekes et al. 2022).[3] There is emerging evidence that teacher training courses aiming to reduce harsh disciplining methods in schools are effective (see Devries et al. 2017; Kaltenbach et al. 2018; Nkuba et al. 2018).

4.3.5 Aid and Collective Violence

Unlike the sparse literature on aid and interpersonal violence, the literature on the impact of aid on collective violence is very large. However, the evidence of a conflict-reducing and peace-enhancing effect of aid is mixed. We only briefly summarize the main findings and refer to the in-depth overviews by Zürcher (2017) and Findley (2018). There are many different mechanisms through which aid can impact collective violence, as there can be direct and indirect effects. Timing is also an important consideration, and prevention or conflict initiation, reduction in conflict intensity, ending conflicts, and stabilizing post-conflict situations should be distinguished. Finally, the aid delivery mode may be important, that is, whether funds are provided to the recipient government or whether they are bypassed, and the aid is delivered through non-state actors. We discuss these possible mechanisms in turn.

Aid can have direct effects on armed conflict by increasing the government's budget. Assuming that aid is fungible, some of the budget increase can be used to increase military expenditure (Collier and Hoeffler 2006) in order to deter collective violence or to suppress it. Alternatively, aid can be used to 'buy off' potential rebel groups by spending it on addressing their grievances (Azam and Mesnard 2003). Fungibility and spending on the opposition would result in less violent conflict, but there is no evidence of a direct effect of development aid on the reduction of collective violence. It has been hypothesized that specific types of aid could be directly conflict-enhancing because rebel groups could misappropriate it to strengthen their military capability. Food aid has been identified as a significant determinant in extending civil wars (Nunn and Qian 2014), but food aid makes up just over 1 per cent of total aid (DAC, average 2019–22) and is therefore unlikely to have a large impact on the risk and duration of conflict in general.

Although there is no evidence that aid directly affects collective violence, aid may have an indirect impact via growth and poverty reduction. Low income and growth have been identified as important drivers of armed conflict (e.g., Fearon and Laitin 2003; Collier and Hoeffler 2004b), but the vast literature on aid and growth suggests that there is no evidence of a robust growth-enhancing effect of

[3] For more information on legal bans, see https://endcorporalpunishment.org (accessed 14 June 2023).

aid (Rajan and Subramanian 2008 and references within). A reason why aid is not growth enhancing is that many aid recipients are fragile states and thus most in need of additional resources but least capable of making good use of them (Bauer 1976). Furthermore, much of development aid is not directly growth enhancing, or at least not in the short run (e.g., aid for education, health, and emergency relief). A notable exception in the aid and growth literature is post-conflict countries. Here, aid can enhance the peace dividend that typically arises at the end of the conflict, that is, aid increases post-conflict growth (Collier and Hoeffler 2004a).

There are several studies analysing whether different modes of aid delivery can also improve local governance and thus support the peace process. Community-driven development (CDD) programmes aim to do just that and have been implemented in many countries, for example, Liberia, the DRC, the Philippines, and Afghanistan. The evaluation of CDDs provides a mixed picture, although they can improve inclusion and participation at the local level, and they have little impact on institutional capacity at the state level (King and Samii 2014; Justino 2019). Another popular mode of aid delivery is through cash transfer programmes. Aid is paid directly to poor individuals, either unconditionally or on certain conditions, for example, their children attending school and health programmes. While some cash transfer programmes have a conflict-reducing effect, others have a destabilizing effect by encouraging predatory behaviour from outside groups (Blattman et al. 2014, 2017; Crost et al. 2016).

4.4 How Much Aid Is Targeted at Violence Prevention and Reduction?

We now turn to the question how much of the total development aid is actually spent on preventing, reducing, and treating violence.

Unfortunately, there are no ready-made statistics on how much aid is provided for this purpose. In order to answer this question, we sift through the information supplied by the data bank AidData3 (Tierney et al. 2011). We use this data source because it comprehensively covers development aid and provides information on aid projects and activities from over 90 multilateral and bilateral donors. This level of detailed information is not available from the OECD aid database. The advantage of the AidData3 data source is that it is the most comprehensive, but the disadvantage is that the most recent year covered is 2013.

A report by the AidData Lab examines how much aid is spent on each SDG, suggesting that during 2000–13, the highest spending category is aid for SDG 16 at about US$342.5 billion (Sethi et al. 2017). This is conceptually very close to our quest to find out how much aid is targeted at the prevention, reduction, and treatment of violence because SDG 16 aims to 'Promote peaceful and inclusive societies for sustainable development, provide access to justice for all and build effective, accountable, and inclusive institutions at all levels'. However, this includes many aid projects aimed at improving institutions. They make up almost 60% of the SDG16 projects (Sethi et al. 2017: 29). This includes not only the building of institutions intended to reduce violence, such as security and legal reforms, but also healthcare and educational reforms. Thus, aid aimed at achieving SDG 16 is not equivalent to reducing violence; it also does not allow us to distinguish between aid targeted at the different categories of violence.

We therefore conduct our own analysis of the AidData3 database to find out how much aid is targeted at violence reduction. AidData3 has over 1.5 million entries, and our data analysis proceeds in three steps:

1. We bundle all the data entries into 16 large spending categories.
2. We examine one of the categories, 'Government and Social Infrastructure', in more detail and derive an estimate of aid spent on the reduction of interpersonal violence (Table 4.2).
3. Building on steps 1 and 2, we construct an estimate of aid spent on the reduction of collective violence (Table 4.3).

4.4.1 Step 1: Categorizing All Aid Projects

Every entry in the database has a project title, a description, and a purpose code. Based on this code, we divide all the entries in the database into 16 large spending categories akin to the OECD aid statistics by sector. These categories range from big spending categories on infrastructure to small categories, such as food aid. One of the categories that is clearly targeted towards dealing with the consequences of armed conflict is 'Emergency' aid, which covers aid for humanitarian assistance after man-made and natural disasters (the former cause is much more prevalent).

From this first categorization of aid, it is not obvious which other types of aid are targeted towards violence reduction. The largest categories of aid are 'Infrastructure' and 'Budget & Debt'. These relate to physical infrastructure, budgetary support, and debt relief, which are not violence related.[4]

Our category 'Government and Social Infrastructure' is a combination of projects from sectors 'Government & Civil Society, general', 'Conflict prevention and resolution, peace, and security', and 'Other Social Infrastructure & Services'.[5] This combined category is most likely to contain activities to address violence-related issues.

[4] This is a rather strong statement. Aid for infrastructure may include some aid for reconstruction after armed conflict. Likewise, governments may use budget support programmes for activities aimed at violence reduction, but we have no further information on which aid project was a post-conflict reconstruction project. Debt relief is also granted to many post-conflict countries.

[5] OECD DAC 5 Sectors 151, 152, and 160, respectively.

Table 4.2 Aid for the prevention, reduction, and treatment of interpersonal violence in the government and social infrastructure category, 2000–13

Sector	Total (US$)	Other (US$)	Other (%)	Interpersonal (US$)	Interpersonal/other (%)	Interpersonal of total in category (%)
Social/welfare services	102,458	101,848	25.72	610	0.60	0.60
Dev. policy/planning	80,162	77,852	19.66	2,309	2.97	2.88
Govt. & social	73,605	72,835	18.39	770	1.06	1.05
Govt. administration	57,777	57,663	14.56	115	0.20	0.20
Legal & judicial dev.	33,664	26,661	6.73	7,002	26.26	20.80
Conflict/post-conflict	31,059	31,059	7.84	0	0.00	0.00
Housing policy	10,293	10,293	2.60	1	0.01	0.01
Employment policy	10,052	10,015	2.53	38	0.38	0.38
Security system reform	8,570	7,735	1.95	835	10.80	9.75
Human rights	15	15	0.00	0	0.07	0.07
Media	2	2	0.00	0	0.00	0.00
Elections	2	2	0.00	0	0.00	0.00
Women's equality orgs.	1	1	0.00	0	0.00	0.00
Totals	407,660	395,980	100.00	11,680	2.95	2.87

Note: US$ are constant US dollars in millions.
Source: author's calculations based on AidData3.

Table 4.3 Aid for the prevention, reduction, and treatment of collective violence, 2000–13

Purpose	Activity	US$
Emergency		180,848
Conflict/post-conflict	Civilian peacebuilding, conflict prev. & resol.	14,220
Conflict/post-conflict	Post-conflict peacebuilding (UN)	4,739
Conflict/post-conflict	Reintegration and SALW control	4,412
Conflict/post-conflict	Land mine clearance	4,865
Conflict/post-conflict	Child soldiers (prevention and demobilization)	202
Security sys. reform		7,735
Total		217,021

Note: US$ are constant US dollars in millions. SALW stands for small arms and light weapons.
Source: author's calculations based on AidData3.

While we are confident that most of the emergency aid is spent on problems resulting from collective violence, it is not so obvious how much of 'Government and Social Infrastructure' aid is targeted at violence-related problems. We therefore take a closer look at this category.

4.4.2 Step 2: Examining Aid for 'Government and Social Infrastructure'

Aid in the category 'Government and Social Infrastructure' is spent to meet social and welfare needs that may or may not be the result of violence. We therefore examine all the subcategories of 'Government and Social Infrastructure' more closely in Table 4.2. Out of these subcategories, only a small number are directly aimed at violence. One obvious subcategory is aid for 'conflict prevention and resolution, peace, and security', and we refer to this aid as 'Conflict/Post-Conflict'. Out of the total aid for 'Government and Social Infrastructure', almost 8 per cent is spent on problems arising from conflict and post-conflict.

Another subcategory that is likely to be aimed at violence-related issues is 'Security System Reform'. However, here it is more difficult to tell which type of violence this aid is targeting. While there are many post-conflict reforms, which we would count as spending on collective violence, it also includes police reform in peaceful countries, in which case it would be spending that we would count as spending on interpersonal violence. Another subcategory that is very likely to contain aid for violence reduction is 'Legal and Judicial Development' because it includes support to institutions, systems, and procedures of the justice sector, such as the police, the judicial system, and prisons. Other subcategories that potentially address interpersonal violence are: 'Human rights', 'Media', 'Elections', and support for 'Women's equality organizations'.

So how much aid is targeted at the problem of interpersonal violence? To identify the aid spent on the reduction of interpersonal violence, we went through all 275,670 aid projects in the category 'Government and Social Infrastructure' for the years 2000–13. We searched the titles and short descriptions for keywords including the relevant stems of 'violence', 'police', 'crime', and a number of other pertinent keywords (in different languages). Table 4.2, column 1 lists the US dollar amounts spent on all the projects within the subcategories. Column 4 lists the US dollar amounts spent on projects that were picked up in our keyword search, that is, we identify these as projects aimed at reducing interpersonal violence. Column 6 provides the proportion of 'Government and Social Infrastructure' aid spent on these violence-reducing projects. As a result of this exercise, we find that the total amount of aid spent on problems associated with interpersonal violence during the period 2000–13 was about US$11.7 billion, or around 2.9% of aid for 'Government and Social Infrastructure', as reported in the bottom right-hand corner of Table 4.2.

How does this compare to the amount spent on reducing collective violence? The last step of our data inquiry provides an answer to this question.

4.4.3 Step 3: Summarizing Aid for the Reduction of Collective Violence

We now turn to summarizing the amount of aid spent on the prevention, reduction, and treatment of collective violence. In step 1, we identified 'Emergency' aid (US$181 billion) and in step 2 'Conflict/Post-Conflict' aid (US$31 billion) and parts of 'Security System Reform' (US$7.7 billion).

Our calculations show that the approximate US$217 billion of aid spent on collective violence dwarf the US$11.7 billion spent on interpersonal violence. In other words, the international community spends about 19 times more aid on collective than interpersonal violence. This is despite the fact that interpersonal violence is more prevalent and is associated with much higher costs.

Given these large differences between aid spending on collective and interpersonal violence, we are asking ourselves whether we are calculating these numbers in the correct way. Perhaps there are some computational or conceptual mistakes in our calculations? In order to assess the magnitude of our numbers, we consider whether we are missing important aid projects—those that are not intended to reduce violence directly but are likely to have an indirect effect on violence.

As discussed above, development aid aimed at reducing collective violence is relatively straightforward to identify. It includes aid for emergency situations, conflict resolution and prevention, and security system reform. However, it is much more difficult to trace aid intended to reduce interpersonal violence. We were very careful when we searched the database, but we are likely to have missed projects aimed at reducing violence. Take projects targeted at 'Narcotics Control'. The main aim of these narcotics controls is the improvement of public health (UN Single Convention on Narcotic Drugs from 1961), but the illegal trade in narcotics fuels violence and therefore a reduction in this trade would also have positive effects on violence reduction. How much aid is spent on narcotics control? We searched for keywords such as 'drugs', 'narcotics', and related keywords and found that about US$23.7 billion are associated with these projects. However, in the absence of further information on these projects, we were unable to decide how much of the narcotics control could reasonably be counted as violence reducing. If we assumed that *all* of this aid for narcotics control is violence reducing, the proportion of aid in the category 'Government and Social Infrastructure' spent on the reduction of interpersonal violence would increase from 2.9 to 8.7% (or to 1.1% of total aid).

To summarize, we suggest that international agencies spend about US$217 billion on the reduction of collective violence—about 6.6% of total development aid. These numbers demonstrate that aid agencies consider armed conflict to be a development concern. However, very little aid is provided with the explicit aim of reducing interpersonal violence. No exact figures exist, and, as we discussed above, it is somewhat a matter of definition of what should be included in violence-reduction aid. We suggest that only about US$11.7 billion, equivalent to 0.3% of total development aid, is spent on the treatment and reduction of interpersonal violence. As discussed in Section 4.2, interpersonal violence is highly prevalent in low-income countries, but given the small allocation of aid targeted at the reduction of interpersonal violence, it appears that the international aid agencies do not perceive interpersonal violence as a pressing challenge to societal development. Unfortunately, we only have detailed AidData3 project data for the period 2000–13. Perhaps the focus has changed since 2013? We can only speculate here. Examining the OECD database by ODA sectoral categories shows that the allocation by main categories is not markedly different, except for budget aid and debt relief (down by about 16 percentage points) and emergency aid (up by about 8 percentage points). However, the main category of interest, 'Government and Social Infrastructure', changed only slightly (up by 4 percentage points). Thus, nothing in these more recent aid statistics points towards a dramatic shift of an increased use of aid for the prevention and treatment of interpersonal violence.

In this section, we focused on aid targeted at collective and interpersonal violence. However, we also conducted a similar search exercise for projects aimed at the reduction of suicide and self-harm and more broadly projects to address mental health issues. We only found very few projects for suicide and self-harm (11 projects) and some projects aimed at the improvement of mental health (1,274). Taken together, aid spent on suicide/self-harm and mental health only amount to 0.006% of total aid.

4.5 Discussion and Conclusion

We provide a novel investigation of how much aid is spent on violence reduction. Our analysis suggests that, while 6.6% of total aid is targeted at collective violence, less than 1 per cent is targeted at interpersonal violence and almost none at self-directed violence. Although our estimations come with some caveats, the big gap between the percentage of aid spent on collective versus interpersonal and self-directed violence suggests that donors have identified collective violence as a major development concern, while interpersonal and self-directed violence does not have the same status. This supports previous advocacy work by Mikton (2008). Based on our findings, the international community should reconsider the allocation of aid, in particular because low- and middle-income countries have high prevalence rates of interpersonal violence. Furthermore, suicide is an enormous global public health problem. Although well documented by health experts and international organizations, this has so far not been recognized by donors.

We discuss the evidence on whether aid is effective in reducing violence. There is a large and active literature on aid and collective violence; however, the evidence on the impact of aid on armed conflict is mixed and depends on a number of different conditions (Zürcher 2017; Findley 2018). In contrast, our review demonstrates that there is hardly any literature on the impact of aid on interpersonal violence. In a sense this is not surprising, given how little aid is spent on the reduction of interpersonal violence. Either donors do not seem to perceive this type of violence as important, or they assume that aid cannot be effectively used to reduce interpersonal violence. Given that there is so little discussion, it is not possible for us to decide *why* such a small amount of aid is spent on interpersonal violence prevention. For high-income countries, there is already a large literature on the prevention, reduction, and treatment of interpersonal violence, but there is emerging evidence from low- and middle-income countries. However, this emerging literature has so far not examined whether aid is effective in reducing interpersonal violence. There is no a priori reason to assume that aid-financed interventions targeted at violence prevention, reduction, and treatment are less efficient than national spending. But so far there is little evidence, and this would make an interesting area of future research.

Another under-researched area is the connection between different forms of violence. Collective violence impacts interpersonal violence (e.g., Saile et al. 2014; Stojetz and Brück 2023), and both types of violence increase self-directed violence. More knowledge on these links would help to leverage synergy effects of violence-reduction interventions and potentially help to persuade donors to address the so-far-neglected forms of interpersonal and self-directed violence.

The main contribution of this chapter is to highlight that donors spend little aid on interpersonal and self-directed violence, despite the overwhelming need. The focus has been very much on what donors do, but what is the role of recipients within the aid-effectiveness principles? Building on a series of agreements in Rome (2003), Paris (2005), and Accra (2008), the Busan Partnership for Effective Development Co-operation was set out in 2011 setting out four main principles: (1) country ownership, (2) focus on results, (3) inclusive partnerships, and (4) transparency and accountability. Progress towards achieving these principles is monitored and documented in reports by the OECD and the UNDP (OECD-UNDP 2014, 2016, 2019). We offer a brief reflection on the principles of ownership and results. Security is a key condition for development and legitimate governments have the right to maintain their monopoly on violence. International intervention falls outside the remit of development aid since aid explicitly excludes military assistance. Thus, the Busan principles are not applicable for these types of security concerns. A notable exception consists of post-conflict situations where donors provide aid to address specific problems such as security sector reforms, land mine clearance, and the reintegration of ex-combatants. Given that aid can have a stabilizing effect in these situations (Collier and Hoeffler 2004a), post-conflict aid appears to be an effective use of resources, reflecting the priorities of post-conflict governments. In contrast, our analysis shows that aid is not targeted at the security needs arising from violent crime. It is unclear whether this is not a priority for recipient governments or whether donors are reluctant to provide aid to address these types of security concerns. In addition, self-directed violence is an immense problem, but it is unclear why this is not addressed. None of the three progress reports (OECD-UNDP 2014, 2016, 2019) mention interpersonal or self-directed violence.

Monitoring aid effectiveness and measuring progress are impossible if there are no data. Some donors provide support to collect data and make them publicly available, such as the Demographic and Health Surveys (DHS) financed by USAID or UNICEF's Multiple Indicator Cluster Surveys (MICS). These surveys include questions on violence at home and in the community. Evidence from standardized victimization surveys is rare and would provide important information on the prevalence of (violent) crime. On homicide the evidence base is also very poor. In the sub-Saharan Africa region, 44 countries do not provide any statistics and data are estimated (UNODC 2019). Given the lack of data, progress is very hard to measure and donors should strengthen systems of vital registration and crime recording. The collection of data on self-harm should also be supported, but cultural sensitivities around mental health and self-harm may cause conflicts between the principles of ownership and results.

To conclude, our estimates of aid aimed at the prevention, reduction, and treatment of the various forms of violence show that little is spent on the problems of interpersonal and self-directed violence. This is despite high prevalence rates and enormous human suffering. Thus, we call into question why donors as well as recipients do not use more aid to ensure the physical integrity of citizens, which is arguably the fundamental prerequisite for economic development.

References

Abramsky, T., K. Devries, L. Kiss, J. Nakuti, N. Kyegombe, E. Starmann, B. Cundill, L. Francisco, D. Kaye, T. Musuya, L. Michau, and C. Watts (2014). 'Findings from the SASA! Study: A Cluster Randomized Controlled Trial to Assess the Impact of a Community Mobilization Intervention to Prevent Violence against Women and Reduce HIV Risk in Kampala, Uganda'. *BMC Medicine*, 12(1): 1–17. https://doi.org/10.1186/s12916-014-0122-5.

Abramsky, T., K. M. Devries, L. Michau, J. Nakuti, T. Musuya, N. Kyegombe, and C. Watts (2016). 'The Impact of SASA! A Community Mobilisation Intervention, on Women's Experiences of Intimate Partner Violence: Secondary Findings from a Cluster Randomised Trial in Kampala, Uganda'. *Journal of Epidemiology and Community Health*, 70(8): 818–25. https://doi.org/10.1136/jech-2015-206665.

Acarturk, C., E. Uygun, Z. Ilkkursun, T. Yurtbakan, G. Kurt, J. Adam-Troian, I. Senay, R. Bryant, P. Cuijpers, N. Kiselev, D. McDaid, N. Morina, Z. Nisanci, A. L. Park, M. Sijbrandij, P. Ventevogel, and D. C. Fuhr (2022). 'Group Problem Management Plus (PM+) to Decrease Psychological Distress among Syrian Refugees in Turkey: A Pilot Randomised Controlled Trial'. *BMC Psychiatry*, 22: 1–11. https://doi.org/10.1186/s12888-021-03645-w.

Acemoglu, D., and M. O. Jackson (2017). 'Social Norms and the Enforcement of Laws'. *Journal of the European Economic Association*, 15(2): 245–95.

Afrobarometer (2020). Afrobarometer (R7 2016/2018) (Benin, Botswana, Burkina, Cameroon, Cape Verde, Côte d'Ivoire, Gabon, Gambia, Ghana, Guinea, Kenya, Lesotho, Liberia, Madagascar, Malawi, Mali, Mauritius, Morocco, Mozambique, Namibia, Niger, Nigeria, Sao Tome and Principe, Senegal, Sierra Leone, South Africa, Sudan, Swaziland, Tanzania, Togo, Tunisia, Uganda, Zambia, Zimbabwe). Tech. Rep. Washington, DC: World Bank. Available at: https://bookdown.org/paul/applied-causal-analysis/ accessed 31 May 2021.

Auriol, E., G. Camilotti, and J.-P. Platteau (2018). 'Eradicating Women-Hurting Customs: What Role for Social Engineering?' In S. Anderson, L. Beaman, and J.-P. Platteau, editors, *Towards Gender Equity in Development* (pp. 319–65). Oxford: Oxford University Press. https://doi.org/10.1093/oso/9780198829591.003.0015.

Azam, J.-P., and A. Mesnard (2003). 'Civil War and the Social Contract'. *Public Choice*, 115(3): 455–75. https://doi.org/10.1023/A:1024265631528.

Backhaus, S., P. Leijten, J. Jochim, G. Melendez-Torres, and F. Gardner (2023). 'Effects over Time of Parenting Interventions to Reduce Physical and Emotional Violence against Children: A Systematic Review and Meta-Analysis'. *eClinicalMedicine*, 60(June): 102003. https://doi.org/10.1016/j.eclinm.2023.102003.

Banerjee, A., R. Chattopadhyay, E. Duflo, D. Keniston, and N. Singh (2021). 'Improving Police Performance in Rajasthan, India: Experimental Evidence on Incentives, Managerial Autonomy, and Training'. *American Economic Journal: Economic Policy*, 13(1): 36–66. https://doi.org/10.1257/pol.20190664.

Banerjee, A., E. L. Ferrara, and V. Orozco (2019). 'Entertainment, Education, and Attitudes toward Domestic Violence'. In *AEA Papers and Proceedings* (Vol. 109, pp. 133–7). https://doi.org/10.1596/31722.

Bauer, P. T. (1976). *Dissent on Development*. Cambridge, MA: Harvard University Press.

Bekoe, D. (2012). 'Elusive Gains: Policing and Security Sector Reform in Liberia'. In D. J. Francis (ed.), *Policing in Africa* (pp. 37–52). Springer. https://doi.org/10.1057/9781137010582_2.

Blair, G., J. M. Weinstein, F. Christia, E. Arias, E. Badran, R. A. Blair, A. Cheema, A. Farooqui, T. Fetzer, G. Grossman, D. Haim, Z. Hameed, R. Hanson, A. Hasanain, D. Kronick, B. S. Morse, R. Muggah, F. Nadeem, L.L. Tsai, M. Nanes, T. Slough, N. Ravanilla, J. N. Shapiro, B. Silva, P. C. L. Souza, and A. M. Wilk (2021). 'Community Policing Does Not Build Citizen Trust in Police or Reduce Crime in the Global South'. *Science*, 374(6571): eabd3446. https://doi.org/10.1126/science.abd3446.

Blattman, C., N. Fiala, and S. Martinez (2014). 'Generating Skilled Self-Employment in Developing Countries: Experimental Evidence from Uganda'. *The Quarterly Journal of Economics*, 129(2): 697–752. https://doi.org/10.1093/qje/qjt057.

Blattman, C., J. C. Jamison, and M. Sheridan (2017). 'Reducing Crime and Violence: Experimental Evidence from Cognitive Behavioral Therapy in Liberia'. *American Economic Review*, 107(4): 1165–1206. https://doi.org/10.1257/aer.20150503.

Brankamp, H. (2020). 'Refugees in Uniform: Community Policing as a Technology of Government in Kakuma Refugee Camp, Kenya'. *Journal of Eastern African Studies*, 14(2): 270–90. https://doi.org/10.1080/17531055.2020.1725318.

Brogden, M., and P. Nijhar (2013). *Community Policing*. London: Routledge. https://doi.org/10.4324/9781843925798.

Buller, A. M., A. Peterman, M. Ranganathan, A. Bleile, M. Hidrobo, and L. Heise (2018). 'A Mixed-Method Review of Cash Transfers and Intimate Partner Violence in Low- and Middle-Income Countries'. *The World Bank Research Observer*, 33(2): 218–58. https://doi.org/10.1093/wbro/lky002.

Chalfin, A., and J. McCrary (2017). 'Criminal Deterrence: A Review of the Literature'. *Journal of Economic Literature*, 55(1): 5–48. https://doi.org/10.1257/jel.20141147.

Collier, P., and A. Hoeffler (2004a). 'Aid, Policy and Growth in Post-Conflict Societies'. *European Economic Review*, 48(5): 1125–45. https://doi.org/10.1016/j.euroecorev.2003.11.005.

Collier, P., and A. Hoeffler (2004b). 'Greed and Grievance in Civil War'. *Oxford Economic Papers*, 56(4): 563–95. https://doi.org/10.1093/oep/gpf064.

Collier, P., and A. Hoeffler (2006). 'Military Expenditure in Post-Conflict Societies'. *Economics of Governance*, 7(1): 89–107. https://doi.org/10.1007/s10101-004-0091-9.

Cools, S., and A. Kotsadam (2017). 'Resources and Intimate Partner Violence in Sub-Saharan Africa'. *World Development*, 95: 211–30. https://doi.org/10.1016/j.worlddev.2017.02.027.

Crost, B., J. H. Felter, and P. B. Johnston (2016). 'Conditional Cash Transfers, Civil Conflict and Insurgent Influence: Experimental Evidence from the Philippines'. *Journal of Development Economics*, 118(January): 171–82. https://doi.org/10.1016/j.jdeveco.2015.08.005.

Devries, K. M., L. Knight, E. Allen, J. Parkes, N. Kyegombe, and D. Naker (2017). 'Does the Good Schools Toolkit Reduce Physical, Sexual and Emotional Violence, and Injuries, in Girls and Boys Equally? A Cluster-Randomised Controlled Trial'. *Prevention Science*, 18(7): 839–53. https://doi.org/10.1007/s11121-017-0775-3.

Devries, K. M., J. Y. Mak, C. Garcia-Moreno, M. Petzold, J. C. Child, G. Falder, S. Lim, L. J. Bacchus, R. E. Engell, L. Rosenfeld, C. Pallitto, T. Vos, N. Abrahams, and C. H. Watts (2013). 'The Global Prevalence of Intimate Partner Violence against Women'. *Science*, 340(6140): 1527–28. https://doi.org/10.1126/science.1240937.

Di Tella, R., and E. Schargrodsky (2004). 'Do Police Reduce Crime? Estimates Using the Allocation of Police Forces after a Terrorist Attack'. *American Economic Review*, 94(1): 115–33. https://doi.org/10.1257/000282804322970733.

Draca, M., S. Machin, and R. Witt (2011). 'Panic on the Streets of London: Police, Crime, and the July 2005 Terror Attacks'. *American Economic Review*, 101(5): 2157–81. https://doi.org/10.1257/aer.101.5.2157.

Eggers Del Campo, I., and J. I. Steinert (2020). 'The Effect of Female Economic Empowerment Interventions on the Risk of Intimate Partner Violence: A Systematic Review and Meta-Analysis'. *Trauma, Violence, & Abuse*, 23(3): 1524838020976088. https://doi.org/10.1177/1524838020976088.

Engelsma, B., G. Mackie, and B. Merrell (2020). 'Unprogrammed Abandonment of Female Genital Mutilation/Cutting'. *World Development*, 129: 104845. https://doi.org/10.1016/j.worlddev.2019.104845.

Stojetz, W. and T. Brück. (2023). 'Exposure to Collective Gender-Based Violence Causes Intimate Partner Violence'. *Journal of Development Economics*, 164: 103054. https://doi.org/10.1016/j.jdeveco.2023.103054

Farrington, D. P., H. Gaffney, and H. White (2022). 'Effectiveness of 12 Types of Interventions in Reducing Juvenile Offending and Antisocial Behaviour'. *Canadian Journal of Criminology and Criminal Justice*, 64(4): 47–68. https://doi.org/10.3138/cjccj.2022-0022.

Fearon, J. D., and A. Hoeffler (2018). 'Beyond Civil War: The Costs of Interpersonal Violence'. In B. Lomborg (ed.), *Prioritizing Development: A Cost Benefit Analysis of the United Nations' Sustainable Development Goals* (pp. 67–88). Cambridge, UK: Cambridge University Press. https://doi.org/10.1017/9781108233767.006.

Fearon, J. D., and D. D. Laitin (2003). 'Ethnicity, Insurgency, and Civil War'. *American Political Science Review*, 97(1): 75–90. https://doi.org/10.1017/S0003055403000534.

Findley, M. G. (2018). 'Does Foreign Aid Build Peace?' *Annual Review of Political Science*, 21: 359–84. https://doi.org/10.1146/annurev-polisci-041916-015516.

Francis, D. J. (2012). *Policing in Africa*. Berlin: Springer. https://doi.org/10.1057/9781137010582.

Garcia-Hombrados, J. (2022). 'Child Marriage and Infant Mortality: Causal Evidence from Ethiopia'. *The Journal of Population Economics* 2022(35): 1163–1223. https://doi.org/10.1007/s00148-021-00873-y.

Geneva Declaration (2015). *Global Burden of Armed Violence 2015: Every Body Counts. Geneva Declaration* 11 May 2015. http://www.genevadeclaration.org/measurability/global-burden-of-armed-violence/global-burden-of-armed-violence-2015.html accessed 12 April 2020.

Gupte, J. (2015). *Four Glaring Holes in Modi's 'Vikas' Agenda. The Wire*, 13 November 2015. Available at: https://thewire.in/politics/four-glaring-holes-in-modis-vikas-agenda.

Hamdani, S. U., A. Rahman, D. Wang, T. Chen, M. van Ommeren, D. Chisholm, and S. Farooq (2020). 'Cost-Effectiveness of WHO Problem Management Plus for Adults with Mood and Anxiety Disorders in a Post-Conflict Area of Pakistan: Randomised Controlled Trial'. *The British Journal of Psychiatry*, 217(5): 623–9. https://doi.org/10.1192/bjp.2020.138.

Heekes, S.-L., C. B. Kruger, S. N. Lester, and C. L. Ward (2022). 'A Systematic Review of Corporal Punishment in Schools: Global Prevalence and Correlates'. *Trauma, Violence, & Abuse*, 23(1): 52–72. https://doi.org/10.1177/1524838020925787.

Heilmann, A., A. Mehay, R. G. Watt, Y. Kelly, J. E. Durrant, J. V. Turnhout, and E. T. Gershoff (2021). 'Physical Punishment and Child Outcomes: A Narrative Review of Prospective Studies'. *The Lancet*, 398(10297): 355–64. https://doi.org/10.1016/S0140-6736(21)00582-1.

Hoeffler, A. (2017). 'What Are the Costs of Violence?' *Politics, Philosophy & Economics*, 16(4): 422–45. https://doi.org/10.1177/1470594X17714270.

Jordans, M. J., B. A. Kohrt, M. Sangraula, E. L. Turner, X. Wang, P. Shrestha, R. Ghimire, E. Van't Hof, R. A. Bryant, K. S. Dawson, K. Marahatta, N. P. Luitel, and M. van Ommeren (2021). 'Effectiveness of Group Problem Management Plus, A Brief Psychological Intervention for Adults Affected by Humanitarian Disasters in Nepal: A Cluster Randomized Controlled Trial'. *PLoS Medicine*, 18(6): e1003621. https://doi.org/10.1371/journal.pmed.1003621.

Justino, P. (2019). 'Governance Interventions in Conflict-Affected Countries'. *The Journal of Development Studies*, 55(7): 1364–78. https://doi.org/10.1080/00220388.2018.1487053.

Kabia, J. M. (2012). 'A Force for Good? Police Reform in Postwar Sierra Leone'. In D. J. Francis (ed.), *Policing in Africa* (pp. 33–72). Springer. https://doi.org/10.1057/9781137010582_3.

Kaltenbach, E., K. Hermenau, M. Nkuba, K. Goessmann, and T. Hecker (2018). 'Improving Interaction Competencies with Children—A Pilot Feasibility Study to Reduce School Corporal Punishment'. *Journal of Aggression, Maltreatment & Trauma*, 27(1): 35–53. https://doi.org/10.1080/10926771.2017.1357060.

King, E., and C. Samii (2014). 'Fast-Track Institution Building in Conflict-Affected Countries? Insights from Recent Field Experiments'. *World Development*, 64: 740–54. https://doi.org/10.1016/j.worlddev.2014.06.030.

Klick, J., and A. Tabarrok (2005). 'Using Terror Alert Levels to Estimate the Effect of Police on Crime'. *The Journal of Law and Economics*, 48(1): 267–79. https://doi.org/10.1086/426877.

Klugman, J., L. Hanmer, S. Twigg, T. Hasan, J. McCleary-Sills, and J. Santamaria (2014). *Voice and Agency: Empowering Women and Girls for Shared Prosperity*. Washington, DC: World Bank. https://doi.org/10.1596/978-1-4648-0359-8.

Latinobarómetro (2020). Latinobarómetro 2020 (Argentina, Bolivia, Brasil, Chile, Colombia, Costa Rica, Rep. Dominicana, Ecuador, El Salvador, Guatemala, Honduras, México, Nicaragua, Panamá, Paraguay, Perú, Uruguay, Venezuela). Available at: https://www.latinobarometro.org/latContents.jsp.

Lessing, B. (2017). *Making Peace in Drug Wars: Crackdowns and Cartels in Latin America*. Cambridge, UK: Cambridge University Press. https://doi.org/10.1017/9781108185837.

Lessing, B. (2021). 'Conceptualizing Criminal Governance'. *Perspectives on Politics* 19(3): 854–73. https://doi.org/10.1017/S1537592720001243.

Mikton, C. (2008). 'Preventing Violence and Reducing Its Impact: How Development Agencies Can Help'. *Injury Prevention*, 14(4): 279. https://doi.org/10.1136/ip.2008.019554.

Nemeroff, C. B. (2004). 'Neurobiological Consequences of Childhood Trauma'. *The Journal of Clinical Psychiatry*, 65(Suppl 1): 18–28.

Nkuba, M., K. Hermenau, K. Goessmann, and T. Hecker (2018). 'Reducing Violence by Teachers Using the Preventative Intervention Interaction Competencies with Children for Teachers (ICC-T): A Cluster Randomized Controlled Trial at Public Secondary

Schools in Tanzania'. *PLoS One*, 13(8): e0201362. https://doi.org/10.1371/journal.pone.0201362.

Nunn, N., and N. Qian (2014). 'US Food Aid and Civil Conflict'. *American Economic Review*, 104(6): 1630–66. https://doi.org/10.1257/aer.104.6.1630.

OECD (2018). *Official Development Assistance – Definition and Coverage*. Available at: https://www.oecd.org/dac/financing-sustainable-development/development-finance-standards/officialdevelopmentassistancedefinitionandcoverage.htm (accessed 12 June 2023)

OECD-UNDP (2014). Making Development Co-operation More Effective: 2014 Progress Report. Paris: OECD.

OECD-UNDP (2016). Making Development Co-operation More Effective: 2016 Progress Report. Paris: OECD.

OECD-UNDP (2019). Making Development Co-operation More Effective: 2019 Progress Report. Paris: OECD.

Osafo, J., K. O. Asante, and C. S. Akotia (2020). 'Suicide Prevention in the African Region'. In E. Arensman D. De Leo, and J. Pirkis, editors, *Suicide and Suicide Prevention from a Global Perspective* (pp. S53–S71). Hogrefe Publishing. https://doi.org/10.1027/0227-5910/a000668.

Pinheiro, P. S. (2006). *World Report on Violence against Children*. Geneva: UN Secretary-General's Study on Violence Against Children.

Platteau, J. P., and Z. Wahhaj (2014). 'Strategic Interactions between Modern Law and Custom'. In A. V. Ginsburgh and D. Throsby, editors, *Handbook of the Economics of Art and Culture* (Vol. 2, pp. 633–78). Oxford: Elsevier. https://doi.org/10.1016/B978-0-444-53776-8.00022-2.

Prinsloo, M., D. Bradshaw, J. Joubert, R. Matzopoulos, and P. Groenewald (2017). 'South Africa's Vital Statistics Are Currently Not Suitable for Monitoring Progress towards Injury and Violence Sustainable Development Goals'. *South African Medical Journal*, 107(6): 470–1. https://doi.org/10.7196/SAMJ.2017.v107i6.12464.

Rajan, R. G., and A. Subramanian (2008). 'Aid and Growth: What Does the Cross-Country Evidence Really Show?' *The Review of Economics and Statistics*, 90(4): 643–65. https://doi.org/10.1162/rest.90.4.643.

Saile, R., V. Ertl, F. Neuner, and C. Catani (2014). 'Does War Contribute to Family Violence against Children? Findings from a Two-Generational Multi-Informant Study in Northern Uganda'. *Child Abuse & Neglect*, 38(1): 135–46. https://doi.org/10.1016/j.chiabu.2013.10.007.

Sanders, M. R., J. N. Kirby, C. L. Tellegen, and J. J. Day (2014). 'The Triple P-Positive Parenting Program: A Systematic Review and Meta-Analysis of a Multi-Level System of Parenting Support'. *Clinical Psychology Review*, 34(4): 337–57. https://doi.org/10.1016/j.cpr.2014.04.003.

Sanghavi, P., K. Bhalla, and V. Das (2009). 'Fire-Related Deaths in India in 2001: A Retrospective Analysis of Data'. *The Lancet*, 373(9671): 1282–8. https://doi.org/10.1016/S0140-6736(09)60235-X.

Sethi, T., S. Custer, J. Turner, J. Sims, M. DiLorenzo, and R. Latourell (2017). *Realizing Agenda 2030: Will Donor Dollars and Country Priorities Align with Global Goals?* Williamsburg, VA: AidData at the College of William & Mary.

Straus, M. A., E. M. Douglas, and R. A. Medeiros (2013). *The Primordial Violence: Spanking Children, Psychological Development, Violence, and Crime*. London: Routledge. https://doi.org/10.4324/9780203808856.

Tierney, M. J., D. L. Nielson, D. G. Hawkins, J. T. Roberts, M. G. Findley, R. M. Powers, B. Parks, S. E. Wilson, and R. L. Hicks (2011). 'More Dollars than Sense: Refining Our Knowledge of Development Finance Using AidData'. *World Development*, 39(11): 1891–1906. https://doi.org/10.1016/j.worlddev.2011.07.029.

UNICEF (2014). 'Hidden in Plain Sight: A Statistical Analysis of Violence against Children'. New York: United Nations Children's Fund.

UNICEF (2017). 'A Familiar Face: Violence in the Lives of Children and Adolescents'. Tech. Rep. New York: United Nations Children's Fund. Available at: https://www.unicef.org/reports/familiar-face.

UNODC (2005). *Crime and Development in Africa*. Vienna: United Nations Office on Drugs and Crime (UNODC). Available at: https://gsdrc.org/document-library/crime-and-development-in-africa/ (accessed in November 2024).

UNODC (2014). *Global Study on Homicide 2014*. Vienna: United Nations Office on Drugs and Crime.

UNODC (2019). *Global Study on Homicide 2019*. Vienna: United Nations Office on Drugs and Crime.

Usdin, S., N. Christofides, L. Malepe, and A. Maker (2000). 'The Value of Advocacy in Promoting Social Change: Implementing the New Domestic Violence Act in South Africa'. *Reproductive Health Matters*, 8(16): 55–65. https://doi.org/10.1016/S0968-8080(00)90187-3.

Webb, R. T., S. Antonsen, M. J. Carr, L. Appleby, C. B. Pedersen, and P. L. Mok (2017). 'Self-Harm and Violent Criminality among Young People Who Experienced Trauma-Related Hospital Admission during Childhood: A Danish National Cohort Study'. *The Lancet Public Health*, 2(7): e314–22. https://doi.org/10.1016/S2468-2667(17)30094-4.

WHO (1996). WHO Global Consultation on Violence and Health Violence: A Public Health Priority (Document WHO/EHA/SPI.POA.2). Geneva: World Health Organization.

WHO (2002). *World Report on Violence and Health*. Geneva: World Health Organization.

WHO (2014). *Preventing Suicide: A Global Imperative*. Geneva: World Health Organization.

WHO (2018). *National Suicide Prevention Strategies: Progress, Examples and Indicators*. Geneva: World Health Organization.

WHO (2019). *Female Genital Mutilation*. Tech. Rep. Geneva: World Health Organization.

WHO (2020a). *Global Health Estimates 2019: Death by Cause, Age, Sex, by Country and by Region 2000–2019*. https://www.who.int/data/gho/data/themes/mortality-and-global-health-estimates. Geneva: World Health Organization.

WHO (2020b). *Global Status Report on Preventing Violence against Children*. Geneva: World Health Organization.

WHO (2021). *Violence against Women Prevalence Estimates 2018: Global, Regional and National Prevalence Estimates for Intimate Partner Violence against Women and Global and Regional Prevalence Estimates for Non-Partner Sexual Violence against Women*. Geneva: World Health Organization.

World Bank (2011). *World Development Report 2011: Conflict, Security, and Development*. Washington, DC: World Bank.

Zürcher, C. (2017). 'What Do We (Not) Know about Development Aid and Violence? A Systematic Review'. *World Development*, 98: 506–22. https://doi.org/10.1016/j.worlddev.2017.05.013.

PART III

OWNERSHIP AND SOCIAL CONTRACT IN WEAK STATES AND CONFLICT SITUATIONS

5

Southern Perspectives on Effective Development Cooperation

Rethinking Country Ownership

Debapriya Bhattacharya, Towfiqul Islam Khan, and Najeeba Mohammed Altaf

5.1 Introduction

5.1.1 Background

The 'owning' of a foreign aid-supported development intervention is a much-vaunted concept for ensuring development cooperation effectiveness but it has limited operational validation. The present chapter focuses on four issues that underpin this problematique.

First, the discussion about 'ownership' has exclusively focused on the processes and activities at the recipient level. However, ownership of an intervention by the provider may be critical in defining the development intervention outcomes. This issue has acquired a new dimension as international development cooperation loses traction among taxpayers in the provider countries. The recent pandemic and alternative demands for resources have further complicated the predictability of development cooperation. It has become critical to redefine ownership using variables that simultaneously consider the interests of both the provider and recipient. This would improve the effectiveness of the development intervention and could bring more predictability to cooperation, which is one of the weak spots.

The second issue relates to how ownership is often understood as the provider's responsiveness to a recipient government's development priorities as enunciated in its national plan or policy documents. This could be a response by the provider to a recipient's public investment programme, strategic or policy document, and/or a specific request made by the recipient government. The issue is that, notwithstanding the provider's responsiveness to national priorities as enunciated by recipients, ownership can still remain supply driven. This is particularly

Debapriya Bhattacharya et al., *Southern Perspectives on Effective Development Cooperation*. In: *Fragile Aid*.
Edited by: Rachel M. Gisselquist et al., Oxford University Press. © UNU-WIDER (2025).
DOI: 10.1093/oso/9780198960287.003.0005

the case when a recipient country's national priorities are loosely formulated or broadly articulated. However, this can generate a form of 'shared ownership' between provider and recipient countries, even though it does not ensure the effective allocation of resources.

The third issue relates to restricting the concept of ownership only to the purview of the recipient government. This narrow approach has become particularly relevant as the public space for discourse is diminishing in many developing countries that suffer from weak democratic practices. Indeed, national priorities are generally dictated by the political ambitions of the government in a recipient country or are derived through bureaucratic processes without adequate consultation with relevant stakeholders. Moreover, it has been observed in many cases that providers support equating recipient government ownership with country ownership of a development intervention through a lack of encouragement to include other development actors such as civil society, local governments, and the private sector (Stern et al. 2008). However, the 'inclusive' or 'shared' aspect of ownership has also been examined over the last decade. It is understood to indicate that recipient governments will take the lead in shaping the country's development policies while engaging other stakeholders in the development process (Keijzer et al. 2019). The role of 'providers' in this process emerges through support for recipient countries' priorities, investment in the capacity development of individuals and institutions, and utilization of recipient countries' public financial management (PFM) systems (OECD 2008a).

The fourth issue relates to the monitorable indicators that reflect a foreign-aided project's nature and level of ownership in the Global Partnership for Effective Development Co-operation (GPEDC) monitoring exercise. There may be questions about the robustness of the indicators used by the GPEDC monitoring process, such as the quality of a recipient country's PFM system, use of recipient country systems by the provider, proportion of untied aid, and the predictability of development cooperation to examine 'country ownership'. The concept needs to be clarified to elucidate the operational anchor points of the concept of ownership, evolve the appropriate indicators in this regard, and ensure data availability.

It should also be noted that the profiles of both recipients and providers of development cooperation have undergone change in recent decades. As the primary focus in the examination of foreign aid-supported development interventions, recipient countries largely comprise those which are graduating from or have graduated from low-income country and least-developed country status. Furthermore, conflict-affected or fragile countries are also on the rise among the recipients. Thus, it is necessary to round out the group of recipients to include countries that suffer from disadvantages in terms of geography, environmental issues, conflict, and governance issues, among others (Bhattacharya and Khan 2020). These are countries in which the agriculture, health, education, and social protection sectors play a vital role in sustained growth and development. Yet these countries are also seeking to achieve structural change with the support of official development assistance (ODA), specifically ODA grants.

The providers of development cooperation are also undergoing transition. The tightening of ODA budgets, which started from the global economic and financial crisis of 2008, has generally been further constrained by the increase in in-country refugee costs leading to a decline in the disbursed volumes of ODA and its concessionality, followed by a concurrent increase in both investment in global public goods—primarily funding for action against climate change—and the growing multilateralization of bilateral aid (Bhattacharya and Khan 2020; OECD 2022). Indeed, there has been a renewed emphasis on development effectiveness in recent years. This therefore presents an opportune moment to re-examine the concept of ownership and its new underlying elements, given the changes in the priorities of provider countries.

5.1.2 Objectives

In view of the above, in this chapter, we seek to articulate a contemporary understanding of the 'ownership' principle and the various dimensions underpinning it. In line with this we approach 'country ownership' from the global perspective and country-level experiences, and we articulate a forward-looking approach to ownership. To this end, we track the evolution of the ownership concept as reflected in international literature. We also review how ownership manifests across the process chain, and we identify factors that promote or impede the ownership principle in practice at the recipient-country level. In addition, we explore the scope for a 'collective' form of ownership in lieu of 'country' ownership in the context of attaining development cooperation effectiveness.

5.1.3 Methodology, Scope, and Analytical Framework

Methodology and Scope

The chapter draws on the findings from six sector-focused case studies based in Asia, Latin America, and Africa. The case studies explore the application of the Busan Principles in the education, social protection, and agriculture sectors of Bangladesh (Bhattacharya et al. 2022), El Salvador (Sanfeliú et al. 2022), Rwanda (Besharati et al. 2022), Uganda (Kasirye et al. 2022), Tanzania (Killian et al. 2022), and Senegal (Hathie et al. 2022), and their relation to improved sector development outcomes.[1] It is also based on findings articulated in four thematic papers that explore broader themes of effective development cooperation.

Against this backdrop we examine sectoral experiences in the application of the first Busan Principle, that is, 'ownership of development priorities by developing countries', and the related 'effectiveness to impact' initiatives.[2] We identify the initiatives as the means through which the principles are practically applied at the sectoral level and explore the potential of external factors to play a role in facilitating or constraining the effectiveness of the initiatives.

The chapter is based on, inter alia, a review of relevant academic literature, publications from pertinent United Nations (UN) wings and the GPEDC, and other relevant national policy documents which mark the evolution of the ownership concept. Other methods include key informant interviews and workshops with relevant experts within the sectors and countries examined in the case studies and thematic papers. These experts consist of key representatives from international agencies and provider countries, government officials of recipient countries overseeing the execution of the sectoral strategies, representatives from policy-oriented civil society think tanks or organizations, sector development experts, and representatives of sectoral beneficiaries.

The extensive desk research combined with the findings from the key informant interviews and validation workshops served to unpack the relevance of the concept of country ownership and its contribution to improved development outcomes at the recipient-sector level.

Analytical Framework

We began by identifying areas within the development cooperation value chain which could indicate more of a 'collective ownership'. As mentioned previously ownership has conventionally been understood as the commitment made by recipient-country governments to their respective national and sectoral development through the adoption of a development plan, programmes, and/or strategy. Our research explores further the roles that providers may have played or could play to secure ownership and ensure improved effectiveness of development cooperation at the sectoral level. These areas of provider involvement include: (i) the conceptualization process of the sector strategy or plan; (ii) financing—particularly the resource allocation at the programme/project level

[1] These case studies were conducted as part of a multi-country research project titled 'Exploring 'Development Effectiveness' at the Sectoral Level in Southern Countries'. This is a research project funded by the European Commission pertaining to examining the application of the Busan Principles of Development Effectiveness in various sectoral and national contexts. For synthesis of the research findings, please see Bhattacharya et al. (2023).

[2] Six 'Effectiveness to Impact' initiatives were designed by the GPEDC and launched in 2020 to 'support the practical application of the Busan Principles at the sector level'. These include 'inclusive dialogues', 'joint analysis, drafting and review', 'agreed priorities and results framework', 'joint planning and budgeting', 'implementation modalities to strengthen national systems', and 'transparent evaluation and monitoring process' (GPEDC 2022).

and its internalization; (iii) implementation and monitoring processes; (iv) ensuring the sustainability of the development intervention; and (v) inclusivity of other key stakeholders throughout the processes.

5.1.4 Layout of the Chapter

After this introduction (Section 5.1) we review the evolving definitions of ownership by mapping the historical milestones that are pivotal in shaping the narrative (Section 5.2). This is followed by a deep dive into experiences of operationalizing ownership at the sector and country levels across Bangladesh, Rwanda, Tanzania, El Salvador, Senegal, and Uganda (Section 5.3). We then conclude with a concise overview of observed ownership patterns across various stakeholders, including international development partners (IDPs),[3] within recipient countries.

5.2 Looking Back on Ownership in Development Cooperation

'Ownership' of a recipient country is not a recently unveiled concept within the realm of international development cooperation. Its predecessor—borrowing country 'commitment'—was first discussed in the mid-1980s. At that time commitment was understood to mean: (i) the extent of agreement between a lender and borrower in relation to a programme's objectives and methods for achieving them; and (ii) the extent of interest among a borrower's key actors for implementing said programme (Heaver and Israel 1986). However, it was a decade later in the mid-1990s when the concept really took off (Woll 2006). Against this background this section explores the motivations underpinning the necessity of country ownership, the changes in its interpretation, the stakeholders involved, and its indicators or assessment over the years.

The primary motivation for promoting ownership among recipient countries, as stated by Heaver and Israel (1986: 1), was the general understanding that a 'borrower's commitment' to development projects will 'explain the success of a lending operation', and the lack thereof will consequently be 'one of the most commonly quoted cases of unsatisfactory programme or project implementation and lower than expected impact'. As mentioned earlier the renewed focus on country ownership in the mid-1990s was brought about to counteract the criticism of the lenders for their conditionality-heavy lending during the peak structural adjustment era of the 1980s (Woll 2006). However, the concept of attaining ownership by aligning the borrowing country's policy direction with a lender's preference or ideal

[3] The term 'international development partners' (IDPs) is used instead of 'donors'. It is used interchangeably with 'provider(s)' throughout this chapter.

was a precursor to successful programme implementation and, by extension, effective use of foreign aid has remained fairly consistent in the years since the concept was first brought to light (Castel-Branco 2008; Faust 2010; Rahman 2021).

While the main trigger for stressing ownership of recipient countries may have remained somewhat consistent in the last three decades, its interpretation has seen some changes. The 1996 Organisation for Economic Co-operation and Development (OECD) resolution required a recipient country to 'own' its national goals and strategies and 'lead' its development processes through dialogue. The understanding here was that recipient countries would design 'an integrated set of goals' based on targets broadly agreed upon by the international community—a first step to 'committing' their national goals and strategies. In this regard it was suggested that broad consensus and commitment should be sought from all levels of government, the private sector, non-governmental organizations, civil society, and external partners through dialogue (OECD 1996).

In 1999 the World Bank introduced the Poverty Reduction Strategy Papers (PRSPs) in place of the Structural Adjustment Programme, which had been criticized for undermining recipient countries' authority and autonomy. Through SAPs recipients were encouraged to develop their country strategies and policies and the World Bank would then support this ownership through financial support for the nationally derived strategies (Hasselskog and Schierenbeck 2017).

Not long after introduction of the PRSPs, the 'Comprehensive Development Framework' proposed by former World Bank President Wolfensohn was considered a decisive event in emboldening the concept of 'owning'. Echoing the sentiments of 1986, his speech referred to the need for a recipient country to be in the driver's seat: 'they [recipients] must determine goals and the phasing, timing and sequencing of programs' (Wolfensohn 2000; Rahman 2021). It was also acknowledged that development partners would only step in to support this ownership. When possible, this ownership would be fostered through a 'public debate' that would include government officials, members of the international development community, civil society, and the private sector (Wolfensohn 2000).

In 2003 the Rome Declaration on Harmonisation 'attached high importance' to a recipient government's leadership role and subsequently zeroed in on a much narrower approach to country ownership for coordinating aid and owning the country's development results (OECD 2003). Under this understanding development partners would step in to support recipient governments, that is, the central entity of the development process, to strengthen partnerships and engagement with civil society and the private sector (Shimomura and Ohno 2005).

During the second High-Level Forum (HLF) held in Paris in 2005 and in the consequent Paris Declaration, 'ownership' was first introduced as a guiding principle with monitorable indicators[4] (Hasselskog and Schierenbeck 2017). This was defined as 'recipient countries designing their poverty reduction strategies while improving domestic institutions and combatting corruption' (OECD 2005). However, much like the experience following the Rome Declaration, in practice, this principle revealed the general perception and acceptance that the ownership in question referred to recipient government ownership (Besson 2009). This was followed by the Accra Agenda for Action in 2008, which rearticulated the principle to emphasize the necessity of including civil society in development processes and the usage of recipient-country fiduciary systems by development partners (OECD 2008b).

In 2011, following the fourth HLF in Busan, South Korea, understanding of country ownership was adapted to the evolving landscape of international development financing, paving the way for the establishment of the GPEDC to nurture increased inclusivity of development actors. As such the principle was rephrased as: 'Partnerships for development can only succeed if they are led by developing countries, implementing approaches that are tailored to country-specific situations and needs' (OECD 2011). The explicit mention of partnerships and recipient leadership is recognized as leaving 'no space for donors to ignore the perspectives of recipient countries' (Rahman 2021: 359). The aspect of ownership as a prerequisite for attaining both improved and sustainable development outcomes was further reinforced in the Addis Ababa Action Agenda[5] (UN DESA 2015).

By the close of the second GPEDC High-Level Meeting in Nairobi, the centrality of the national government in leading the country's development strategies was once more reaffirmed with the understanding that the national parliament would review and scrutinize them. Local government and civil society would play a role alongside in encouraging transparency and accountability and would foster an enabling environment for 'inclusive participation of people to expand their democratic ownership over policies and development strategies ... with an emphasis on the poor and marginalised' (GPEDC 2016).

Despite early mentions of local ownership and including recipient-country stakeholders (in addition to the government) in development processes, the successive milestones in shaping ownership have revealed that country ownership has continued to prevail as the recipient government in the 'driver's seat' of

[4] The indicators presented in connection with assessing recipient-country ownership included three qualitative proxy indicators comprising: (i) Quality of country national development strategies (Indicator 1); (ii) Quality of country public financial management (PFM) systems (Indicator 2a); and (iii) Quality of country public procurement systems (Indicator 2b) (OECD 2008b.)

[5] The Addis Ababa Action Agenda is the document prepared following the conclusion of the Third International Conference on Financing for Development in Addis Ababa, Ethiopia from 13th to 16 July 2015.

development; see Figure 5.1. Stakeholders beyond development partners (e.g., civil society organizations (CSOs) and non-governmental organizations (NGOs)) have continued to participate as outsiders within recipient countries, only to be called upon in a consultative manner when needed. Notwithstanding the introduction of qualitative proxy indicators for monitoring ownership from 2005 onwards, these indicators focus more on the quality of country systems in anticipation of use by implementing bodies and, specifically, the development partners. However, the reality indicates an alternative scenario wherein the quality of

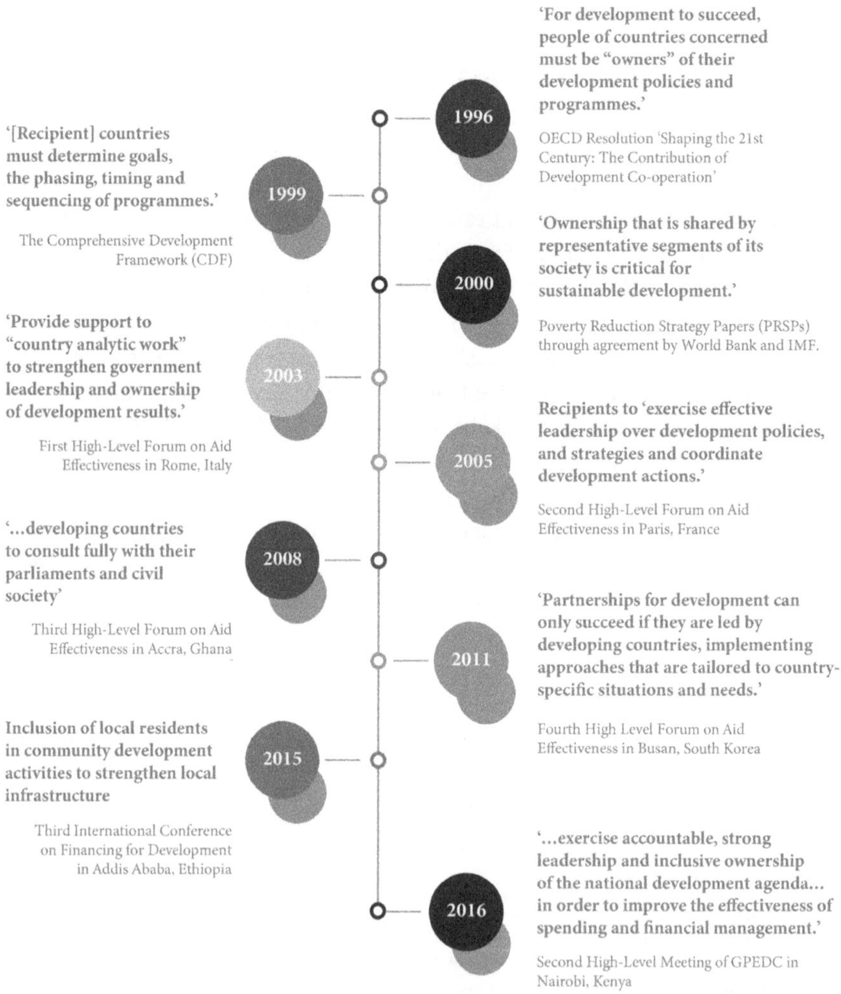

Figure 5.1 Historical milestones in shaping ownership of development processes

Source: authors' compilation from OECD (2005, 2008c, 2011), Hasselskog and Schierenbeck (2017), and Rahman (2021).

country systems does not actually correlate with the frequency of use. Indeed, the frequency of usage is reportedly affected by other external factors, namely the type of aid financing in consideration. Craviotto and Poel (2019) noted that loans are 'administered through country systems as opposed to grants'. As such the marginal increase in the usage of country systems can be attributed to the increase in loans in ODA over the last decade. This may be indicative of an already prevailing sentiment that country ownership and its underlying proxy indicators lend themselves to creating further vagueness surrounding the concept (Castel-Branco 2008).

The question that begs to be asked is: What are the indicators of a more 'collective' form of ownership? Research shows that true country ownership would encompass a slew of political factors including: (i) the recipient country's commitment to its development; (ii) the intellectual conviction of the recipient's key policy makers; (iii) the endorsement or support of the political leaders; and (iv) conscious and visible efforts to engage with multiple stakeholders to gain broad consensus (Kim et al. 2013).

The current GPEDC monitoring framework comprises a set of ten indicators to track the progress of stakeholders' commitment towards the four Effective Development Co-operation Principles. Five of these indicators have been designated to track the 'ownership of developing countries'.[6]

However, indicators such as 1a (Development partners use country-led results frameworks) and 1b (Countries strengthen their national results frameworks) reflect the overlapping contribution of the indicators to all four principles, particularly the 'ownership' principle, built into the monitoring framework. In this connection the following section explores the experiences of recipient countries in owning and leading their development strategies at the sectoral level, the stakeholders that have been involved and how, and the conditions under which attaining this ownership has been possible.

5.3 Exploring Ownership at the Country Level

At the country level ownership essentially means that a recipient country's national priorities play the central role in the selection, design implementation, and monitoring processes of development cooperation. This chapter argues for a more meaningful and effective role of the ownership principle of the Busan Partnership agreement by introducing the concept of collective ownership. The experience of development effectiveness at the recipient-country level suggests

[6] The indicators that underpin ownership in the Global Partnership's Monitoring Framework include: Indicator 5a (Development co-operation is predictable: annual predictability); Indicator 5b (Development co-operation is predictable: medium-term predictability); Indicator 9a (Quality of countries' public financial management systems); Indicator 9b (Development partners use country systems); and Indicator 10 (Aid is untied).

that operationalizing collective ownership would comprise three elements. The first element involves identifying the key stakeholders (e.g., relevant government agencies of the recipient country, IDPs, local government bodies, CSOs, targeted beneficiaries, and local communities). The second requires meaningful consultation with the key stakeholders identified as regards determining the development priorities at the national, sectoral, and local levels. The third element calls for the use of a development framework that aligns itself with the priorities determined at the national, sectoral, and local levels. Hence, we consider that a development cooperation initiative in a country adheres to the ownership principle adequately only when it is aligned with the recipient country's national, sectoral, and local development plans and meaningfully engages all key stakeholders at all stages, including at the selection, design implementation, and monitoring stages. From this perspective and taking account of the six aforesaid country studies, this chapter discusses defining and measuring ownership, examining participation of various key stakeholders throughout the development cooperation process chain, the application of ownership in various political contexts, and the roles of key stakeholders in upholding ownership.

5.3.1 Defining and Measuring Ownership

Establishing ownership requires a definite conceptualization at the recipient country level. At present the ownership principle is limited to bringing the central government of the recipient country onboard. There is very limited recognition of other stakeholders being integral to the concept. Also, how ownership is measured varies from country to country. A review of the experience of six developing countries across three continents suggests that stakeholders can conceptualize ownership in four different ways, which can be identified as the characteristics of ownership in the context of development cooperation initiatives.

First, in some Southern countries, the level of ownership is defined through specific mention of development priorities in their policy, plan, or strategy documents. This should ensure the alignment of the development cooperation initiative with the recipient country's development priorities. However, plan, policy, and strategy documents are often sponsored and guided by the IDPs.[7] Hence, while the documents in question may be endorsed by the government agency, there may only be partial commitment at the operational level.

Second, in some Southern countries, ownership may be measured through the prism of financing arrangements. The simplest indicator in this context is increased budgetary allocations from the recipient country, either in absolute or

[7] It is assumed that the IDPs operate within their democratic context and consult with their own key stakeholders.

relative terms. However, often, such increased budgetary allocations may not provide predictability. The government budget may generally increase in terms of operational expenditure but not necessarily in terms of development expenditure. Hence, the budgetary allocations may only have the life span of the development project.

This is also relevant for IDPs. The external financing flows from IDPs are usually committed for a project or programme life cycle. It is true that in many countries several IDPs finance a sector over the medium to long term. This often assures their ownership and commitment to the specific sector in a country. However, this can also change very rapidly, sometimes due to changes in the political commitment at the headquarters of the IDPs. One of the most recent such experiences is the withdrawal of financing in many countries by the UK's former Department for International Development, which has been replaced by the Foreign, Commonwealth & Development Office (FCDO). It has also been seen that financing can be increased in sector programmes but not necessarily in the sector as a whole. Hence this may signify a diversion of funds rather than increased ownership. This phenomenon may be true for both the recipient government and IDPs.

The level of ownership often determines the sustainability of project results. For example, in Senegal in the context of the agriculture sector, project results are found to be ephemeral (Hathie et al. 2022). It is understood that as the IDP funding is likely to stop, the activities will also stop, and even the temporary outcomes may disappear. Indeed, there are no efforts to scale up the innovations introduced by IDP-funded projects throughout the country, primarily due to a lack of ownership by the line ministry. In contrast in Uganda, following the withdrawal of funding from the FCDO (and Irish Aid) in June 2022, the government took on responsibility for fully funding the Social Assistance Grants for Empowerment programme (Kasirye et al. 2022). However, it should be noted that coverage of this programme is very low against its need.

Nevertheless, it is often seen that the IDPs that provide grants (usually the bilateral providers) demonstrate more ownership as regards the outcomes. In contrast the IDPs that provide credits (usually multilateral providers) are more interested in the process indicators (Bhattacharya et al. 2022). This suggests that the types of financing flows also influence the shape of the ownership. Even when a development cooperation initiative is fully funded by IDPs, if the recipient government is leading and it is aligned with a broader national development agenda, the recipient's ownership is upheld. For example, the Northern Uganda Social Action Fund was part of the broader Northern Uganda Reconstruction Program, and the Office of the Prime Minister in Uganda takes the lead despite the programme being fully funded by IDPs (Kasirye et al. 2022).

Third, in some countries, greater use of country systems may indicate enhanced ownership. This is relevant for both recipient countries and IDPs. There is indeed an enhanced practice of using the country system in designing and implementing development cooperation initiatives. However, the country system is sometimes not followed.

Fourth, ownership can be measured in terms of the meaningful participation of the key stakeholders. However, the extent of participation varies from country to country. It can also be the case that not all government agencies adequately participate in the development cooperation processes. Also, the participation of all the key stakeholders may not be ensured, while identifying the key stakeholders is often inadequate. Indeed, this characteristic is often found to be the weakest of the four.

To uphold the ownership principle in the development cooperation process, it is critical that all these characteristics are involved. Indeed, these characteristics—alignment with national development priorities, financing commitments, use of the country system, and participation of all key stakeholders—can meaningfully define the ownership of a development initiative from the perspective of a Southern recipient country.

5.3.2 Ownership at Different Stages of the Development Cooperation Process

The analyses in six country studies suggest that the participation of key stakeholders varies from country to country and is linked to the capacities of Southern governments. For example, in Senegal, national ownership is still weak and the dominant influence of IDPs on the projects they finance is very evident. Indeed, the Senegal government does not have the necessary capacity and tools to ensure permanent monitoring of programme execution (Hathie et al. 2022). On the other hand, in most cases, the governments in Bangladesh and Rwanda are found to be more dominant players compared to their IDP counterparts (Besharati et al. 2022; Bhattacharya et al. 2022). For example, in Rwanda, the national government initiated the 'division of labour' in 2010 and implemented it in 2012, while for the education sector the CSOs are also managed under the Rwanda Education NGO Coordination Platform (Besharati et al. 2022).

When ownership is defined through the participation of all key stakeholders, the level of ownership is found to be different from country to country. However, more importantly, the participation varies at different stages of the development cooperation process. Participation is generally stronger at the selection and the design stage of the project. In most countries recipient country government agencies, IDPs and some CSOs participate at this stage. At the implementation and monitoring stages, there is almost no involvement by CSOs. Meaningful involvement of IDPs also often declines at these stages. More importantly, the feedback loop is almost absent in all the countries under review. For example, in Senegal, various joint reviews were undertaken between 2014 and 2018 in the agriculture sector through inclusive dialogue between relevant stakeholders (Hathie et al. 2022). However, there was a very low level of uptake of the recommendations in the implementation of agricultural policies at a later stage, which eventually resulted in stakeholders having a reduced level of interest in such reviews.

5.3.3 Ownership in Different Political Realities

The political realities in the recipient country often shape the state of ownership principle in a country and in a sector within the country. It is conventionally understood that more democratic political realities in recipient countries are likely to better facilitate the inclusive participation of all key stakeholders. This also promotes better and more transparent monitoring, review, and feedback processes compared to other recipient countries. In the context of joint dialogue involving all key stakeholders, there is less likelihood of an IDP provider disagreeing with a recipient country's government. However, in contrast, the likelihood of an IDP enforcing its own standards in the case of a development cooperation initiative increases when there is misalignment between the priorities of a recipient country and those of the IDP. Indeed, stronger recipient-country governments, in terms of being either democratic or authoritarian, are more likely to play a stronger role. However, more-authoritarian governments may ignore the roles of other stakeholders, particularly those at the national level. It is also found that the countries with better development stages have a stronger say in development cooperation initiatives. The presence of alternative and non-conventional financing sources also influences the bargaining power of recipient countries.

Political stability is also often recognized as a critical factor for successful development cooperation initiatives (Dercon 2022). The political realities also shape the development cooperation initiatives. For example, in post-2019 El Salvador, the Technical Secretariat of the Presidency, which had been in charge of the technical coordination with IDPs over the preceding decade, was dissolved when there was a change in the political party in power and led to the establishment of the El Salvador Co-operation Agency under the office of the president (Sanfeliú et al. 2022). This critical strategic change was not discussed with the 'permanent three-party dialogue commission' and is an indication of the participation of key stakeholders being more limited. Political leadership is indeed a critical element for shaping development cooperation initiatives. In Tanzania the establishment of the Tanzania Social Fund was a strong political wish of the country's then president (Killian et al. 2022). The fund was initiated after the president's visit to Malawi and his exposure to the Malawi Social Action Fund (MASAF). The president requested the same World Bank team which had set up MASAF (Jacob and Pedersen 2018).

As development cooperation initiatives fully or partially funded by IDPs are generally considered to be public goods, it is thought that it is within the purview of the recipient government to design and utilize them as required. Hughes and Hutchinson (2012) argued that politics in the recipient country should be critically considered to ensure the effectiveness of a development cooperation initiative. Masaki (2018), citing the example of Zambia, argued that, over 16 years, IDP-funded projects were directed towards districts with substantial support for opposition parties, partly due to limited information about swing states and with an intention to generate support in the districts with weaker support for the ruling party. It is believed that the use of development cooperation for electoral political motives may weaken coordination between a recipient country's government and IDPs and may discourage use of country results frameworks, which has recently been a concern in some cases (OECD/UNDP 2019). The multiplicity arising from IDP procedures, along with the absence of harmonization with the country system, ultimately cause cost and time overruns in implementation (Hathie et al. 2022).

5.3.4 Role of Non-state Actors in Establishing Ownership Principles

Operationalizing the ownership principle by ensuring the meaningful participation of all key stakeholders at all stages of the development cooperation chain is a collective responsibility. To this end it is the recipient government that will be in the driving seat. The government of the recipient country must ensure that all national stakeholders, including the relevant government agencies, local government, CSOs, private sector, and local communities, have adequate space at all stages.

IDPs should also encourage participation and ensure this during negotiations. It is also the responsibility of other stakeholders (e.g., local government, CSOs, private sector, and local communities) to keep pushing for their space as part of their ownership exercise. They will also need to invest in their capacities so that they can meaningfully contribute, while the IDPs and the recipient government should also support such endeavours. The capacities of recipient governments are also a key determinant for them to lead development cooperation initiatives (Hathie et al. 2022). Also, the IDPs situated at the recipient-country level should be able to negotiate with their headquarters counterparts to uphold national priorities and align IDP priorities accordingly. It is the case that almost every IDP in every recipient country has its own country programming document. Although these programming documents are generally aligned with the recipient country's priorities, the IDP is often likely to follow its own priorities (Hathie et al. 2022).

The sectoral experiences discussed thus far reveal that upholding the ownership principle greatly depends on the capacity of the recipient government and the nature of the IDP particularly to stress national development priorities in policy, programme, or strategic documents, positively influence consistent key stakeholder participation at all levels in the development cooperation process, and ensure the sustainability of sector development outcomes.

5.4 Conclusion and Recommendation

The ownership principle is undoubtedly crucial for upholding the remaining principles, but it is possibly one of the most complicated to achieve in practice. Discussions at successive high-level forums and meetings in the last two decades have continually reiterated the need for inclusivity when implementing development cooperation initiatives. However, the sectoral experiences of operationalizing country ownership have revealed that the current GPEDC framework's provisions for monitoring ownership at the country level is a rather closed-off model, often disconnected from the realities on the ground.

This chapter unpacked and revisited the key elements that underpin the concept of ownership. It examined its operationalization from four angles, namely across countries and sectors, across various stages of the development cooperation process, in various political contexts, and the roles of key stakeholders.

Five key messages emerge as pertinent to shaping new views on the ownership concept in the context of effective development cooperation. The first of these is that ownership is conventionally understood to be attained through an explicit statement of development priorities in a national policy, plan, or strategy document. However, sectoral experiences reveal that, more often than not, IDPs play a key role in formulating these documents. Their involvement at this stage does not reflect whether the document has been prepared through a reasonable consultative process between the IDP's headquarters and the country office. Moreover, although preparing a policy, plan, or strategic document may indicate adequate endorsement by the recipient government, this may not be fully translated at the operational level.

Second, an increase in the share of recipient government financing in a programme/project has been used to indicate an increase in a recipient country's ownership of an initiative. However, this has been met with substantial scepticism by relevant stakeholders. As an increase in budgetary allocation may also be the result of an increase in operational expenditure rather than capital expenditure, an increase in government financing does not always reflect an increase in recipient ownership. In some cases, it is considered to occur to the detriment of the sustainability of the results.

The third message relates to the declining level of inclusivity along the development cooperation process. The process can be divided into three broad stages: conceptualization and design, implementation and management, and assessment and feedback. In Southern countries the involvement of relevant key stakeholders—representing the recipient government, CSOs, NGOs, the private sector, and IDPs—dominates in the first stage. While the recipient government remains in the driver's seat throughout the process, the space for the non-state actors gradually shrinks as it reaches the implementation stage. There is also a broken feedback loop, but it can be argued that this is the result of a lack of capacity and space for non-state actors to provide feedback adequately. This leaves only one foreseeable option, that is, that actors will need to demand this space, which can only occur in an enabling institutional environment within recipient countries. In these circumstances, it is equally important for IDPs to negotiate an enabling environment for meaningful key stakeholder participation and to assess the extent to which feedback is absorbed.

Fourth, the enabling environment required for meaningful multistakeholder participation throughout the development cooperation process depends on political leadership and political stability within a recipient country. In cases where the government takes an authoritarian stance, the voices of the non-state actors are ignored. IDPs are more likely to impose their development inclinations, particularly in situations where there is misalignment between their development priorities and those of the recipient. In these cases, the experiences reveal that along with an increase in alternative sources of development financing, recipient countries have also seen an increase in their bargaining power.

The case studies also point to a certain degree of disregard by providers of political economy realities within recipient countries. The expressed desire to not disrupt political relations may have played a pivotal role in diminishing IDP ownership of development cooperation processes within recipient countries. The decline in IDP ownership is further exacerbated by the inadequate exposure of IDP country offices to the GPEDC monitoring framework and its relevance, thus indicating the need to allocate staff time and to design an effective work plan to enable IDP offices to become familiar with the relevance of the GPEDC framework in recipient countries.

The reality, though, is that the roles undertaken by IDP country offices have weakened due to deviating interests at IDP headquarters as a result of increased geopolitical tensions, humanitarian crises, and constrained finances. In tandem with shrinking spaces for non-state actors, this reality has led to decreased interest in the GPEDC principles facilitating effective use of development cooperation across the board. In view of this there is a need to incentivize IDP country offices to attain desired development outcomes within a recipient country.

Finally, the fifth and potentially the most interesting message relates to the modality of development cooperation. Whether the recipient receives grants or loans, it plays a substantial role when designing the results framework and indicators for a programme or project. It was previously found that the increase in usage of recipient-country systems was concurrent with an increase in loans (as a share of ODA) disbursed through recipient-country systems (Craviotto and Poel 2019). However, in our case studies, the experiences reveal that the loan providers generally operate under pressure to disburse loans as the cost of prolonging a programme or project outweighs its benefit. Thus, creditors are more lenient about achieving results than their counterparts. On the other hand, the grant providers are far more inclined to exert pressure on recipient countries to achieve desired sustainable development outcomes.

Based on the sector experiences explored throughout this chapter, upholding ownership involves four key elements.[8] Of the four, the extent of key stakeholder participation throughout the development cooperation process was identified as particularly critical for strengthening ownership.

5.4.1 A New(er) Approach to Ownership

Although pertinent to monitoring ownership, the current GPEDC framework indicators[9] present a very recipient-country and process-oriented approach to measuring the concept. As the evidence from consecutive GPEDC monitoring rounds has revealed, there has been a decline in the alignment between providers' and recipients' development priorities, usage of results frameworks, and the predictability of development cooperation. The findings highlight several factors beyond the purview of the current GPEDC framework, but which play a critical role in delivering improved development outcomes. A particular factor is the changes at the provider-country level which spill over from geopolitical and geoeconomic issues and lead to changes in development priorities and approaches.

In this vein, this chapter argues that the active and substantive participation of three key stakeholder groups in successive development cooperation processes is critical to achieving ownership. It identifies 'participation' as its core basis and rearticulates the first principle as 'collective ownership' in place of 'country ownership'. Thus, collective ownership is defined as the meaningful participation of key stakeholders at all stages in the development cooperation process. These key[10] stakeholders comprise: (i) the recipient country's government; (ii) international providers; and (iii) the remaining non-state actors, particularly the private sector, CSOs, and NGOs. Ensuring their meaningful participation will begin with identifying key stakeholders relevant to the process in which they may be engaged and will end with an assessment of the effectiveness of their involvement.

[8] The four elements are all focused at the recipient-country level and are: (i) the recipient government taking up the leadership role; (ii) an increase in (absolute or relative) recipient financing in a programme or project; (iii) type of ODA financing; and (iv) key stakeholder participation.

[9] The current indicators of ownership in the GPEDC monitoring framework broadly comprise obtaining the political endorsement of budgeted development cooperation, using the national results framework and recipient country systems, and attaining predictability of foreign financing.

[10] The word 'key' here is used to emphasize that not all stakeholders, despite their relevance, can be engaged at all levels.

Provider ownership throughout the process is crucial for encouraging and ensuring key stakeholder participation. In terms of their own engagement, provider representations can be identified and engaged according to the sectoral relevance of their role in conceptualization and design, implementation, and management, or results assessment and feedback processes, and their capacity to do so.

The complexity of attaining ownership to facilitate effective development cooperation requires the active and meaningful participation of multiple key stakeholders at different levels of the development cooperation process and these are aspects that must be embedded in the GPEDC monitoring framework.

References

Besharati, N., S. Uwera, and C. B. Berwa (2022). 'Impact of GPEDC Principles on Education, Training and Youth Employment in Rwanda'. Rwanda: European Commission. https://capacity4dev.europa.eu/library/exploring-development-effectiveness-sectoral-level-southern-countries_en.

Besson, P. (2009). 'Country Ownership and Aid Effectiveness: Why We All Talk About It and Mean Different Things'. Politorbis 46–1. Bern: Swiss Federal Department of Foreign Affairs. Available at: https://css.ethz.ch/content/specialinterest/gess/cis/center-for-securities-studies/en/services/digital-library/publications/publication.html/114277 (accessed 19 September 2022).

Bhattacharya, D., and S. S. Khan (2020). 'Rethinking Development Effectiveness: Perspectives from the Global South'. Dhaka: Southern Voice. Available at: http://southernvoice.org/rethinking-development-effectiveness-perspectives-from-the-global-south/ (accessed 15 April 2022).

Bhattacharya, D., T. I. Khan, N. M. Altaf, M. Alam, and I. Kabir (2022). 'The Primary Education Sector in Bangladesh: Exploring the Effectiveness of Development Co-operation'. Bangladesh: European Commission. https://capacity4dev.europa.eu/library/exploring-development-effectiveness-sectoral-level-southern-countries_en.

Bhattacharya, D., T. I. Khan, N. M. Altaf, and L. Alcázar (2023). 'Key Findings and Message'. Brussels: European Commission. https://capacity4dev.europa.eu/library/exploring-development-effectiveness-sectoral-level-southern-countries_en.

Castel-Branco, C. N. (2008). 'Aid Dependency and Development: A Question of Ownership? A Critical View'. Maputo: Instituto de Estudos Sociais e Económicos (IESE). Available at: https://www.iese.ac.mz/lib/saber/ead_34.pdf (accessed 10 September 2022).

Craviotto, N., and J. V. Poel (2019). 'Global Partnership on Effective Development Co-operation: Will This Weekend's Senior Level Meeting Turn the Tide on Effective Development?'. Brussels: European Network on Debt and Development (EURODAD) Available at: https://www.eurodad.org/global_partnership_on_effective_development_cooperation (accessed 11 October 2022).

Dercon, S. (2022). *Gambling on Development: Why Some Countries Win and Others Lose.* London: Hurst Publishers.

Faust, J. (2010). 'Policy Experiments, Democratic Ownership and Development Assistance'. *Development Policy Review*, 28(5): 515–34. https://doi.org/10.1111/j.1467-7679.2010.00496.x.

GPEDC (2016). *Nairobi Outcome Document.* Nairobi: Global Partnership for Effective Development Co-operation.

GPEDC (2022). *Effectiveness to Impact Initiatives: Sector Needs Assessment.* New York, NY: Global Partnership for Effective Development Co-operation.

Hasselskog, M., and I. Schierenbeck (2017). 'The Ownership Paradox: Continuity and Change'. *Forum for Development Studies*, 44(3): 323–33. https://doi.org/10.1080/08039410.2017.1384530.

Hathie, I., N. Cissé, A. Ly, L. Tall, and A. Seck (2022). 'Exploring "Development Effectiveness" at the Sectoral Level in Southern Countries: Case of Crop Production Sector in Senegal'. Senegal: European Commission. https://capacity4dev.europa.eu/library/exploring-development-effectiveness-sectoral-level-southern-countries_en.

Heaver, R., and A. Israel (1986). *Country Commitment to Development Projects.* Washington, DC: The World Bank.

Hughes, C., and J. Hutchison (2012). 'Development Effectiveness and the Politics of Commitment'. *Third World Quarterly*, 33(1): 17–33. Available at: https://www.jstor.org/stable/41341209 (accessed 5 November 2022).

Jacob, T., and R. H. Pedersen (2018). 'Social Protection in an Electorally Competitive Environment (1): The Politics of Productive Social Safety Nets (PSSN) in Tanzania'. Working Paper 109. Manchester: The University of Manchester. Available at: https://www.effective-states.org/working-paper-109/ (accessed 20 October 2022).

Kasirye, I., F. Nakazi, S. Ainomugisha, and T. Akurut (2022). 'An Assessment of the Role of Busan's Effective Development Co-operation Principles in Delivering Uganda's Social Protection Sector Outcomes'. Uganda: European Commission. https://capacity4dev.europa.eu/library/exploring-development-effectiveness-sectoral-level-southern-countries_en.

Keijzer, N., S. Klingebiel, C. Örnemark, and F. Scholte (2019). 'Seeking Balanced Ownership in Changing Development Cooperation Relationships'. Sweden: Expert Group for Aid Studies (EBA). Available at: https://papers.ssrn.com/sol3/papers.cfm?abstract_id=3310599# (accessed 10 April 2022).

Killian, B., W. J. Walwa, R. F. Sambaiga, and L. R. Mugisha (2022). 'Effectiveness of Development Co-operation Principles: An Inquiry into the Dimension of Health Sub-Sector under the Social Protection Programme in Tanzania'. Tanzania: European Commission. https://capacity4dev.europa.eu/library/exploring-development-effectiveness-sectoral-level-southern-countries_en.

Kim, E. M., P. H. Kim, and J. Kim (2013). 'From Development to Development Co-operation: Foreign Aid, Country Ownership, and the Developmental State in South Korea'. *The Pacific Review*, 26(3): 313–36. https://doi.org/10.1080/09512748.2012.759263.

Masaki, T. (2018). 'The Political Economy of Aid Allocation in Africa: Evidence from Zambia'. *African Studies Review*, 61(1): 55–82. https://doi.org/10.1017/asr.2017.97.

OECD (1996). *Shaping the 21st Century: The Contribution of Development Co-operation.* Paris: OECD Publishing.

OECD (2003). *HLF1: The First High Level Forum on Aid Effectiveness, Rome.* Paris: OECD Publishing. Available at: https://www.oecd.org/dac/effectiveness/hlf-1thefirsthighlevelforumonaideffectivenessrome.htm (accessed 20 September 2022).

OECD (2005). *Paris Declaration on Aid Effectiveness.* Paris: OECD Publishing. Available at: https://www.oecd.org/dac/effectiveness/parisdeclarationandaccraagendaforaction.htm (accessed 20 September 2022).

OECD (2008a). *2008 Survey on Monitoring the Paris Declaration.* Paris: OECD Publishing.

OECD (2008b). *The Paris Declaration on Aid Effectiveness and the Accra Agenda for Action.* Paris: OECD Publishing.

OECD (2008c). *The Accra Agenda for Action (AAA).* Paris: OECD Publishing.

OECD (2011). *Busan Partnership for Effective Development Co-operation: Fourth High Level Forum on Aid Effectiveness, Busan, Republic of Korea.* Paris: OECD Publishing. https://doi.org/10.1787/54de7baa-en.

OECD (2022). *International Development Statistics Database.* Available at: https://stats.oecd.org/qwids/ (accessed 20 September 2022).

OECD/UNDP (2019). *Making Development Co-Operation More Effective: 2019 Progress Report.* Paris: OECD Publishing. https://doi.org/10.1787/26f2638f-en.

Rahman, M. M. (2021). 'Development Aid and the "Ownership" Principle in Development Policy'. In H. Zafarullah and A. S. Huque, editors, *Handbook of Development Policy.* Cheltenham: Edward Elgar Publishing Limited. https://doi.org/10.4337/9781839100871.00040.

Sanfeliú, M. B., C. Gómez, G. Hernández, and Y. Sánchez (2022). 'Exploring "Development Effectiveness" at the Sectoral Level in Southern Countries: The Crop Production Sector in El Salvador'. El Salvador: European Commission. https://capacity4dev.europa.eu/library/exploring-development-effectiveness-sectoral-level-southern-countries_en.

Shimomura, Y., and I. Ohno (2005). 'Introduction and Overview'. In I. Ohno, Y. Shimomura, K. Ohno, and M. Nagasu, editors, *True Ownership and Policy Autonomy: Managing Donors and Owning Policies.* Tokyo: GRIPS Development Forum, National Graduate Institute for Policy Studies: 1–20.

Stern, E., L. Altinger, O. Feinstein, M. Marañón, D. Ruegenberg, N.-S. Schulz, and N. S. Nielsen (2008). 'Thematic Study on the Paris Declaration, Aid Effectiveness and Development Effectiveness'. Copenhagen: Ministry of Foreign Affairs. Available at: https://daraint.org/dara_evaluations/thematic-study-on-the-paris-declaration-aid-effectiveness-and-development-effectiveness/ (accessed 19 September 2022).

UN DESA (2015). *Addis Ababa Action Agenda of the Third International Conference on Financing for Development (Addis Ababa Action Agenda).* Addis Ababa: United Nations Department of Economic and Social Affairs.

Wolfensohn, J. D. (2000). *The Comprehensive Development Framework.* Washington, DC: The World Bank.

Woll, B. (2006). 'The Ownership Paradox: The Politics of Development Co-operation with Bolivia and Ghana'. London: London School of Economics and Political Science. Available at http://etheses.lse.ac.uk/856/ (accessed 11 October 2022).

6

Rethinking the Relationship between Community-Driven Reconstruction and the Social Sciences

Lessons from Afghanistan

Jennifer Brick Murtazashvili

6.1 Introduction

The Government of the Islamic Republic of Afghanistan fell from power on 15 August 2021, when President Ashraf Ghani hopped on a helicopter in the middle of the day and flew away to neighbouring Uzbekistan, without telling even some of his closest aides or staff. Hours later, the Taliban, who had had fought a 20-year insurgency against this government, waltzed into the presidential palace and took over. Not a shot was fired.

This was not a failure of the Afghanistan National Security Forces (ANSF), as some military experts and strategic thinkers have suggested. Rather, politics undid the Republic. Public opinion in Afghanistan showed how the Afghan Army, which was leading the charge against the Taliban, was among the most trusted public institutions in the country (The Asia Foundation 2018, 2020). While the vast majority of the analysis on Afghanistan in Western media focused on the failure of the security forces to defend the capital and supply chain challenges, the collapse of the army was a consequence—not a cause—of political failures (Murtazashvili 2022).

The fundamental problem was that the Afghan government lost legitimacy in the eyes of its people (Bizhan 2022: 24–63). The ANSF stopped fighting because soldiers no longer believed in their leaders. After decades of fighting hard—and losing tens of thousands of brothers-in-arms—they simply gave up. They saw a confused and isolated regime in Kabul that seemed more interested in preserving its control vis-à-vis rivals within the government than it was in fighting the insurgency (Murtazashvili 2021b).

In the wake of the Republic's calamitous fall to the Taliban in 2021, the world witnessed a flurry of academic and policy discussions regarding the effectiveness of post-conflict reconstruction efforts, particularly in Afghanistan. These debates

Jennifer Brick Murtazashvili, *Rethinking the Relationship between Community-Driven Reconstruction and the Social Sciences*. In: *Fragile Aid*. Edited by: Rachel M. Gisselquist et al., Oxford University Press. © UNU-WIDER (2025).
DOI: 10.1093/oso/9780198960287.003.0006

also revealed a significant paradox in the literature on development. On the one hand was a vast body of literature that lauded reconstruction efforts and found many local-level interventions to be very successful and even sustainable. On the other hand were claims that the billions of dollars spent on these micro-level interventions did not yield a legitimate or sustainable government.

This chapter critically explores this paradox. It argues that academic research focused on the intervention studied the effectiveness (or lack thereof) of the intervention but failed to understand the broader political context in which these projects operated. Rather than support efforts to build the state, many of these projects undermined it. This is particularly the case for most of the local-level interventions that sought to strengthen communities and local-level development.

These conclusions are based on extensive field observations conducted in Afghanistan during the two decades of the US intervention to assess perceptions of aid as individuals and communities were coming to terms with the scope and scale of the international interventions in their country. The cumulative lesson from this evidence is that to come to terms with the outcomes and challenges of post-conflict reconstruction in Afghanistan, it is imperative to see the effectiveness of aid as a political project. What is necessary to improve prospects for post-conflict reconstruction is to more deeply integrate political considerations into grassroots development. A more nuanced and effective course for reconstruction, not only in Afghanistan but also in conflict-affected regions worldwide, can be made possible by shedding light on the overlooked complexities of local governance and politics.

For more than a decade, development practitioners have discussed the centrality of Political Economy Analysis and the importance of having a political lens on development (Fritz et al. 2014; Denney 2016). Yet so many interventions in Afghanistan failed to account for politics.

This chapter joins an emergent literature that acknowledges the importance of a local lens—but also one that is politically attuned and astute—to approach the challenge of promoting development. We have witnessed a concerted call for micro-level analysis of violent conflict (Justino et al. 2013). As Justino (2018) explains, the idea is that international interventions should empower local governance and local opportunities for collective action, as well as improve state institutions and invest to change social norms.

Despite broad agreement on this approach, there appear to be flaws in its implementation. Ashley Jackson has detailed the challenges with international service delivery in Afghanistan and why individuals and communities were willing to turn to the Taliban as an alternative (Giustozzi and Jackson 2012; Jackson 2018; Jackson and Weigand 2020). I argue that one reason for this failing is that several of the key tools in the repertoire of micro-level analysis, including community-driven development (CDD) and randomized control trial (RCT) methods, are in many instances inappropriate to such analysis. This is because the methodological orientation they adopt—an emphasis on narrow interventions with a clean causal story—leads to certain blind spots. In this regard, what is necessary is to further reflect on the challenges and to criticize micro-level analysis, and to see whether it can be, in a sense, made more legitimately 'micro'. In the case of Afghanistan, there was a move towards interventions at the local level, but these activities were driven more by central actors, in response to external incentives, than local ones. Finally, many of these local-level approaches were paradoxically orthogonal to what was happening on the ground.

These failings occurred despite recent research highlighting the importance of a need for a 'local turn' in the study of peacebuilding (MacGinty and Richmond 2013; Hughes et al. 2015). While a turn to local dynamics is key to counterinsurgency and building local peace, too often paradigms of international relations and international organization prioritize an examination of the role of international actors and their work at the local level, rather than the endogenous work of local actors. This is reflected in the work of Séverine Autesserre, for example, who has stressed the importance of international organizations engaging more effectively in local conflicts (Autesserre 2010). But this approach still prioritizes the importance and centrality of international actors. It is less a local turn than a causal inference turn, and the key players are not local but foreign. We are shown the world through their incentive structures and their lenses, without adequate attention to the degree to which such interventions are embedded in local institutions. Scholars and policy-makers impose blinkers on themselves when they prioritize the study of their own work rather than the centrality of local institutions, actors, and incentives. Studying global organizations at the local level is a very incomplete study of local peacebuilding. It may be the case that international actors and their interventions are in fact tangential to local politics. They may be effective to their bureaucratic stakeholders but make very little difference to the local communities they purport to be supporting.

6.2 The Obsession with Community in Aid

The international donor community entered Afghanistan under the premise that the country was a *tabula rasa*, a blank slate without effective local governance structures following the fall of the Taliban. This led to a concentrated focus on community-level engagement, often overlooking the existence and efficacy of customary governance systems that had persisted and adapted over time. Without having to worry about pre-existing structures, the international community and some Afghan politicians—like Ashraf Ghani, who had long been involved in such efforts during his tenure at the World Bank—pushed for CDD projects that could establish entirely new structures at the village level from scratch. Donors missed the fact that customary systems not only had survived decades of conflict but also continued to play a critical role in local governance, even after significant political upheaval (Murtazashvili 2021a).

In their pursuit of goals like gender equality and the Millennium Development Goals, international efforts at times promoted new forms of local governance that did not align with the customary practices embedded within rural Afghan society. This mismatch led to the creation of parallel structures and governance systems that were externally driven and often incongruent with the nuanced social and political fabric of rural Afghan communities (Sharan 2013). Furthermore, the donors' focus on community-level aid often led to the neglect of larger-scale public goods and services that communities needed but could not provide themselves. This approach also created distortions, as the introduction of aid projects sometimes led to cycles of corruption and unintended consequences (Murtazashvili 2016).

The most significant community-driven programme in Afghanistan during the era of post-conflict reconstruction was The National Solidarity Program (NSP). This programme was initiated by the Afghan government to provide support to around 15,000 villages in rural Afghanistan. Launched in 2003 with a budget of US$600 million, the NSP aimed to establish local, democratically elected institutions called Community Development Councils (CDCs) to lead reconstruction and development efforts. The programme drew inspiration from the Kecamatan Development Program in Indonesia and was implemented by the Ministry of Rural Rehabilitation and Development (MRRD) with funding from various international sources including the World Bank and aid agencies from the UK, Denmark, Canada, and the United States. The NSP intended to engage rural populations, which comprise around 80% of Afghanistan's population, in development and to foster the rule of law and community-managed projects.

Rather than let it be implemented by the MRRD itself, however, the government and the World Bank chose to have international NGOs play the primary role facilitating the programme, providing technical support and managing the elections of CDC leadership councils. The programme unfolded in phases, with the objective of expanding CDCs to cover 80–90% of Afghanistan's rural communities and improving the institutional quality, sustainability, and governance of these local bodies (MRRD 2006).

The NSP aimed to establish, strengthen, and maintain CDCs as effective institutions for local governance and socio-economic development, with an explicit goal of promoting gender equality as well (Beath et al. 2013a). The first phase in the NSP was community mobilization and training in inclusive and transparent decision-making, leading to the election of community councils. These councils were then tasked with creating local development plans.

The implementation phase involved block grants spent on sub-projects chosen by the community, consistent with their training and using the newly established institutions. The intention was that the participatory community processes would continue into other activities beyond the lifespan of the CDD programme, with the aim of institutionalizing norms of good governance and social cohesion (King and Samii 2014).

In conflict-affected areas like Afghanistan, the idea was that such CDD programmes could serve as a mechanism for service delivery where the state's administrative reach was limited. Donors and implementing agencies did not merely focus on immediate service delivery but also sought to build local governance capacity, fostering social cohesion, and creating stable communities capable of self-management and conflict resolution. The NSP's institutional outputs were designed to encourage broad-based participation in the process, potentially altering existing power dynamics to be more inclusive, and giving community members a positive experience of collaboration. This was expected to foster a sense of ownership over local development activities, which would then act as an incentive for community members to hold implementers accountable (Goodhand and Sedra 2010).

The CDCs also sought to create an institutional infrastructure, such as development plans, community bank accounts, and local audits, that could make future collective actions less costly and more manageable after the project ended, thus seeking to have a lasting impact on community organization and governance.

A midline evaluation of the programme indicated a significant rise in women's participation in community councils and enhanced perceptions that community assemblies were providing services, thus indicating progress towards the programme's main goals during its term (Beath et al. 2013b). However, the NSP exhibited significant structural and operational shortcomings that revealed its true nature as a top-down initiative even though it was framed as a way to empower communities.

6.3 The Illusion of a Bottom-up Approach

Ostensibly designed to empower local governance through the creation of CDCs, the NSP inadvertently mirrored earlier state-driven efforts, notably those from the communist era, thus perpetuating a legacy of centralization under the guise of localism.

Local perceptions of the NSP were shaped by historical experiences of state interventions. Afghans had witnessed a series of governance initiatives that, despite their varied ideological underpinnings, commonly sought to extend the reach of the central government into the rural fabric of the nation. During the communist period (1978–92), for instance, efforts to establish village-level councils were part of a broader agenda to consolidate state control and mobilize the rural populace in support of state policies (Edwards 2002). These councils, rather than acting as independent entities reflecting the will of the communities, functioned as conduits for central policy implementation, often disrupting traditional power structures and local autonomy.

The NSP's approach echoed these earlier interventions by promoting structures that, while nominally community-based, depended heavily on guidance and resources from the central government and international donors. The selection of projects, the allocation of funds, and the very design of the CDCs often followed a predetermined agenda set by external actors, leaving little room for genuine community initiative. In the eyes of many Afghans, the NSP was less about development and more about the government's desire to project its influence and authority into the rural hinterlands.

The programme was viewed through a political lens, with its evident continuity from past government initiatives, especially the communist policies. During the time I spent in rural Afghanistan working to understand community governance, I was surprised to hear complaints from residents that the programme was the work of 'communists'. It turns out that some of the key players implementing the project were communists (or 'former' communists). Many whom I interviewed suggested that the programme reminded them of similar programmes rolled out during the rule of Daoud Khan in the 1970s; others said that the communists during their rule sought to implement such councils as part of their attempts to rule the countryside in the 1990s. They saw the NSP as an extension of communist-backed approaches to link communities to the state. Several residents mentioned that the Minister of Rehabilitation and Rural Development, Hanif Atmar, who played a major role in implementing the programme, was a 'communist' who was simply trying to control villages and tie them to the state. Atmar was a known agent of the Khad, the secret police of the Afghan communist party. In fact, Atmar lost one of his legs fighting with a Khad special-operations unit against mujahedeen fighters in the 1980s. When the communists lost control of Kabul, he left for the UK, where he earned a degree in post-conflict recovery (Burns 2008). In the minds of several of the people I spoke with, his efforts to promote community development councils were a natural outgrowth of his disdain for the countryside and a desire to centralize power.

The similarity of NSP to previous attempts to establish state-affiliated bodies within communities were again met with resistance or ambivalence by local populations wary of state intrusion into their customary systems of governance. By not adequately differentiating itself from the political strategies of previous regimes, the NSP struggled to gain the full trust and engagement of the communities it aimed to serve. This historical resonance highlighted the importance of understanding the intricate tapestry of local governance and the potential pitfalls of ignoring the lessons of the past when designing development interventions.

6.4 Afghanistan as a Laboratory for Experiments

Rather than a *tabula rasa*, rural Afghanistan at the time reconstruction began was rich in social capital, embodied in a complex and trusted system of customary governance (Miakhel 2006; Miakhel and Coburn 2010). For instance, customary assemblies like *jirgas* and *shuras* played a crucial role in maintaining order and resolving conflicts at the community level. These indigenous institutions, reflecting a robust system of social norms and collective action, were indicative of a society that was far from a blank slate. They highlighted the capacity for self-organization and mutual trust within communities, essential components of social capital that were unfortunately overlooked in the reconstruction process.

The execution of the NSP encapsulated this misjudgement. Rather than support existing community governance systems and their activities, funds were primarily used to support the implementation of the new project. It was reported that for every dollar spent directly on community projects, approximately another dollar was spent on facilitation, administration, and oversight, raising questions about the programme's balance between external control and community empowerment. The funnelling of funds to a new bureaucracy created locally was one of the reasons why these projects reminded so many of the earlier efforts by the communist governments to use development programmes as a political strategy to control communities rather than to empower them.

The shortcomings of international reconstruction efforts were not limited to programme design and implementation but also extended to their impact on community cohesion. The duplication of roles and creation of parallel structures often conflicted with existing traditional authority systems, resulting in community tensions. This disruption was exacerbated by the manipulation of project selections and aid distribution by local elites, leading to increased corruption and conflict—precisely the opposite of the intended objectives of fostering unity and development.

My reading of the local context was that the reconstruction efforts in Afghanistan, exemplified by the NSP, demonstrated a disconnect between the international community's assumptions and the on-the-ground realities of Afghan society. These efforts failed to build on a strong foundation of local governance but, in some cases, contributed to its erosion, inadvertently fuelling further conflict and instability. My conclusion after assessing the NSP was that there was a need for reconstruction policies to be grounded in a nuanced understanding of local governance and social dynamics (Murtazashvili 2016).

The NSP could have empowered communities, for example by providing them with oversight over local projects and establishing opportunities for them to control their revenue sources. They had little input over spending and no authority to raise taxes of any sort.

The World Bank's evaluations of the projects hinted at the uneven and even negative impact of the programme. Despite some positive short-term impacts, the programme undermined perceptions of local governance in the country and the ability of communities to resolve disputes—thus undermining local social cohesion (Beath et al. 2013c). While the NSP initially appeared to enhance local governance through the creation of CDCs and increased participation, its long-term impacts were negligible or even negative (King and Samii 2014).

Some findings were more positive. For instance, the creation of CDCs more than doubled the proportion of local assemblies that included at least one female member. This was a significant development, especially considering the traditional male dominance in local governance structures in Afghanistan. Additionally, the CDCs increased the provision of local governance services, the activity level of customary authorities, and the role of representative assemblies in governance during the project's lifespan. These changes indicated a temporary shift towards more inclusive and active local governance. However, these improvements were fleeting. While there was a durable increase in the number of meetings held annually by representative assemblies, the overall quality of local governance as perceived by male villagers declined. At the endline of the study, the NSP was found to have negatively impacted the perceived quality of local governance, reducing satisfaction with the work of local leaders by 8% and almost doubling dissatisfaction with recent decisions or actions of village leaders (Beath et al. 2015: 59). This outcome suggests that the NSP, despite its community-driven facade, did not fundamentally alter the existing power dynamics within villages. The CDCs, while initially increasing the provision of local governance services and participation in governance, failed to sustain these improvements in the long term (Beath et al. 2015: 61).

These findings indicate that the creation of new institutions in parallel to customary structures without well defined roles and sustained support may not achieve the desired effect in community-driven development initiatives, particularly in fragile and conflict-affected contexts like Afghanistan. Billions of dollars were spent on a project that ultimately undermined local governance in Afghanistan, yet for years it was heralded as a great success by international NGOs implementing the programme and the politicians outside Afghanistan who funded it (Kerry 2010).

6.5 A Case Study of Property Rights 'Reform'

Secure property rights are considered critical to economic development, as they encourage investment and the improvement of assets, rather than a focus on their protection. This principle is particularly pertinent in contexts like Afghanistan, where land ownership is often established but not legally recognized. Hernando de Soto's influential argument that unlocking economic potential lies in recognizing the de facto rights of individuals and communities to land has led to a focus on formalizing property rights in international development efforts (2003). Major organizations, including the World Bank and the United States Institute for Peace, have adopted this approach, supporting extensive legal titling projects in post-conflict areas like Afghanistan (Wily 2003, 2013).

The response to these initiatives in Afghanistan, especially from 2001 to 2021, was notably subdued. This lukewarm reaction can be attributed to the centralized nature of formalization efforts, which depend on government implementation and enforcement. In a country where the government and legal capacities are perceived as lacking, it is more practical for people to continue relying on their informal, traditional, and customary methods for property issues (Murtazashvili and Murtazashvili 2016, 2021).

In Afghanistan, while legal title is rare, the majority of landowners have customary deeds (Murtazashvili 2012). These documents, not recognized in the legal property rights regime, are nevertheless signed by local administrators and function as proof of ownership. In the event of disputes, landowners turn to local *shuras* or *maliks*, indicating a robust system of community-based dispute resolution.

Legal titling projects were complementary to the NSP. Like the NSP, the legal titling projects were designed without sufficient consideration of the preexisting community structures that provided for conflict resolution, including conflicts over property rights. The legal titling projects were also like the NSP in that they operated through formal, higher-level administrative structures. In the case of property reforms, this involves a substantial role for the courts in the process of land registration. In Afghanistan, where courts are widely regarded as corrupt and government institutions ineffective, these assumptions were fundamentally flawed. The disconnection between the formal legal system and the customary practices prevalent in Afghan society further alienated communities from state-led initiatives.

An alternative approach, focusing on community-based land adjudication and recording, recognizes the existing local systems' strengths and legitimacy. This method seeks to empower and enhance community mechanisms for resolving land disputes, aligning more closely with the realities on the ground. This approach contrasts sharply with the failures of top-down initiatives, highlighting the importance of respecting and leveraging existing social capital and customary practices.

The experience in Afghanistan, particularly with legal titling and programmes like the NSP, underscores the importance of understanding and working within community governance structures—not replacing them with alternatives. These lessons emphasize the need for a genuinely bottom-up approach, one that respects and builds upon the existing social fabric or what development scholars call 'working with the grain' (Levy 2014), for future economic and developmental initiatives in Afghanistan and similar contexts. Only by recognizing and integrating the established customary systems can sustainable progress be achieved in areas where formal government structures are either weak or mistrusted.

6.6 The Political Failures of Reconstruction

The centralization of development interventions was part of a more general emphasis on establishing a centralized state. The main reason for the collapse of the Islamic Republic of Afghanistan in August 2021 was the culmination of a series of failures rooted in the political strategies adopted by the international community and the state's own governance practices organized around a goal of establishing a highly centralized Afghan state. Contrary to the perception of Afghanistan as inherently ungovernable, it was the policy choices made by the United States and its partners over two decades that significantly contributed to a failed reconstruction project.

State-building efforts led by the international community were based on a series of flawed assumptions. The primary approach centred on establishing a Weberian state, which emphasized the consolidation of state power and the establishment of a monopoly on violence. This strategy involved the formation of a heavily centralized government system, which was contrary to Afghanistan's historical and cultural context of decentralized governance and initial distribution of power in 2001 (Barfield 2010, 2012).

The 2004 Constitution created a governance system that offered Afghan citizens limited participation and oversight, widening the gap between the rhetoric of the US intervention and the realities experienced by citizens. Additionally, the international coalition's focus on counter-insurgency and power consolidation often contradicted the goals of democracy-building. Vast resources were invested with minimal oversight, leading to the creation of parallel governance structures that further undermined state legitimacy (Noelle-Karimi 2013).

President Ashraf Ghani's rule from 2014 to 2021 hastened the state's collapse. His administration was marked by over-centralization, micromanagement, and discrimination against ethnic minorities. Ghani's authoritarian tendencies, coupled with his narrow base of support, alienated many, including those within his government. This alienation was compounded by Ghani's efforts to sideline regional powerbrokers and warlords, who were replaced by loyalists, often exacerbating regional tensions and violence (Murtazashvili 2022).

Moreover, the international community's interventions often directly undermined customary governance structures, which had historically provided public goods and services and served as forums for community deliberation.

The implementation of programmes like the NSP, aimed at building local-governance structures, often led to increased disputes and undermined established social norms about community governance (Murtazashvili 2016, 2021c). By the end of Ghani's presidency, the Afghan government had lost much of its legitimacy, and the Taliban had made significant territorial gains. Ghani's focus on subduing internal opposition rather than addressing governance issues or combating the Taliban contributed to the rapid territorial losses to Taliban forces. By mid-2021, the government controlled only a fraction of Afghan territory, and many districts fell to the Taliban without resistance (Murtazashvili 2021b).

These approaches failed to acknowledge and integrate Afghanistan's historical context of decentralized governance and undermined existing social and political structures, ultimately contributing to the state's loss of legitimacy and effectiveness. Community-driven efforts not only failed to contribute to the stability of the state; they undermined them because they worked against the grain of society. These centralized CDD efforts also fit nicely with the international community's preoccupation with creating centralized structures and its willingness to work through the remnants of centralized structures as they went about implementing their preferred projects.

6.7 Letting Tools of Social Science Drive Our Lenses on Development

Besides failing to appreciate the political challenge confronting development, the international aid and assessment community maintained an almost surgical focus on narrow interventions that they could assess using quantitative, causal methods. Afghanistan was a fertile ground for experiments for an academic community increasingly preoccupied with using RCTs to study community-level interventions in development.

The emphasis on controlled interventions such as RCTs constituted a methodological bias. One aspect of this bias is a myopic understanding of development processes. This bias is particularly evident in complex socio-political contexts like Afghanistan, where the nuances of local politics, power dynamics, and societal structures play a crucial role in shaping development outcomes (Pritchett 2023).

RCTs, with their controlled settings and emphasis on isolating variables, provide valuable insights into the specific impacts of interventions. However, this scientific precision comes at a cost. The inherently apolitical nature of RCTs means that they often fail to account for the broader political environment, which is a critical determinant of the success or failure of development efforts. By focusing on quantifiable outcomes within controlled community settings, RCTs overlook the larger political, cultural, and social factors that influence these outcomes (Spears et al. 2020).

In Afghanistan, for example, the focus on RCTs has led to an oversimplified understanding of the effectiveness of CDCs. While RCTs might show that CDCs are enduring or effective in certain specific metrics, this approach neglects how these councils are perceived and integrated within the wider political landscape. If CDCs are viewed as tools of external influence or as mechanisms of state control, their endurance, as measured by these evaluation tools, merely reflects the extent of their backing by international donors rather than genuine community acceptance or effectiveness. They also reflect the ability of donors to use them to measure and control.

This critical oversight is not just a matter of academic concern but also has real-world implications. Development programmes that are designed and evaluated primarily on the basis of RCT-driven findings can lead to interventions that are disconnected from the political, economic, and social realities and needs of the communities they aim to serve. Such programmes may persist not because they are effective or beneficial to the communities, but because they align with the interests and narratives of external donors and state actors. Furthermore, the RCT approach's detachment from political realities can inadvertently contribute to the reinforcement of existing power structures. By failing to consider how interventions might be co-opted by local elites or used as instruments of state control, RCTs can contribute to the perpetuation of inequalities and the undermining of genuine grassroots empowerment.

The reliance on RCTs in development studies therefore raises fundamental questions about the nature and objectives of development interventions. Are these interventions genuinely aimed at empowering communities and addressing their needs, or are they primarily designed to produce quantifiable outcomes that satisfy donor requirements and academic curiosity? The answer to this question has profound implications for the future of development practice, especially in politically complex environments like Afghanistan. While RCTs offer methodological rigour, their limited scope and apolitical nature render them insufficient for understanding the full spectrum of development challenges. To truly grasp the complexities of development, especially in contexts shaped by intricate political and social dynamics, a more holistic approach is required—one that integrates political analysis and considers the broader impacts of interventions beyond the immediate outcomes measured by RCTs.

Samii (2023) presents a positive evaluation of Community-Driven Reconstruction (CDR) in fragile states, emphasizing its efficiency, adaptability, and durability in comparison with other strategies. Samii argues that CDR has been successful in establishing localized networks for administering reconstruction aid and highlights the adaptability of CDR institutions in contexts like Afghanistan, where they have been able to take on new roles beyond their original scope.

However, a critical analysis of these findings raises concerns about the inherent nature of these 'successes'. In the context of Afghanistan, for instance, the persistence of CDR institutions, as lauded in Samii (2023), is not necessarily a marker of their success or desirability from the community's perspective. While the NSP was not an especially robust institution, the analysis above demonstrates that it was not a good match for many communities.

Nonetheless, it was the case that the NSP stuck around even after the fall of the Republic of Afghanistan. The Taliban were more than happy to be handed keys to one of the most centralized states in the world along with a burgeoning infrastructure that provided the central government (not elected provincial or district governments) with the ability to link directly to communities. This is exactly what the NSP was intended to be: a mechanism to transfer funds directly to communities. While such a mechanism may have been efficient for donors and central authorities, such ties were never constrained by electoral politics or even other layers of subnational oversight.

There are risks of relying on RCTs to evaluate the impact of CDR interventions without a comprehensive political analysis or, at the very least, a basic political economy analysis. RCTs can provide valuable insights into specific, measurable outcomes of interventions, but they may not capture the broader political and social dynamics at play. In Afghanistan, CDR's impact on bottom-up collective action and social inclusiveness was limited, indicating a gap between the measured outcomes and the broader institutional and societal context. The endurance of CDR institutions, while noteworthy, is in many ways less significant than the extent to which the programmes are perceived and interact with existing power structures and community dynamics.

Despite these challenges, it is significant that such effort has been devoted to assessments of Afghanistan's projects—not only by the World Bank and other organizations (e.g., Crost et al. 2014), but also within more general meta studies of such projects, as noted above.

But there is always a limitation with these sorts of interventions and the ways that they are assessed. The RCTs can only speak to the specific intervention, with its specific design. They do not tell us what might have been tried, and do not necessarily offer insight into why the projects do not live up to expectations. In Afghanistan, a deeper appreciation for local contexts suggests the value of strengthening local autonomy by working with the enduring institutions of Afghan society, rather than experimenting with new institutions. There is a massive range of possibilities for institutional design. There are many more possible interventions to consider, and the focus on one approach, and on dozens of evaluations of those approaches, denies much of the creative imaginings of development policy.

6.8 Policy Recommendations

Policy-makers and practitioners have many ways to incorporate lessons from the failings of Afghanistan and internalizing the false promise of community-driven development. One shift in orientation is to consider projects that tackle the biggest challenges (which are often unaddressed). In Afghanistan, the oft-unaddressed problem was fostering inter-communal cooperation. If communities are the most robust source of cooperation, we should find the places where community cooperation breaks down. This is often at the edges of communities. Donors can encourage initiatives that facilitate collaboration between different communities. This involves creating platforms for dialogue and joint projects that require cooperation across traditional community boundaries. By doing so, interventions can address more complex and contentious issues that are often avoided due to their difficulty.

Donors have spoken extensively about taking politics seriously in their work. By utilizing tools of political economy analysis to understand the broader political context in which development interventions are implemented, well intentioned donors can take politics seriously and understand the environment in which their interventions operate. Too often, community interventions fail to address the political challenges of development. This approach can help identify potential political barriers and opportunities, ensuring that interventions are more politically informed and contextually appropriate.

Donors can also take local ownership seriously by promoting genuine local ownership. In Afghanistan, donors claimed to be giving communities ownership over community development projects, but as illustrated above, these projects were simply national projects implemented locally. They did not provide any meaningful oversight over local governments or their tax dollars, which mattered more to citizens than use of donor funds.

Interventions can shift the focus from donor-driven, top-down approaches to strategies that genuinely empower local communities. This means not only involving communities in decision-making processes but also ensuring that they have the necessary resources and support to drive their own development agendas with their local governments. It may be the case that communities never have the resources to fully own the kinds of interventions donors intend because they do not have the political means to do so. If communities cannot afford to sustain and support development interventions in the long-term and they cannot hold funders to account for their decisions, then donors may be wise to rethink the viability of such programmes.

Rather than seeing organizations rooted in custom and tradition as an obstacle to development, donors can leverage customary governance structures into their programmes. In Afghanistan, the creation of CDCs was driven by a political desire by Afghan politicians to replace such structures with new, state-structured bodies, giving the state more control over communities. This not only led to ineffective outcomes, but also undermined governance in communities where such programmes were implemented. It is vital to take politics seriously and recognize and integrate existing customary governance systems into development programmes, however imperfect they may be. The challenge for donors is that the norms and values embedded in these organizations may be at odds with universal values promoted by external actors. This represents a serious challenge, but one that cannot be neglected. These traditional institutions have a deep-rooted legitimacy and can play a crucial role in maintaining order and resolving conflicts.

Finally, donors can adopt flexible and adaptive programming that can respond to changing political and social contexts (C. Andrews 2008; M. Andrews 2013; M. Andrews et al. 2013). This involves continuous monitoring and evaluation, allowing for adjustments to be made as needed to ensure the effectiveness and relevance of interventions.

It is imperative to rethink our approach to external interventions in an era where conflict-affected regions continue to grapple with instability, development challenges, and the need for sustainable peace. Micro-level interventions, while well intentioned, often fall short of achieving their intended outcomes due to unintended consequences that undermine inter-communal cooperation and neglect the intricate political dynamics at the grassroots level. A holistic approach, integrating political considerations into grassroots development, is essential for forging a path toward lasting peace and prosperity. These well intentioned local interventions will continue to struggle without a more careful consideration of politics (Ferguson 1994). In Afghanistan, they did indeed struggle because of the lack of attention to the political context, but also because they were preoccupied with a specific type of intervention and ways of assessing it. Donors and scholars have been too ready to focus on form over function and to spend time gazing at their own work, thereby not seeing the wood for the trees. That is exactly what happened in Afghanistan.

The first pillar of this holistic approach emphasizes the need to delve deeply into the local political dynamics of conflict-affected regions. Communities in these areas are not isolated entities but are embedded within complex political landscapes. Recognizing this reality allows us to grasp the nuances of power structures, historical context, traditional governance systems, informal institutions, and the often-overlooked influence of external actors. By understanding the intricate web of politics, we gain valuable insights that can inform development strategies. In Afghanistan, this means that if you are going to create new community councils, which are governance entities, they must have political power. Providing people with money, without the accountability resources to oversee it is not empowerment. In Afghanistan, the purpose of local donor interventions was to channel donor funds to communities and allow the government to have a direct route to communities. There was now two-way accountability. As the Afghan government was increasingly focused on centralization of its authority, these councils became a vehicle to transfer patronage to communities.

The second pillar underscores the importance of conflict sensitivity in development interventions. This entails acknowledging existing tensions and actively working to mitigate potential conflicts. It involves a nuanced understanding of the root causes of conflicts and their interplay with development initiatives. By addressing conflicts at their core and adopting preventive measures, we can ensure that development efforts do not inadvertently exacerbate instability but, instead, contribute to its resolution.

At the heart of a holistic approach lies the empowerment of local communities. It recognizes that communities are not passive recipients of aid but active agents in their own development. Empowering these communities involves facilitating their participation in decision-making processes and equipping them with the tools and resources needed to address their unique challenges (Rostami Povey 2003). By fostering ownership and agency at the grassroots level, development interventions become more responsive and sustainable (Easterly 2006). In Afghanistan, creating local development councils were at odds with one of the most centralized government structures in the world. These councils were entirely dependent upon outside funding and thus behaved like rentier organizations, not as vehicles for local empowerment.

By focusing on political dynamics, we create interventions that are inclusive and do not inadvertently reinforce existing power imbalances. In doing so, we pave the way for governance structures that are able to receive projects, but also able to constrain political power (Ibrahimi 2019).

Looking ahead, the implications of embracing this holistic approach are profound. Development strategies in conflict-affected regions should adopt adaptive programming, recognizing the evolving political contexts and community needs. Local ownership should be prioritized, with communities taking the lead in shaping their development trajectories. But donors working locally and in communities is not the same as communities behind the wheel, driving their own development (Labonne and Chase 2009). By addressing political dynamics, we contribute to conflict prevention, identifying and resolving potential sources of tension before they escalate.

A holistic approach that integrates political considerations into grassroots development is not a mere shift in strategy but a fundamental reimagining of how we engage with conflict-affected regions. It holds the promise of promoting intercommunal cooperation, mitigating conflict, and empowering communities on their journey towards recovery and development. By recognizing and navigating the intricate tapestry of political dynamics at the grassroots level, we can collectively work towards a future where sustainable peace and prosperity thrive in even the most challenging of contexts.

6.9 Caveats and Cautions

There is a tendency to group states into categories, such as 'fragile' or 'failed' state. The Afghan case illustrates that applying blueprints can be dangerous. The development community was content to try the sorts of interventions that had been tried many times before. Like those previous attempts, they did not dramatically improve development prospects but in some sense undermined them.

A better way may be to proceed by considering a strategy to empower local governance—real local governance that is constitutionally accountable—and to promote local ownership of development policy. There are, of course, downsides to local ownership. In economics, there is the idea of the Nirvana Fallacy, which is that we often compare a preferred alternative to an unrealistic standard. One might critique centralized interventions and then see local ownership as an idealized situation. The Nirvana Fallacy applies particularly to Afghanistan. Local ownership does not mean perfect governance, since governance institutions at any level can fail. Rather, as we have seen, to compare centralized and local ownership it is necessary to create space for local ownership to have something to compare it with. That aspect of creating local autonomy has been missing from development policy.

Relatedly, there is the meta-political question of the political feasibility of the reforms above. One argument is that the development community, by taking Afghanistan 'as it was', did what was politically feasible and pragmatically necessary. To some extent, pragmatism must inform development policy, though it is not clear that the donor community understood the country as it really was. Rather, it selectively focused on interventions because they were politically and bureaucratically attractive, rather than making a dispassionate calculation that those sorts of interventions were the best for that particular situation.

References

Andrews, C. W. (2008). 'Legitimacy and Context: Implications for Public Sector Reform in Developing Countries'. *Public Administration and Development*, 28(3): 171–80. https://doi.org/10.1002/pad.495.

Andrews, M. (2013). *The Limits of Institutional Reform in Development*. Cambridge: Cambridge University Press. https://doi.org/10.1017/CBO9781139060974.

Andrews, M., L. Pritchett, and M. Woolcock (2013). 'Escaping Capability Traps through Problem Driven Iterative Adaptation (PDIA)'. *World Development*, 51: 234–44. https://doi.org/10.1016/j.worlddev.2013.05.011.

Autesserre, S. (2010). *The Trouble with the Congo: Local Violence and the Failure of International Peacebuilding*. New York: Cambridge University Press. https://doi.org/10.1017/CBO9780511761034.

Barfield, T. J. (2010). *Afghanistan: A Cultural and Political History*. Princeton, NJ: Princeton University Press. https://doi.org/10.23943/princeton/9780691145686.001.0001.

Barfield, T. (2012). 'Centralization/Decentralization in the Dynamics of Afghan History'. *Cliodynamics*, 3(1). https://doi.org/10.21237/C7CLIO3112219.

Beath, A., F. Christia, and R. Enikolopov (2013a). 'Democratization, Division of Responsibilities and Governance Quality: Experimental Evidence on Local Institutions in Afghanistan'. SSRN Scholarly Paper ID 2202563. Rochester, NY: Social Science Research Network. https://doi.org/10.2139/ssrn.2202563.

Beath, A., F. Christia, and R. Enikolopov (2013b). 'Empowering Women through Development Aid: Evidence from a Field Experiment in Afghanistan'. *American Political Science Review*, 107(3): 540–57. https://doi.org/10.1017/S0003055413000270.

Beath, A., F. Christia, and R. Enikolopov (2013c). 'Randomized Impact Evaluation of Afghanistan's National Solidarity Programme'. Report 81107. Washington, DC: World Bank. Available at: https://documents1.worldbank.org/curated/en/114831468197966566/pdf/812510BRI00P110Box0379833B00PUBLIC0.pdf (accessed 20 June 2024).

Beath, A., F. Christia, and R. Enikolopov (2015). 'The National Solidarity Programme: Assessing the Effects of Community-Driven Development in Afghanistan'. *International Peacekeeping* 22(4): 302–20. https://doi.org/10.1080/13533312.2015.1059287.

Bizhan, N. (2022). 'Building Legitimacy and State Capacity in Afghanistan'. In N. Bizhan (ed.), *State Fragility*. London: Routledge: 24–63. https://doi.org/10.4324/9781003297697-2.

Burns, J. F. (2008). 'Afghan President, Pressured, Reshuffles Cabinet'. *The New York Times*, 11 October. Available at: https://www.nytimes.com/2008/10/12/world/asia/12afghan.html (accessed 20 June 2024).

Crost, B., J. Felter, and P. Johnston (2014). 'Aid under Fire: Development Projects and Civil Conflict'. *American Economic Review*, 104(6): 1833–56. https://doi.org/10.1257/aer.104.6.1833.

Denney, L. (2016). 'Using Political Economy Analysis in Conflict, Security and Justice Programmes'. ODI Toolkit. London: Overseas Development Institute.

Easterly, W. (2006). *The White Man's Burden: Why the West's Efforts to Aid the Rest Have Done So Much Ill and So Little Good*. New York: Penguin Press.

Edwards, D. B. (2002). *Before Taliban: Genealogies of the Afghan Jihad*. Berkeley, CA: University of California Press.

Ferguson, J. (1994). *The Anti-Politics Machine*. Minneapolis, MN: University of Minnesota Press.

Fritz, V., B. Levy, and R. Ort (eds) (2014). 'Problem-Driven Political Economy Analysis: The World Bank's Experience'. Washington, DC: World Bank. https://doi.org/10.1596/978-1-4648-0121-1.

Giustozzi, A., and A. Jackson (2012). 'Talking to the Other Side: Taliban Perspectives on Aid and Development Work in Afghanistan'. HPG Policy Brief 50. London: Humanitarian Policy Group. Available at: https://policycommons.net/artifacts/4778499/talking-to-the-other-side/5614795/ (accessed 20 June 2024).

Goodhand, J., and M. Sedra (2010). 'Who Owns the Peace? Aid, Reconstruction, and Peacebuilding in Afghanistan'. *Disasters*, 34(January): S78–102. https://doi.org/10.1111/j.1467-7717.2009.01100.x.

Hughes, C., J. Öjendal, and I. Schierenbeck (2015). 'The Struggle versus the Song—the Local Turn in Peacebuilding: An Introduction'. *Third World Quarterly*, 36(5): 817–24. https://doi.org/10.1080/01436597.2015.1029907.

Ibrahimi, S. Y. (2019). 'Afghanistan's Political Development Dilemma: The Centralist State Versus a Centrifugal Society'. *Journal of South Asian Development*, 14(1): 40–61. https://doi.org/10.1177/0973174119839843.

Jackson, A. (2018). 'Life under the Taliban Shadow Government'. London: Overseas Development Institute.

Jackson, A., and F. Weigand (2020). 'Taliban Courts in the West and North-West of Afghanistan'. Briefing Note. London: Overseas Development Institute.

Justino, P. (2018). 'The Need to Be Governed: Governance and Violence in Conflict Contexts'. *The Economics of Peace and Security Journal*, 13(1). https://doi.org/10.15355/epsj.13.1.5.

Justino, P., T. Brück, and P. Verwimp (eds) (2013). *A Micro-Level Perspective on the Dynamics of Conflict, Violence, and Development*. Oxford, New York: Oxford University Press. https://doi.org/10.1093/acprof:oso/9780199664597.001.0001.

Kerry, John F. (2010). 'Chairman Kerry Statement at Hearing on Civilian Strategy for Afghanistan'. US Senate Committee on Foreign Relations, 21 January. Available at: https://www.foreign.senate.gov/imo/media/doc/Afghan%20Governance.Civilian%20Stratey.pdf (accessed 20 June 2024).

King, E., and C. Samii (2014). 'Fast-Track Institution Building in Conflict-Affected Countries? Insights from Recent Field Experiments'. *World Development*, 64: 740–54. https://doi.org/10.1016/j.worlddev.2014.06.030.

Labonne, J., and R. S. Chase (2009). 'Who Is at the Wheel When Communities Drive Development? Evidence from the Philippines'. *World Development*, 37(1): 219–31. https://doi.org/10.1016/j.worlddev.2008.05.006.

Levy, B. (2014). *Working with the Grain: Integrating Governance and Growth in Development Strategies*. Oxford: Oxford University Press. https://doi.org/10.1093/acprof:oso/9780199363803.001.0001.

Mac Ginty, R., and O. P. Richmond (2013). 'The Local Turn in Peace Building: A Critical Agenda for Peace'. *Third World Quarterly*, 34(5): 763–83. https://doi.org/10.1080/01436597.2013.800750.

Miakhel, S. (2006). 'Importance of Tribal Structure and Pakhtoonwali in Afghanistan: Its Role in Security and Governance'. Available at: https://pashtoonkhwa.com/files/articles/Miakhel%20-%20Importance%20of%20Tribal%20Structures%20in%20Afghanistan.pdf (accessed 20 June 2024).

Miakhel, S., and N. Coburn (2010). 'Many Shuras Do Not a Government Make: International Community Engagement with Local Councils in Afghanistan'. Washington, DC: United States Institute for Peace, 8 September. Available at: https://www.usip.org/publications/2010/09/many-shuras-do-not-government-make-international-community-engagement-local (accessed 20 June 2024).

MRRD (Ministry of Rural Rehabilitation and Development), Islamic Republic of Afghanistan (2006). 'The Expansion of the National Solidarity Program: Empowering Communities to Deliver the I-ANDS Benchmarks. Proposal for a 3-Year Program Extension'. Kabul, Afghanistan: National Solidarity Program.

Murtazashvili, I., and J. B. Murtazashvili (2016). 'The Origins of Private Property Rights: States or Customary Organizations?'. *Journal of Institutional Economics*, 12 (01): 105–28. https://doi.org/10.1017/S1744137415000065.

Murtazashvili, J. B (2012). 'Survey on Political Institutions, Elections, and Democracy in Afghanistan'. Washington, DC: Democracy International and United States Agency for International Development.

Murtazashvili, J. B. (2016). *Informal Order and the State in Afghanistan*. Cambridge: Cambridge University Press. https://doi.org/10.1017/CBO9781316286890.

Murtazashvili, J. B. (2023). 'Local Political Organization in Afghanistan'. In M. Reeves and J. Feaux De LaCroix, editors, *Central Asia in Context*. Pittsburgh: University of Pittsburgh Press.

Murtazashvili, J. B. (2021b). 'Northern Afghanistan Once Kept out the Taliban. Why Has It Fallen So Quickly This Time?'. *Washington Post*, 28 July. Available at: https://www.washingtonpost.com/politics/2021/07/28/northern-afghanistan-once-kept-out-taliban-why-has-it-fallen-so-quickly-this-time/ (accessed 20 June 2024).

Murtazashvili, J. B. (2021c). 'The Endurance and Evolution of Afghan Customary Governance'. *Current History*, 120(825): 140–5. https://doi.org/10.1525/curh.2021.120.825.140.

Murtazashvili, J. B. (2022). 'The Collapse of Afghanistan'. *Journal of Democracy*, 33(1): 40–54. https://doi.org/10.1353/jod.2022.0003.

Murtazashvili, J. B., and I. Murtazashvili (2021). *Land, the State, and War: Property Institutions and Political Order in Afghanistan. Cambridge Studies in Economics, Choice, and Society*. New York: Cambridge University Press. https://doi.org/10.1017/9781108642217.

Noelle-Karimi, C. (2013). 'Jirga, Shura and Community Development Councils: Village Institutions and State Interference'. In C. Schetter (ed.), *Local Politics in Afghanistan: a Century of Intervention in Social Order*, pp. 39–58. New York: Columbia University Press. https://doi.org/10.1093/acprof:oso/9780199327928.003.0003.

Pritchett, L. (2023). '"Rely (Only) on the Rigorous Evidence" Is Bad Advice'. *Review of Development Economics*, Speical Issue: 1–15. https://doi.org/10.1111/rode.13037.

Rostami Povey, E. (2003). 'Women in Afghanistan: Passive Victims of the Borga or Active Social Participants?'. *Development in Practice*, 13(2–3): 266–77. https://doi.org/10.1080/09614520302950.

Samii, C. (2023). 'Revisiting Community-Driven Reconstruction in Fragile States'. WIDER Working Paper 2023. Helsinki: UNU-WIDER. https://doi.org/10.35188/UNU-WIDER/2023/334-5.

Sharan, T. (2013). 'The Dynamics of Informal Political Networks and Statehood in Post-2001 Afghanistan: A Case Study of the 2010–2011 Special Election Court Crisis'. *Central Asian Survey*, 32(3): 336–52. https://doi.org/10.1080/02634937.2013.843301.

Soto, H. de (2003). *The Mystery of Capital: Why Capitalism Triumphs in the West and Fails Everywhere Else*. New York: Basic Books.

Spears, D., R. Ban, and O. Cumming (2020). 'Trials and Tribulations: the Rise and Fall of the RCT in the WASH Sector'. In F. Bédécarrats, I. Guérin, and F. Roubaud, editors, *Randomized Control Trials in the Field of Development: A Critical Perspective*, pp. 166–85. Oxford: Oxford University Press. https://doi.org/10.1093/oso/9780198865360.003.0008.

The Asia Foundation (2018). 'A Survey of the Afghan People: Afghanistan in 2018'. Washington, DC: The Asia Foundation.

The Asia Foundation (2020). 'A Survey of the Afghan People: Afghanistan in 2019'. Washington, DC: The Asia Foundation.

Wily, L. A. (2003). 'Land Rights in Crisis: Restoring Tenure Security in Afghanistan.' Issues Paper Series. Kabul: Afghanistan Research and Evaluation Unit.

Wily, L. A. (2013). 'Land, People, and the State in Afghanistan.' Kabul: Afghanistan Research and Evaluation Unit. Available at: https://www.baag.org.uk/sites/default/files/resources/attachments/AREU%20Land%2C%20People%2C%20and%20the%20State%20in%20Afghanistan%202002-2012.pdf (accessed 20 June 2024).

7

Why Is It Important to Use a Social Contract Lens for Donor Interventions in Somalia?

Gaël Raballand, Deborah Isser, Hodan Hassan, and Mathieu Cloutier

7.1 Background and Introduction

Since the collapse of the Somali state in 1991, recurrent cycles of conflict and instability have often threatened the achieved progress.[1,2] Clan-based conflicts remain a common form of violent contestation in Somalia. These conflicts usually revolve around scarce resource allocation and access, and they remain a key source of mistrust across the Somali population. Al-Shabaab, the terrorist group that has been plaguing Somalia for more than a decade, capitalizes on these local conflicts. Thus, long-standing grievances and memories of past marginalization impede the progress towards reconciliation.

Finding a political settlement that supports a stable, central government has been a core challenge for Somalia. In 2000, a Transitional National Government (TNG) was launched, but failed to establish legitimate institutions and effective security measures. In 2004, a new interim government, the Transitional Federal Government (TFG), was established in Nairobi under the auspices of the Inter-Governmental Authority on Development (IGAD). The TFG was largely sustained by the African Union's deployment of a peacekeeping mission, the African Mission to Somalia (AMISOM) in 2007. This occurred at a time when Al-Shabaab was becoming a significant factor in Somalia. In 2012, after a devastating famine, the Federal Government of Somalia (FGS) emerged from the Provisional Constitution agreed upon in 2011 (World Bank 2018).

Since 2012, Somalia has made strides in deepening federalism, with successive FGS administrations developing key federal institutions and advancing

[1] The authors thank Jens-Peter Dyrbak, Brian Frantz, Kate Greany, Nimo Jirdeh, Thomas Oertle, Natasha Sharma, Nicola Smithers, and the participants to the presentation to the donor group on 22 April 2021 for their excellent comments and suggestions.

[2] The findings, interpretations, and conclusions do not necessarily reflect the views of the World Bank, the executive directors of the World Bank, or the governments they represent.

Gaël Raballand et al., *Why Is It Important to Use a Social Contract Lens for Donor Interventions in Somalia?*.
In: *Fragile Aid*. Edited by: Rachel M. Gisselquist et al., Oxford University Press. © UNU-WIDER (2025).
DOI: 10.1093/oso/9780198960287.003.0007

state formation, leading to the emergence of Galmudug, Hirshabelle, Jubbaland, and South West as Federal Member States (FMS).[3] However, the first decade of the FGS's existence saw ongoing conflicts with FMS due to undefined roles and responsibilities in the federal system, especially regarding security and revenue sharing. President Hassan Sheikh Mohamud, elected in 2022, prioritized inclusive politics, focusing on the Constitution, federalism, and security architecture.

President Mohamud convened a series of National Consultative Council (NCC) meetings that brought together the FGS and most FMS (except Puntland) and led to political agreements on power-sharing, fiscal federalism, national security, and electoral models.[4] On 30 March 2024, the Somali Federal Parliament passed amendments to the first four chapters of the Provisional Constitution, updating executive power-sharing and transitioning from indirect to popular elections. However, Puntland and other key figures rejected these amendments, calling for broader consultations.

This chapter uses social contract analysis[5] to reflect on Somalia's development challenges and the role of donor engagement. Building on the framework developed in a World Bank study on social contracts in sub-Saharan Africa (Cloutier et al. 2021), the social contract in Somalia is analysed in relation to security, education,[6] and taxes. Security is the sine qua non condition of a social contract; at its most fundamental level, citizens submit to state rule in return for basic security. Education is a proxy for the nature of social outcomes and the extent to which it is provided in ways that meet expectations demonstrate the level of resilience. Taxation is a critical element of state capacity, while tax compliance is an important measure of the quality of the bargaining mechanism.

Political scientists and anthropologists have demonstrated that a social contract approach is important to better understand what can/should be done from donors perspective (Lemay-Hébert 2009, 2020; Ismail 2016). State legitimacy is crucial and non-economic factors, such as justice or state fairness vis a vis citizens play a major role in this regard.

[3] [1] The FMS of Puntland had already been established (c.1998) by the time the Provisional Constitution was adopted in 2012.

[4] [2] Puntland's President Said Deni, initially participated in the first NCC but later boycotted subsequent meetings due to fiscal and political disputes with the FGS.

[5] The focus of the classical social contract on individuals leads largely to a liberal set of values that may be disconnected from core issues needing attention in African conflicts, including the relationship that communities (rather than individuals) have with the state (Leonard 2013). However, it does not mean that improving accountability of the state to the clan or citizens are mutually exclusive. They can be complementary, although the state and clans in Somalia have tended to have exclusionary aspects.

[6] Security and education are respectively the first and second highest priorities for citizens in the emerging FMS (USAID 2017).

The main messages of the chapter are the following:

1. There are multiple and overlapping social contract relationships in Somalia. At the national level the citizen–state relationship is heavily mediated by alternative authorities both at the local level through clans, militias, and member states, and at the transnational level through donor interventions.
2. The most resilient social contracts tend to be at the most local level, which is primarily within a clan. The clan intercedes on behalf of its members in interacting with other clans and the state and is the authority most looked to for accountability and protection in most Somali communities (Menkhaus 2007).[7] Since 1991, Somalia has seen the re-emergence of the clan as a protector against violence. The strength of the contract within the clan is based upon clan capacity to utilize informal tax collection[8] to keep its residents safe and solve some conflicts. But the clan is less effective as a mediator of citizen relations with larger entities (FGS or even FMS in some cases).
3. At the federation level, Somalia's social contract is characterized by a weak bargaining mechanism. On the state capacity side, measures of state efficiency in Somalia are among the lowest as compared with its regional neighbours.[9] Citizen capacity in terms of cohesion and collective action is weak and indirect. The formal bargaining mechanism—that of elections—gives citizens limited voice and is mediated by an electorate of elites. Poor social outcomes and low levels of trust indicate weak resilience. Given the extremely limited service provision capacity of the FGS/FMS, it is unsurprising that the social contract between the state and citizens is weak.[10]
4. The chronic political instability and insecurity that characterizes Somalia is deeply rooted in the short-term and exclusionary aspects of the elite bargain.[11] As an example, federal elections have been based upon an indirect electoral model that places a premium on financial means, political connectedness, and clan strength. At the same time, it excludes de facto women

[7] Leonard (2013: 3) notes that 'fundamental social contracts in Africa are not between the state and individuals alone, but by individuals with their communities and by communities with the state'. This is what Bandula-Irwin (2019) calls the social contract between local powerbrokers and the state.

[8] Van den Boogaard and Santoro (2022) show the importance of informal taxation in Gedo district compared to official taxation (FGS and FMS).

[9] Comparable data for Somalia is also limited.

[10] According to Leonard (2013), bargains exist only when they produce immediate benefits for all parties, which makes them particularly unstable in fragile, conflict, or violence-affected states (FCVs). In such countries, individual allegiance to a community/state is often dependent on protection.

[11] This is what Bandula-Irwin (2019) calls the social contract between the international community and the Somali state.

candidates (despite the 30% quota in the Parliament) (Affi 2020). It also limits those who can participate to mainly clan elders and a narrow group of electors determined by political leadership and clans. The exclusion of large parts of the Somali population (including the poor, women, and marginalized clans) from political and economic life has fostered a set of grievances that have been exploited by armed groups. Inclusion has been increasingly integrated in the policy and programmatic circles, but much less in practical terms for learning and implementation on the ground (Majid and Menkhaus 2019).

5. Dependence on aid flows has historically undermined the formation of a strong social contract between the citizen and state in Somalia because service delivery is attributed to non-state actors (McLoughlin 2015). De facto heavy mediation from the international community of the social contract between citizens and the federal state in Somalia has probably contributed to a persistent weak legitimacy. The Somali state authorities lack the ability and legitimacy to gain sufficient state revenues through taxation. The taxation level is very low and as such fiscal bargaining hardly exists, with related low expectations of citizens from the federal state. Thus, it largely depends on foreign resources and is beholden and responsive to the demands of the international community as opposed to its own citizens (Bandula-Irwin 2019).
6. With the relative exception of Puntland and Somaliland,[12] the FMS do not have the whole control of their territories, in some cases failing to provide the most basic element of the social contract—that of security. They are more often restricted to the capitals and larger towns, with limited reach in rural areas. Somaliland and Puntland both seem to have a stronger social contract with their citizens, given the bottom-up nature of the state-building exercises in both regions (USAID 2017).[13] For instance, the relative higher levels of state investment in public education and growing efforts to provide oversight of private schools have been reflected in higher levels of satisfaction with the provision of education.

This chapter is organized as follows: Sections 7.2 and 7.3 provide qualitative analysis of the social contract from a historical perspective, followed by an analysis of the current situation, with a focus on the security, education, and taxation. The final section presents the main implications for donor interventions in Somalia and how civil society could play a stronger role in strengthening the social contract.

[12] Somaliland does not consider itself an FMS.
[13] This was also confirmed by Gallup surveys; 2016 for Somalia.

7.2 A Brief History of Social Contracts in Somalia

Development partners have been integrating socio-political frameworks into their strategies and programmes to address development challenges and to better inform them. In this regard, the World Bank's 2017 *World Development Report* (WDR) on governance and the law argues that 'policies that should be effective in generating positive development outcomes, are often not adopted, are poorly implemented, or end up backfiring over time', and that the radically uneven character of public policy formulation, implementation, and enforcement is a matter of governance: namely, 'the process through which state and non-state actors[14] interact to design and implement policies within a given set of formal and informal rules that shape and are shaped by power' (World Bank 2017c: 41).

To understand the current setting of the social contract in Somalia, a historical perspective on the provision of two key social outcomes—security and education—is instructive. Somalia has been described as *a nation in search of a state*. Until the emergence of the Republic of Somalia in 1960 the vast majority of Somalis did not live under a 'state' (Laitin and Samantar 1987; Leonard and Samantar 2011). Siad Barre's regime is viewed paradoxically today: on the one hand, under the ideology of scientific socialism, investments in social sectors in the 1960s through the early 1980s was unprecedented and progress was made in ensuring the rights of marginalized groups in society, such as women or marginalized clans (Majid and Menkhaus 2019). On the other hand, accusations of clan favouritism and the perceived use of the government to oppress dissident clans contributed to societal fracture and ultimately to the collapse of the state in 1991. In addition, the tendency of the Barre government to concentrate government investments and public services in Mogadishu deepened a sense of centre–periphery inequities that persists today.

Regarding security, it is crucial to note that the clan has provided the defining social system for the traditionally nomadic-pastoral and agro-pastoral communities since long before independence. The *Xeer*, the unwritten customary law, has formed the backbone of a set of mutual obligations that was designed to promote peace and prevent conflict between the clans (Lewis 1961).[15] Clan-based identity persists because Somalis believe that in view of the weak or non-existent governmental institutions, it is the only way to protect oneself. The clan system

[14] A non-state actor is usually defined as an actor with sufficient power to influence politics at the local or national levels, despite not belonging to any established state institution. As such, 'non-state actors' may refer to national and international non-governmental organizations (NGOs), business or religious leaders, traditional authorities, workers' organizations, media, local community-based groups and networks, or diasporas (McCullough and Saed 2017).

[15] Members of a sub-clan can usually trace their lineage to a common ancestor up to eight generations.

is perceived as a network that fosters individual survival in an environment characterized by failing, inadequate, or repressive formal institutions (Affi 2020). The group mediates conflicts, negotiates compensation, and/or carries out revenge for perceived wrongdoings committed by outsiders (Gundel 2009).[16] At the community level, clan elders utilize the revenues from *qaaraan* (clan 'dues') to cover the convening of clan meetings, conflict resolution, compensation to clan members in case of loss of property or life, as well as support for the most vulnerable members. Whether or not an individual is able to pay *qaaraan*, she or he is still able to receive the benefits from the collective resources at the disposal of clan leadership (van den Boogaard and Santoro 2021).

The military coup of 1969 that brought Siad Barre into power also raised the profile of the security organs in the state-building process and the 'militarization' of the state. In the mid-1970s, there were approximately 15,000 police officers divided among the 18 regional districts. Officers were focusing on the basic rule of law and security, such as patrolling, criminal investigations, and traffic duties (Hills 2014). The armed forces grew from an estimated 22,000 in 1976 to 123,000 in 1985 (Adam 1998).[17] Throughout the 1980s, Barre replaced many of the key positions within the military with people close to him. As a result, many Somalis viewed the army as an extension of Barre's clan networks. This perception eventually tarnished the military's reputation as a national institution (Africa Confidential 1986).

After the collapse of the central government in the early 1990s, the provision of basic security and justice reverted fully to kinship and customary law. Somaliland was able to develop a nascent social contract with relative security, and Puntland followed. The south-central regions have remained more fragmented, with a fluid set of actors and contestants. At the community level, clan elders worked alongside religious leaders to resolve conflicts and adjudicate claims. Clan militias stepped in to provide protection for communities and the business sector (Keating and Abshir 2017). The clan thus re-emerged as the most legitimate and reliable authority.

However, the limitations of the clan as the sole providers of community protection became apparent in the 1990s and 2000s, particularly in south and central Somalia as conflicts (and the growth of warlords) contributed to widespread insecurity. In this vacuum, Islamist organizations emerged, seeking to restore some semblance of law and order. Across Mogadishu, and in the surrounding areas, Sharia-based courts began to emerge and to attract the support of the business

[16] The clan structure is nominally divided into clan family (largest unit), followed by clan (political unit), and sub-clan (blood-paying unit). Somali clans are indigenous to the Horn and can be found in Somalia, Ethiopia, Djibouti, and Kenya.

[17] In the 1980s there was a strong shift to increase government spending on defence- and security-related areas, which reduced the available funding for other sectors. In 1974, spending on economic and social services was 24% and 16%, respectively. By 1988 that had been reduced to 11% and 4% (Raballand et al. 2021).

community. Due to their ability to maintain sufficient order to allow for a relative normalcy of activity, the court grew in popularity and influence, forming a union in early 2006 under the banner of the United Islamic Courts (UIC) (Hassan 2017). In December 2006, Ethiopian troops entered Somalia and recaptured Mogadishu from the UIC. Al-Shabaab took advantage of this vacuum, and the inability of the TFG to provide basic security led to the deployment of several thousand Ugandan and Burundian troops to Mogadishu under the banner of AMISOM. The 2011 Provisional Constitution led to the establishment of subsequent governments (federal and then FMS). A more relative stability among the clans through power-sharing arrangements and gradual development of a federal structure was reached. However, this unfinished and still fragile effort at state-building has failed to curb the ongoing threat from Al-Shabaab.

In pre-colonial Somalia elders took the responsibility to educate the children through the informal transmission of social and cultural values using examples and storytelling. In addition, communities prioritized the teaching of the Quran and Islamic practices. During the colonial period in Somalia, the colonial powers targeted their education investments mainly to the elite to fill positions within the administrations. When colonial governments partnered with Somali religious leaders and communities, their efforts to introduce non-religious education were successful but still mostly focused on elites (Cassanelli and Abdulkadir 2007).

After independence, the education sector in Somalia developed relatively rapidly. Both the civilian and military governments invested in the construction of schools, hiring and training of thousands of teachers, as well as a successful campaign to formalize Somali script while carrying out a nation-wide literacy campaign (Abdi 1998). Under the Siad Barre regime, the textbooks and a harmonized curriculum were designed to strengthen a pan-Somali identity and to possibly limit the influence of clans (World Bank 2017a). The Barre regime made education free and compulsory for all children between the ages of 6 and 14. During the first decade of Barre's rule (1970–79), primary school enrolments increased significantly, from 40,000 in 1970 to nearly 300,000 in 1979. The percentage of female school children also rose from 20% of all primary school children in 1970 to closer to 40% in 1979. The number of female teachers also increased from 10% in 1969 to 30% in 1979 (Cassanelli and Abdulkadir 2007).

Somalia decreased funding for the education sector in the 1980s when the regime became increasingly militarized and spending focused increasingly on security. This resulted in a decrease in the number of primary schools country-wide, from 1,407 in 1980 to 644 by 1990. The public funds allocated per pupil declined from US$27 in 1982 to US$3.50 in 1990, in large part due to increased military spending and declining economic output (UNESCO 2000).

In the immediate aftermath of the state collapse in 1991, the provision of education all but stopped in most areas of the country, as communities experienced a descent into violence and displacement. When communities realized that the reconstitution of the state would take longer, they started to organize themselves to ensure that basic elements of the state, such as education and security, would be provided. The expectation of the state's ability to provide for these services gradually declined (Abdinoor 2008). In the early 2000s, the more stable areas of Somaliland and Puntland re-emerged as the primary providers of education. By 2001 there were over 70,000 students enrolled in primary and secondary schools in Somaliland. In Puntland there were an estimated 50,000 students enrolled in primary and intermediate schools in 2004 (Cassanelli and Abdulkadir 2007).

7.3 The Current Setting: A Weak and Exclusionary Citizen–State Bargaining Mechanism Results in a Thin Social Contract

Using the examples of security, education, and taxation, the current social contract between the authorities and the population in Somalia is thin and largely exclusionary. It can be largely explained by a weak state–citizen bargaining dynamic characterized by very poor state capacity and low demand for services.[18]

7.3.1 A Thin Social Contract

A critical characteristic of both security and education provision in Somalia is the very limited role of the formal state. Put another way, to the extent these outcomes are delivered, it is necessarily through a co-production of an array of actors, public and private, community- and clan-based, and local and international resources. These actors in turn have varying levels of representation, authority, and legitimacy, and are at times complementary and at times in conflict with each other. This has some negative consequences on state legitimacy, including perceptions of the state by the populations. As explained by McLoughlin (2015: 341), the common wisdom is that the provision of vital public services necessarily improves the legitimacy of a fragile, conflict, or violence-affected state (FCV). In practice, however, the relationship between a state's performance in delivering services and its degree of legitimacy is nonlinear. 'This relationship is conditioned by expectations of what the state should provide, subjective assessments of impartiality and distributive justice [...] how easy it is to attribute (credit or blame) performance to the state, and the characteristics of the service.' In many FCVs, 'unpopular' functions such as taxation are attributed to the state, whereas 'popular' functions are perceived to stem solely from donors or NGOs.

[18] This section will not focus on state capacity and low demand for services. This is developed in more detail in Raballand et al. (2021).

The Key Role of the Clan in Providing Security

Security issues remain crucial in Somalia. Although the FGS spends the bulk of its budget to improve the security situation,[19] insurgents and armed groups have not yet been defeated. Therefore, security spending is costly for the authorities but with incomplete results. Between 2011 and 2016, Al-Shabaab lost control of most of the major towns in the south and central areas of Somalia as a result of Somali National Alliance (SNA)/AMISOM offensives and localized militia efforts. Yet, despite this rapid shrinkage in the administrative control of populations, Al-Shabaab continues to attack civilian government targets, as well as AMISOM and the SNA. In addition, the group maintains a disruptive presence in the areas surrounding major towns and cities across most of the FMS (Hassan 2017). In rural areas, communities still rely almost fully on clans for the provision of security (Hills 2014).

Many of the 'formal' military and police units are composed of former clan militia because of their ability to come into the SNA with their own weapons. Despite being under FGS/SNA administrative and budgetary control, many of these units have informally remained under the command and control of the clan to which they belong (World Bank 2017b). The make-up of Somalia's security forces is not representative of the country's diverse communities.

The few public perception surveys designed to gauge public opinion about the police are undertaken in areas where internationally funded police have been trained and deployed. These surveys suggest that those who perceive the police to be representative of their clan or the different clans within their neighbourhoods are more likely to not only trust the police, but also to rate their performance well. Conversely, in areas where communities have little to no representation in the police, respondents reported dismal ratings of police performance (Sahan Foundation 2019). The SNA has long been accused of engaging in extortion and gender-based violence, especially when deployed in regions that do not reflect the clan make-up of the military units. Communities that have most often accused the SNA of engaging in predatory behaviour come primarily from marginalized or minority groups in south and central Somalia (US State Department 2017).

Some evidence indicates that growing investments in improving civilian–military relationships of the SNA have paid off. During the military campaign undertaken by the SNA between 2019 and 2020 in the Lower Shabelle region aimed at dislodging Al-Shabaab, careful efforts were made to ensure the clan composition of the battalions reflected the communities into which these forces would be inserted. Community members from towns that were recovered from

[19] Somalia spends more on the security sector as a percentage of its budget than any other fragile state, except for Afghanistan. The largest budget item within the security sector is the estimated 40,000–45,000 armed personnel (army, police, paramilitary) who receive some level of compensation from the state (World Bank 2017b).

Al-Shabaab praised the SNA for positively and proactively engaging with residents. The SNA deliberately avoided taxing the town's local natural resources, relying instead on support from stabilization partners to construct new wells (UNSOM 2020). In another major offensive against Al-Shabaab which began in July 2022, the SNA and local forces captured dozens of towns in Hirshabelle and Galmudug. Using its own resources and with support from international partners, the FGS initiated early recovery investments in schools, government buildings, and health centres in former Al-Shabaab strongholds such as Adan Yabal and Haradheere.

The Inability of Authorities to Provide Basic Education Services

Given the relatively limited domestic revenue potential over the mid- to long-term perspective, it is highly likely that the FGS and the FMS will continue to focus on security spending at the expense of social sectors. As such, they will remain a relatively marginal player in delivering social services (Raballand et al. 2021). Citizens instead rely on their local mix of informal clan structures, NGOs, and private sector actors for basic needs and services. As a result, the formal state—the FGS and FMS—produce little by way of social outcomes for the population, and citizen expectations remain low.

Although there have been improvements in basic education indicators over the past decade, Somalia still ranks near the bottom in terms of gross enrolments, with three million children out of school according to UNESCO (out of an estimated 4.7 million school-aged population). One out of every five Somali student-aged children is displaced (USAID 2017). Moreover, education provision is of low quality, mainly due to the high number of unqualified and untrained teachers, multiple curricula, poor education infrastructure, and weak capacity for service delivery (GPE 2020).

The share of students enrolled in government-managed primary schools across all of Somalia is estimated at less than 50%. Apart from Somaliland and Puntland, where most schools are public, only 7.4% of primary students are enrolled in government schools, with the remainder enrolled in some form of private or community schools (World Bank 2017a). Chronic conflict and limited state resources have resulted in uneven access to education in Somalia. This is especially acute in south and central Somalia, where hard-to-reach regions are afforded limited educational support by state or international actors. Extremely high rates of poverty in communities across Somalia also make it difficult for parents to afford school fees. Nomadic pastoralists account for about 65% of the Somali population, and only 22% of pastoralist children receive a formal education (Borgen Project 2018). Furthermore, there are significant inequities in the distribution of educational resources (for example, schools, teachers, learning materials, water facilities) between rural and urban areas.

Girls' participation in education is significantly lower than that of boys. According to Intersos (2016) survey results, the main threats to girls' education are financial challenges (49.5%), child and early marriage (29.2%), insecurity (13.1%), the negative attitude of parents (12.5%), cultural barriers (9.2%), the need to perform household chores (4.3%), and the lack of educational opportunities (1.6%).

By contrast, in Somaliland and Puntland the provision of education has been relatively more inclusive (World Bank 2017b), although investments in urban areas (where population numbers are high) are proportionally much greater than in rural areas. Because resources are still limited, communities raise funds from the diaspora and the business community to pay salaries and/or construct schools in remote areas. In Somaliland and Puntland, the Ministries of Education partially subsidize teacher salaries, ensure harmonized curricula, provide testing certification, and ensure basic infrastructure support. Both regions allocated an estimated 7% of their budgets to the provision of education, while the FGS allocated less than 1%. The FMS and FGS provide limited oversight, depending instead on engagement with private sector and community-led schools (World Bank 2017a).

7.3.2 An Exclusionary and Weak Citizen–State Bargaining Mechanism: The Absence of a Fiscal Contract

Poor social outcomes have tended to reproduce themselves through a feedback loop of low expectations, fragmented capacities, and exclusionary politics. This can be illustrated through examination of taxation and the absence of a fiscal contract, and of the fragile political settlement that relies on a narrow elite bargain.

As in most FCVs, the current tax-based social contract in Somalia between the federal state and its citizens is weak (van den Boogaard and Santoro 2022). It is influenced by the fluid political and security context that limits the writ of the formal state in major population areas, the fractious political relationships between different levels of the state, and the ongoing armed insurgency.

From colonial times through independence, Somalia has had low levels of domestic revenues due to strong resistance from the population as well as limited economic opportunities (Kakwenzire 1986). FGS domestic revenues have grown relatively rapidly from near zero to approximately US$250 million in 2019. Yet, internally generated revenues are still dwarfed by official development assistance to Somalia. Compared to donor funding (including humanitarian aid), domestic revenue amounts to 12.5% of total revenues (25% if Somaliland is included) (World Bank 2020a). A large part of service delivery thus depends on donor financing. Due to a lack of trust and acute capacity constraints, implementation of donor-funded programmes is often achieved through international and local NGOs. The knowledge that it is non-state actors that are largely responsible for services further undermines tax compliance and the broader citizen–state social contract (Baird 2010).

Both the FGS and the FMS source most of their tax revenues from the business community and consumers through the imposition of import and customs duties, which represent more than 50% of total domestic revenues (World Bank 2020a). At the FGS level, tax revenues primarily cover government operations (including salaries) and co-payments to national security forces. Outside the primary tax base of the FGS in Mogadishu, there are usually few visible services provided by the national government.

At the FMS level, the scope of services provided to its residents is limited because of the lack of capacity, resources, and access to rural areas due to the presence of armed groups and poor road networks. Apart from Puntland and Jubbaland (which have large ports) FMS collect at most a few million US dollars, with FGS fiscal transfers to the FMS accounting for 70–90% of the states' total revenues. As a result, the FMS leadership is largely accountable to the FGS—rather than their own citizens—and vulnerable to political pressure.

The misalignment of expectations is evidenced by low rates of federal tax compliance by the private sector.[20] Although business owners acknowledge the critical role that tax revenues can play in the state-building process, they complain that taxes paid to the formal state are not reaping dividends because the government cannot guarantee their safety (Abshir et al. 2020). At the same time, they are forced to pay multiple levels of taxes and fees to an array of state and non-state security actors to allow for the movement of goods. The payment of taxes to Al-Shabaab is seen by many citizens as the most illegitimate and extractive of those made to non-state actors because of the threat of violence—even to businesses located outside their areas of control. Yet, the ability of the group to honour its side of the bargain, especially security for goods and the movement of people along their road networks, makes them a relatively predictable service provider (Hiraal Institute 2020).

Somalia's multiple actors in fees/tax collection reveal a hybrid formal–informal taxing and service delivery arrangement that exists when there are weak or non-existent formal institutions. Non-state actors, whether the private sector or NGOs, are the primary providers of basic social services in large parts of the country (van den Boogaard and Santoro 2021). Partnerships between various local authorities in tax collection are common and Somalia is largely a collection of 'island economies' based on cities and/or districts (World Bank 2020b). At the community level, there are high levels of collaboration in service provision between both formal and informal authorities. For example, local governments often work with

[20] Citizens and private operators pay more to local authorities than formal taxes to federal authorities.

clan elders to supplement security forces through militias. It is not unusual for the local administration and private sector (including the diaspora) to provide in-kind goods or cash for community infrastructure projects. Community members and civil society groups then contribute labour for construction (Jordan 2016).

The practice of paying *qaaraan*, or family contributions to the clan, is seen as a kind of member dues for a social insurance policy. According to perception surveys and studies, of all the informal payments, these payments consistently rate as the most legitimate. That is why some cities/districts collect millions of US dollars per year, whereas FMS have difficulties collecting US$1 million in the same geographical area (World Bank 2021). Contributions at the clan level are also credited with playing a constructive role in building social cohesion. Individuals or families can negotiate the payments, and refusal to pay is rare, given the social sanctions that would be incurred (Jordan 2016).

Payments such as *zakat* (taxes on earnings) and *sadaqa* (alms) are also deeply embedded in Somali society and are considered religious requirements. In addition, citizens provide ad-hoc payments to the religious community for the construction of mosques or religious learning centres. The leaders have high degrees of social trust and are often seen as neutral actors in the community (Abshir et al. 2020).

7.3.3 An Exclusionary Political Settlement

The chronic political instability and insecurity that characterizes Somalia is most probably rooted in the short-term and exclusionary aspects of the elite bargain. The lack of movement on finalizing the Constitution and defining the federalist architecture of the country has resulted in extra-constitutional electoral processes that are prone to disputes, as rules are developed by the parties keen on participating in or influencing the outcome of the election process. This fragile, elite-driven process has the potential to contribute to insecurity, as groups can use the threat of violence to strengthen their bargaining positions (Menkhaus 2018).

At the federal level, Somalia has had successive electoral processes that have resulted in the relatively peaceful transfer of power since 2012. The country has utilized a variation of clan-based, indirect election models to select members of Parliament, who in turn select the federal president. In 2012, the entire electoral process took place in Mogadishu and included 125 clan elders who were elected to the Parliament. In an attempt to widen the enfranchisement of Somalis and to devolve the selection process, the 2016 elections process included 14,000 electors (selected by clan elders) who elected the Parliament from the FMS capitals.

The '4.5' power-sharing formula among the clans has been the basis for the division of seats within the federal Parliament and is also utilized to select members of the federal cabinet and other government institutions.[21] In practice, the (self-declared) four large clan families divide the posts of president, prime minister, deputy prime minister, and speaker of the Parliament. The indirect electoral model places a premium on financial means, political connectedness, and clan strength.[22] It was estimated that up to US$20 million 'changed hands' during the parliamentary elections in 2016, including formal fees for running and informal funds for attracting clan elders and politically connected individuals (Gettleman 2017). The model makes it difficult for women and minority groups to reach leadership positions within the federal government (Affi 2020; McCullough and Saed 2017). Women are largely de facto excluded from political processes, despite the establishment of a 30% quota for women. The exclusion of large parts of the Somali population (the poor, women, and marginalized clans) from political and economic life has led to a set of grievances that have been exploited by armed groups, thereby contributing to an ongoing insurgency that continues to hamper progress.

At the FMS level, electoral processes have followed similar clan-based selection models for legislative and executive positions. Insecurity due to the presence of Al-Shabaab has resulted in the electoral processes occurring primarily in the capitals. The formation of the FMS was based on political settlements between elites.

7.4 Implications for Donor Interventions and Recommendations

Although trust in institutions remains low and the federal model undefined, some new trends are starting to challenge the status quo, namely: (1) a stronger demand from citizens for improved service delivery (starting with security and education) at a time when tax payments have started to increase; and (2) with the heavily indebted poor countries (HIPC) decision point, inflows to the FGS have increased rapidly, significantly changing the power balance in favor of the FGS at the expense of the FMS.

On the demand side, communities have increasingly protested poor service provisions from the police and military. Internally displaced communities in Mogadishu have started to form associations to engage directly with the police to improve access to security and human rights. In Somaliland and Puntland, where tax collection is more robust than in the other regions, citizens have increased expectations of government capacity in the education sector (USAID 2017). In parallel, the increased capacity of the FGS to collect taxes, primarily in Mogadishu, is placing a growing strain on the relationship between the federal government and the residents of the capital, who feel they bear the brunt of the tax burden with little in the way of public services in return (Abshir et al. 2020).

[21] For the historical aspect of this formula and its impact, see Elmi (2010).

[22] In theory, elders should be accountable to citizens. However, as they are unelected, they cannot be directly sanctioned through an electoral process.

The lack of progress in elaborating revenue-sharing arrangements between the FGS and FMS has resulted in double taxation, raising tensions between the various levels of government. By reaching the HIPC decision point in March 2021, the FGS succeeded in generating additional resource flows through the provision of grants from the World Bank, strengthening its financial standing vis-à-vis the FMS. Donors, even unintentionally, have contributed to a change in the balance of power[23] that could potentially create further tensions regarding the social contract in Somalia.

In March 2023, the FGS and FMS (minus Puntland) reached agreement that articulated the fiscal powers and responsibilities between the different levels of government. On 13 December 2023, the IMF and World Bank Executive Boards approved Somalia's HIPC Completion Point which resulted in the granting of US$4.5 billion in debt forgiveness. As a result of this achievement, Somalia has access to more diverse financing options albeit without sustained access to grants which helped plug funding shortfalls. In 2023, the FGS boosted domestic revenue by 16.3%.[24] However, to cope with tighter fiscal conditions, the country must substantially increase domestic revenue generation and rely on highly concessional financing agreements that will test the durability of inter-government fiscal arrangements.

As long as the bulk of donor investments in service delivery are implemented through NGOs and non-state actors, perceptions of the weakness of the state structures and their possible irrelevancy will continue to persist within the population.[25] Foreign aid and external stabilization have become so entrenched that donors and a range of external actors aiming to influence political developments in Somalia have become an integral part of these processes (Hagmann 2016).[26] As emphasized by Van de Walle and Scott (2011: 17), 'service provision is an inherently political process, even more so in fragile or state-building contexts'.

Within the literature on this topic on Somalia, there has been a recurrent call for working more at the local level due to its higher legitimacy and potential for service delivery. Menkhaus (2014b) advocated a strategy based on municipalities. Bandula-Irwin (2019) called for a bottom-up, organic, disjointed negotiation of indigenous governance solutions. However, this approach would not solve a major

[23] Even more so with the HIPC process and budget support operations, which have contributed to a large inflow of funding.

[24] *End-Year Budget Fiscal Performance Report for Fiscal Year 2023*, Ministry of Finance, Somalia, March 2024 https://mof.gov.so/publications/end-year-budget-performance-2023.

[25] Deserranno et al. (2020) also show how aid can sometimes undermine state capacity by 'poaching' government staff (for instance in the health sector) to work for aid agencies at the expense of local state capacity.

[26] The international system grants the privileges of statehood to many countries that are, in fact, unable to exercise a monopoly over their full territory. Therefore, they cannot exercise the legitimate use of force that the concept of statehood requires (Leonard 2013).

problem in Somalia, which is unequal economic and social development and the need to redistribute resources. As highlighted by Leonard and Samantar (2011: 561), 'alternative governance systems [non-state actors] may be less effective than *some* states in delivering certain forms of economic development and aspects of social welfare'. Therefore, state-building in Somalia is the 'art of the possible', and it may have little choice but to work with flawed, contested governments of dubious legitimacy for the time being (Menkhaus 2014a).

The inclination to strengthen what is already working (e.g., focus on enhancing a relatively durable social contract at the community–clan level) is also fraught with potential risks. The tie of kinship is deeply embedded in Somali history and culture, with clear expectations of the reciprocal benefits. The traditional clan elders have played a critical role in providing some level of stability in the aftermath of the state collapse in large part because they are seen as an indigenous institution that continued to exist while most other aspects of the state and society proceeded to rely greatly on international donor efforts. At the FGS and FMS levels, the elders play a formal role in the selection of representatives in Parliament. This context makes it all the more important to exercise maximum caution in how institutions and donors work with elders to avoid the kind of distortions that were common through colonial forms of indirect rule. If elders are seen as an adjunct of politicians in power or donor recipients, they cannot be effective in maintaining peace or addressing justice.

Donor efforts to support more inclusive and resilient social contracts (at the FGS/FMS/district levels) should aim to strengthen the quality of the citizen–state bargaining process—that is, the first main aspect of social contracts set out in the conceptual framework. This requires strengthening citizen collective action capacity, state capacity, and more inclusive political institutions.

There is no clear prescription for achieving this; actions would need to be adaptable and attuned to the complex societal factors that shape outcomes. The following are guiding principles for the design of interventions aiming to strengthen the social contract.

7.4.1 Political Accountability

Move towards a rule-based division of power and resources among the entities by facilitating the definition of a more inclusive and functioning federal model of the state including revenue-sharing arrangements and equalization mechanisms.

- Facilitate movement towards more inclusive and representative election models, including for women, minority clans, and internally displaced persons.[27] A key lesson of recent engagement is that improved political

[27] To ensure compliance with quotas, women should be included in electoral commissions with a mandate to reject male candidates for women's seats (Affi 2020).

inclusion will be achieved gradually and no particular model should be transplanted.

- Policies to strengthen the functioning of media markets can be a crucial part of strategies to foster healthy political engagement. Policies that encourage the provision of information and access to media can improve the political process (Khemani et al. 2016).

7.4.2 Service Delivery and Accountability vis-à-vis Citizens

State service delivery should selectively focus on security/education, given that a full model of public delivery will remain unachievable for years to come.

- Given the robust role of the private sector in social services, donor support should aim to bolster the government's regulatory capacity to enhance quality, access, and targeting.
- There is ample scope for innovative approaches through performance-based contracts and community oversight for locally delivered social services. Transparency is critical to establish expectations and a basis for monitoring performance.
- Support oversight mechanisms at the FGS, FMS parliamentary, and district levels on fiscal allocation, which include representation from elders and civil society organizations. To increase transparency and reduce corruption, both the FGS and the FMS should consistently publish data on governmental decisions and public expenditure (Heritage Institute for Policy Studies 2021).
- Involve the Somalia National Bureau of Statistics in benchmarking progress related to transparency and strengthened citizen–state relations.
- Tackle exclusion in any donor-supported activity. As the sources of instability in Somalia are intimately tied to exclusionary behaviour by the elites, development actors should reflect on how programming can advance the wider enfranchisement of people in political and economic life.
- Donors should limit competition and fragmentation of support to avoid strengthening part of the elite at the expense of others or citizens/clans, which ultimately makes the situation more unstable and fragile.

References

Abdi, A. (1998). 'Education in Somalia: History, Destruction, and Calls for Reconstruction.' *Comparative Education*, 34(3): 327–40. https://doi.org/10.1080/03050069828171.

Abdinoor, A. (2008). 'Community Assumes the Role of State in Education in Stateless Somalia.' *International Education*, 37(2): 43–61.

Abshir, S., K. Abdirahman, and H. Stogdon (2020). 'Tax and the State in Somalia'. Briefing Paper. London and Nairobi: Rift Valley Institute.

Adam, H. (1998). 'Somalia: Personal Rule, Military Rule and Militarism'. In E. Hutchful and A. Bathily, editors, *Military and Militarism in Africa* Dakar: CODESRIA: 355–397.

Affi, L. (2020). '"The Old Men Who Hold Us Back": Clan Elders, Elite Bargaining and Exclusionary Politics'. *Journal of Somali Studies*, 7(2): 125–45. https://doi.org/10.31920/2056-5682/2020/7n2a6.

Africa Confidential (1986). 'Somalia: Military Politics', 26 October.

Baird, M. (2010). 'Service Delivery in Fragile and Conflict-Affected States'. Background Paper for the World Bank's World Development Report (WDR) 2011. Mimeo.

Bandula-Irwin, A. (2019). 'The State and Social Contract in Somalia'. Mimeo.

Borgen Project (2018). '10 Important Facts about Girls' Education in Somalia'. Available at: https://borgenproject.org/facts-about-girls-education-in-somalia (accessed 29 October 2022).

Cassanelli, L., and F. Abdulkadir (2007). 'Somalia: Education in Transition'. *Bildhaan: An International Journal of Somali Studies*, 7(1): 91–125.

Cloutier, M., B. Harborne, D. Isser, I. Santos, and M. Watts (2021). *Social Contracts for Development: Bargaining, Contention, and Social Inclusion in Sub-Saharan Africa*. Washington, DC: World Bank and Paris: Agence française de développement.

Deserranno, E., A. Nansamba, and N. Qian (2020). 'Foreign Aid and State Capacity'. NBER Working Paper 26928. Cambridge, MA: NBER.

Elmi, A. A. (2010). *Understanding the Somalia Conflagration*. Sidmouth: Pluto Press.

Gettleman, J. (2017). 'Fueled by Bribes, Somalia's Election Seen as Milestone of Corruption'. *New York Times*, 7 February.

Global Partnership for Education (GPE)—Somalia (2020). 'Education in Somalia'. Available at: https://www.globalpartnership.org/where-we-work/somalia (accessed 29 October 2022).

Gundel, J. (2009). 'Clans in Somalia'. Report based on a COI Workshop in Vienna. Available at: https://www.ecoi.net/en/document/1193130.html (accessed 29 October 2022).

Hagmann, T. (2016). 'Stabilization, Extraversion and Political Settlements in Somalia'. Research Report. London and Nairobi: Rift Valley Institute.

Hassan, H. (2017). 'The Context of Violent Extremism in Somalia'. Mimeo.

Heritage Institute for Policy Studies (2021). 'Impediments to Good Governance in Somalia'. Report. Mogadishu: Heritage Institute.

Hills, A. (2014). 'Remembrance of Things Past: Somali Roads to Police Development'. *Stability: International Journal of Security & Development*, 3(1): 1–14. https://doi.org/10.5334/sta.di.

Hiraal Institute (2020). 'A Losing Game: Countering Al-Shabab's Financial System'. Report. Mogadishu: Hiraal Institute. Available at: https://hiraalinstitute.org/a-losing-game-countering-al-shababs-financial-system (accessed 29 October 2022).

Intersos (2016). 'Barriers to Girls' Education in South-Central Somalia'. Research Report. Rome: Intersos. Available at: https://www.intersos.org/wp-content/uploads/2017/09/BARRIERS-TO-GIRLS-EDUCATION-IN_SOUTH-CENTRAL-SOMALIA-Annex-1.pdf (accessed 29 October 2022).

Ismail, A. A. (2016). 'The Political Economy of State Failure: A Social Contract Approach', *Journal of Intervention and Statebuilding*, 10(4): 513–29.

Jordan, K. (2016). *Community-Based and Customary Taxation in South-Central Somalia: Possibilities for Hybrid Governance*. Copenhagen: Danish Refugee Council.

Kakwenzire, P. (1986). 'Revenue and Development in Northern Somalia, 1905–1939'. *International Journal of African Historical Studies*, 19(4): 659–77. https://doi.org/10.2307/219139

Keating, M., and S. Abshir (2017). *The Politics of Security in Somalia*. New York: Center on International Cooperation.

Khemani, S., E. Dal Bó, C. Ferraz, F. S. Finan, C. L. Stephenson Johnson, A. M. Odugbemi, D. Thapa, and S. D. Abrahams (2016). *Making Politics Work for Development: Harnessing Transparency and Citizen Engagement*. Washington, DC: World Bank.

Laitin, D., and S. Samantar (1987). *Nation in Search of a State*. Boulder, CO: Westview Press.

Lemay-Hébert, N. (2009). 'Statebuilding without Nation-building? Legitimacy, State Failure and the Limits of the Institutionalist Approach', *Journal of Intervention and Statebuilding*, 3(19: 21–45.

Lemay-Hébert, N. (2020). 'State-Building, State Fragility and Interventions'. In F. O. Hampson, A. Özerdem, J. Kent, editors, *Routledge Handbook of Peace, Security and Development*. London: Routledge: 56–66.

Leonard, D. (2013). 'Social Contracts, Networks and Security in Tropical Africa Conflict States: An Overview'. *IDS Bulletin* 44(1). https://doi.org/10.1111/1759-5436.12003.

Leonard, D., and S. Samantar (2011). 'What Does the Somali Experience Teach Us about the Social Contract and the State?'. *Development and Change*, 42(2): 559–84. https://doi.org/10.1111/j.1467-7660.2011.01702.x.

Lewis, I. M. (1961). *A Pastoral Democracy*. London: Oxford University Press for the International African Institute.

Majid, N., and K. Menkhaus (2019). 'Access and Inclusion'. Roundtable Discussion Paper, mimeo.

McCullough, A., and M. Saed (2017). 'Gatekeepers, Elders and Accountability in Somalia'. Report. London: ODI.

McLoughlin, C. (2015). 'When Does Service Delivery Improve the Legitimacy of a Fragile or Conflict-Affected State?' *Governance*, 28(3): 341–56. https://doi.org/10.1111/gove.12091.

Menkhaus, K. (2007). 'Governance without Government in Somalia: Spoilers, State Building, and the Politics of Coping'. *International Security*, 31(3): 74–106. https://doi.org/10.1162/isec.2007.31.3.74.

Menkhaus, K. (2014a). 'State Collapse and Local Response in Somalia'. In I. Trauschweizer and S. Miner, editors, *Failed States and Fragile Societies*. Athens: Ohio University Press: 142–153.

Menkhaus, K. (2014b). 'If Mayors Ruled Somalia'. Nordic Africa Institute Policy Note 2. Uppsala: Nordic Africa Institute.

Menkhaus, K. (2018). 'Elite Bargains and Political Deals Project: Somalia Case Study'. Report. London: Stabilisation Unit, UK Government. Available at: https://assets.publishing.service.gov.uk/government/uploads/system/uploads/attachment_data/file/766049/Somalia_case_study.pdf (accessed 29 October 2022).

Ministry of Finance, Somalia (2024). *End-Year Budget Fiscal Performance Report for Fiscal Year 2023*. Mogadishu: Ministry of Finance, Federal Government of Somalia. https://mof.gov.so/publications/end-year-budget-performance-2023.

Raballand, G., A. Fiebelkorn, G. Heidenhof, and K. Schmidt (2021). 'Reflections on the Future Role of the State in Somalia from the Perspective of Aid Effectiveness'. *Development Policy Review*, 40(1). https://doi.org/10.1111/dpr.12549.

Sahan Foundation (2019). *FMS Community Perception Report*. Nairobi: Sahan Foundation.

UNESCO (United Nations Educational, Scientific and Cultural Organization) (2000). *Somalia: Year 2000 Education for All Assessment Report*. Paris: UNESCO.

UNSOM (United Nations Assistance Mission in Somalia). (2020). 'Lower Shabelle Stabilization: Lessons from Operation Badbaado 1'. Mimeo.

USAID (US Agency for International Development). (2017). *Somalia Perception Survey*. Report. Washington, DC: USAID.

US State Department (2017). *Human Rights Report: Somalia*. Report. Washington, DC: US State Department. Available at: https://www.state.gov/wp-content/uploads/2019/01/Somalia.pdf (accessed 29 October 2022).

Van den Boogaard, V., and F. Santoro (2021). 'Explaining Informal Taxation and Revenue Generation: Evidence from South-Central Somalia'. ICTD Working Paper 118. Brighton: Institute of Development Studies. https://doi.org/10.19088/ICTD.2021.003.

Van den Boogaard, V., and F. Santoro (2022). 'Financing Governance beyond the State: Informal Revenue Generation in South-Central Somalia'. *African Affairs*. https://doi.org/10.1093/afraf/adac030.

Van de Walle, S., and Z. Scott (2011). 'The Political Role of Service Delivery in Statebuilding: Exploring the Relevance of European History for Developing Countries'. *Development Policy Review*, 29(1): 5–21. https://doi.org/10.1111/j.1467-7679.2011.00511.x.

World Bank (2017a). *Education in Federal Systems: Lessons from Selected Countries for Somalia*. Washington, DC: World Bank.

World Bank (2017b). *Federal Republic of Somalia: Somalia Security and Justice Sector*. Public Expenditure Review. Washington, DC: World Bank.

World Bank (2017c). *World Development Report: Governance and the Law*. Washington, DC: World Bank.

World Bank (2018). *Somalia: Systematic Country Diagnostic*. Washington, DC: World Bank.

World Bank (2020a). *Domestic Resource Mobilization in Somalia*. Washington, DC: World Bank.

World Bank (2020b). *Somalia Urbanization Review*. Washington, DC: World Bank.

World Bank (2021). *Somalia: Country Economic Memorandum*. Washington, DC: World Bank.

8

Local Participation in the Context of National Ownership

The Playing out of Aid Nurtured Ideals in Rwanda and Cambodia

Malin Hasselskog, Vedaste Ndizera, and Joakim Öjendal

8.1 Introduction

An enduring concern in international development cooperation[1] is the inherent inequality between those who receive and those who provide resources (Eyben 2006). As a result, new ideals are continuously formulated to help increase recipient agency, initiative, and influence. Among the most prominent of these ideals are 'local participation' and 'national ownership' (Hasselskog 2020).

With the Paris Declaration in 2005, national ownership gained high-level recognition and for a while came to constitute the core of the aid effectiveness agenda (OECD DAC 2005/2008). The stated ambition was to shift power from those who provide to those who receive aid, and the assumption remains that development priorities and strategies should be domestically determined rather than shaped by external agendas (Harper-Shipman 2020; Hasselskog 2022). Local participation, meanwhile, was rapidly adopted by the mainstream in the 1990s. Over a decade, the World Bank alone allocated almost US$85 billion to local participatory development (Mansuri and Rao 2013: 15), and continued funding reflects a sustained belief that people should influence decisions that concern them rather than being exposed to externally determined interventions (Cornwall 2011; Hasselskog 2016).

These kinds of appealing ideals are easy to agree on and have come to constitute an intrinsic part of development thinking and practice. Employing them, however, is more difficult. Extensive scholarly analysis points to common shortcomings in the operation of local participation as well as national ownership, including excessive focus on technical design with ensuing depoliticization (Hout and Robinson 2009; Hasselskog et al. 2017), and on efficiency with a tendency that responsibility,

[1] In the chapter, 'development co-operation' and 'aid' are used interchangeably, denoting official development assistance (ODA) as defined by OECD (2024)

Malin Hasselskog, Vedaste Ndizera, and Joakim Öjendal, *Local Participation in the Context of National Ownership*. In: *Fragile Aid*. Edited by: Rachel M. Gisselquist et al., Oxford University Press. © UNU-WIDER (2025).
DOI: 10.1093/oso/9780198960287.003.0008

but not control, is transferred to recipients (Arnstein 1969; Whitfield 2009; Cornwall 2011; Harper-Shipman 2020). Throughout—and contrary to the ambition of increased recipient agency—provider influence tends to remain strong.

Still, as measured in large-scale monitoring linked to the aid effectiveness agenda, national ownership increases. Though the rate of progress has levelled off and is mixed between countries, the overall level of national ownership continues to rise (OECD 2007: 16f, 2008: 29ff; OECD/UNDP 2019: 39). Meanwhile, aid recipient countries' policy independence increases also for other reasons than the ownership agenda. As other financial flows and sources of revenue are increasingly available, the importance of 'traditional' aid diminishes, which allows more room to set the development agenda domestically (e.g., Mawdsley 2019).

Irrespective of why national ownership increases, little is known about possible implications for local participation. The two ideals tend to be talked about as a pair, suggesting that they appear conjointly. However, national ownership and local participation are analysed in separate bodies of research, and their interrelation has not been interrogated (Hasselskog 2020). That development priorities and strategies are domestically determined, as prescribed by national ownership, does not necessarily mean that people influence decisions that concern them, in line with local participation. Rather, as depicted by the Organisation for Economic Co-operation and Development (OECD), ownership implies strong government leadership (OECD 2003: 10f; OECD DAC 2005/2008: 15; Booth 2012; OECD/UNDP 2019); as scholarly analysed, it denotes state capacity, commitment, and assertiveness; and according to empirical research, it often coincides with central state control (Whitfield 2009). There are thus indications that national ownership tends to come with a strong state and, accordingly, national policymakers' approach will be crucial for what sort of local participation is welcome and/or possible.

Therefore, we argue, the relation between national ownership and local participation needs to be empirically investigated. This chapter analyses the nature and role of local participation in situations of strong national ownership, asking how prevailing forms of national ownership play out locally and what the experiences are of local participation.

8.2 Research Design and Methods

The examination is designed as a qualitative study of two strategically selected cases of aid recipient countries (Yin 2009). In the mid-1990s, Rwanda and Cambodia were both in dire need of reconstruction. Bad conscience in the international community for not having effectively intervened earlier contributed to massive inflow of aid, which has since then gradually shifted in contents and approach. As a result, the two countries have for three decades been exposed to continuously modified aid trends (Hasselskog 2020), including those of local participation and national ownership.

Rwanda and Cambodia are both historically characterized by patron–client relations, cultures of 'obedience', authoritarian top-down approaches, and absence of political participation (Newbury 1978; Chandler 1983). With international aid, however, activities have been funded that require people's active involvement (Blunt and Turner 2005; Plummer and Tritt 2010; Chemouni 2014; Hasselskog 2016). In both countries, local participation has been promoted through comprehensive decentralization reform, participatory programmes, and support to civil society. Rwanda and Cambodia were also both early, eager, and successful adopters of the ownership agenda, and have moved towards increased policy independence, though for partly different reasons and with Rwanda well ahead of Cambodia (OECD 2012; GPEDC 2016a, 2016b; Hasselskog 2020).

For an analysis of how local participation has fared under the process of increased national ownership, Rwanda and Cambodia constitute critical cases. While sharing the above key characteristics, they display different and changing patterns of national ownership and approaches to local participation and will thus provide illustrative findings on the nature and role of local participation in different situations of national ownership. While obviously not representative of aid recipient countries at large, they will offer varied indications of implications of national ownership for local participation and point to patterns that can be explored further in other cases.

Based on government and donor documentation and previous research, we trace the evolution of national ownership and approach to local participation in the two countries. Based on qualitative content analysis of original empirical material, we analyse how—in the context of decentralization reform and civil society activities with participatory ambitions—national ownership plays out and what experiences of local participation prevail. In Rwanda, during June–August 2022, semi-structured interviews were conducted with 15 representatives of seven civil society organizations (CSOs), five local leaders, and 18 beneficiaries. In Cambodia, during January–August 2022, 20 interviews were conducted with representatives of three CSOs. Interviews focused on CSO relations with national and local governments and international funders, and attitudes to beneficiaries' active involvement as well as obstacles to and instances of such involvement. The interviews were conducted in Kinyarwanda and Khmer respectively, most of them recorded and transcribed, and all translated to English.

As in most qualitative case studies (Yin 2009), the two country cases are rich and diverse. The nature and role of local participation is therefore discussed in Rwanda and Cambodia respectively, before the cases are contrasted and compared in a discussion of wider patterns of implications for different forms of local participation in different situations of national ownership.

8.3 Rwanda

After the 1994 genocide, Rwanda was in a state of political, societal, and economic collapse. Development aid poured in, and the emergency phase was gradually replaced by longer-term development cooperation.

8.3.1 Political Context and the Evolution of National Ownership

Rwandan ownership started early. Already in 1994, that is, several years before the ownership agenda and despite aid dependence, the government emphasized its policy independence (Zorbas 2011). By 2000, there was a firmly formulated development vision (RoR 2000), by 2004 a sophisticated aid coordination structure was in place, and by 2006 an aid policy was adopted, declaring how aid should be used and that the government would assert genuine leadership (RoR 2006).

Since then, the government has expediently followed the Paris agenda in terms of policy formulation, aid coordination, policy dialogue, popular consultation, and more. Development plans and related documents are produced in a timely and professional manner, making up coherent policy frameworks tied to budgets, along with relatively robust systems for public financial management (GoS 2015: 3; GPEDC 2018). There is also an institutional set-up for the government to regularly meet donor, private sector, and civil society representatives (RoR 2017: 30; UN 2017: 46f; Sida 2020: 8). Throughout, Rwanda's diligent assuming of ownership has been reflected in monitoring results and recognized by international observers (OECD 2012; UN 2017: 14; GPEDC 2018).

Early and sustained Rwandan policy independence has been explained by the government's ability to use existing negotiating capital and appease donors, not least by persuasively using the development vocabulary, and by guilt in the international community for not having stopped the genocide along with a desire for African success stories (Hasselskog 2020: O100). Aid providers also appreciate the Rwandan leadership's development orientation and capacity, the efficiency in policy-making and implementation, and the low level of corruption (EU/GoR 2014: 11; GoS 2015: 3; UN 2017: 14). Even when pursuing criticized practices, Rwanda has largely remained popular, enjoying donors' praise and trust, presented as a 'donor darling' or 'poster child' (Zorbas 2011: 105f; Grimm 2013: 87; Gaynor 2016: 779, 782) or at least as belonging to a group of privileged aid recipients (Desrosiers and Swedlund 2019: 436).

The Rwandan government does however not stop at complying with the Paris agenda. It also decisively insists on its priorities and strategies, for example moving ahead with rural resettlement despite donors' reluctance (RoR 2015: 30, 2017: 15), and actively de-emphasizes the role of aid. In its annual report on external development finance (EDF; RoR 2021: 8), development cooperation is singled out in a pie chart of total development resources, and it is stressed that 'most of Rwanda's financing for development came from its own resources'. Graphically and verbally portraying aid as a minor part of development resources is conspicuous for a country where ODA as a share of central government expense is the sixth highest in the world (World Bank 2024).

Throughout, the Rwandan government resolutely manages its aid providers (Grimm 2013). It regulates their role and influence and directs their contributions by assigning sectors among them (Hasselskog et al. 2017; RoR 2021: 35; Sida 2020: 8). Aid providers' room for manoeuvre is thus limited, and some report also feeling subjected to surveillance (Desrosiers and Swedlund 2019: 455). Since 2009, the government closely monitors and assesses the quality of external finance, annually presenting individual donors' performance on 14 indicators, along with comments and a green or red light (RoR 2021: 32–45).

8.3.2 National Ambitions of Local Participation

Alongside its firm claim of national ownership, the Rwandan government persistently articulates its commitment to local participation and related ideals (Hasselskog 2016). In policy documents, participation is promoted to reduce poverty, for 'the culture of people centred participative development to take root' (RoR 2001: 11), 'to enable and reactivate local people to participate in initiating, making, implementing and monitoring decisions and plans that concern them', and to make local leaders directly accountable to the communities they serve (RoR 2001: 8, 2008: 56ff). The 2003 constitution affirms that Rwandans have the duty to participate in the country's development, and in the current strategy for transformation, citizens' participation is declared a priority area (RoR 2017: 19).

Local participation is promoted not least through decentralization, which remains a crucial part of the Rwandan government's political and developmental project (RoR 2000: 12, 2001, 2018: 61; Chemouni 2014; Hasselskog and Schierenbeck 2015; Gaynor 2016). The overall objective of the 2001 decentralization reform was 'to ensure ... empowerment of local populations to fight poverty by participating in planning and management of their development process' and participatory governance was to increase local government responsiveness, accountability, and transparency (RoR 2001: 8–9). Though the focus of the reform has gradually changed, a priority remains to enhance 'citizen participation, empowerment and inclusiveness', for example by engaging 'the citizen at village level in participatory planning/prioritisation as well as budgeting' (RoR 2018: 39f). Throughout, there is a particular focus on women (Nyiransabimana 2018), with the current government vision stating that decentralization will imply 'equal participation of women and men' (RoR 2015: 35).

Within this frame of decentralization, numerous 'home-grown solutions' (HGSs) have been launched, many of which are asserted to revive traditional participatory practices (Hasselskog 2016). *Ubudehe* and *umuganda* are developed specifically to ensure participation in planning and decision-making in the first decentralization phase (Gaynor 2016; RoR 2018: 62) and *imihigo* is in the revised decentralization policy presented as a model for bottom-up planning (RoR 2012b: 17). *Ubudehe* includes a categorization exercise, through which every household is placed in a socio-economic category, while *imihigo* is a comprehensive system of performance contracts, outlining targets for government units as well as households to be achieved within a certain timeframe (Hasselskog 2016, 2018).

Throughout, civil society is recognized as both a participating player and a promoter of popular participation and organizer of consultative forums, and the government asserts to support it in various ways (RoR 2015: 5, 35, 2018: 62; RGB 2022; Hasselskog 2023). A non-governmental organization (NGO) law gives national NGOs the right 'to advocate, protect and promote human rights and other national values; and to express opinions and views on national policies and legislation' (RoR 2012a: 53). This is intended to enable civil society's involvement in policy-making, local governance, and development processes (Kantengwa et al. 2019; ICNL 2024a), while the government will provide financial support and build the capacity of national NGOs (RoR 2012a: 45, 2017: 19). Dialogue with civil society is welcomed (Adamczyk 2012), the possibility of partnerships between the government and national NGOs is established (RoR 2012a: 44f, 58), and a recurrent objective is to strengthen such partnerships (RoR 2017: 11, 15f; RGB 2022). A Joint Action Development Forum (JADF) has also been created to promote public sector cooperation with civil society (RoR 2017: 31), along with a range of other state mechanisms through which CSOs are to engage with decision-makers, thus enhancing citizen participation (Kantengwa et al. 2019: 43f; RGB 2022; Hasselskog 2023).

Despite the government's eloquent commitment to local participation and proclaimed promotion of it through decentralization, HGS, and civil society endorsement—and despite international aid resources—scholars and other observers find the quality of participation in Rwandan governance and development processes inadequate (GoS 2015: 2; UN 2017: 26; Kantengwa et al. 2019: 5). The decentralization reform is seen as top-down, strengthening upwards rather than downwards accountability, extending the reach of the central state, and not providing for citizens to participate in local planning and decision-making (Chemouni 2014; Hasselskog and Schierenbeck 2015; Gaynor 2016). Ostensibly participatory development programmes are found to imply mainly labour and cash contributions and to serve to 'sensitize' people on national policies rather than allowing them to express needs and suggestions (Chemouni, 2014; Gaynor 2016; Hasselskog 2018). Rwandan civil society is seen as largely controlled by national authorities (van Leeuwen 2008: 405, 414ff; EU/GoR 2014: 26f; GoS 2020:

2), which promote a service delivery—rather than 'watchdog'—function of civil society and make CSOs align their work with government policies (Adamczyk 2012: 68; ICNL 2024a; Protik et al. 2018; RoR 2018: 22; Hasselskog 2023).

8.3.3 CSO Experiences of National Ownership and Local Participation

So, in this context of ownership claims and participation vocabulary by the government, and critique of participation practices by observers, how do prevailing forms of national ownership play out and what are the experiences of local participation?

CSO Relations with the Government and Foreign Funders

CSO respondents recurrently emphasize that they follow national priorities. 'Everything is aligned with government policies' (Rwa int 25). Local authorities may also ask CSOs to adjust their activities by providing certain input, prioritizing certain areas, or including certain people, and the CSOs apparently accept such requests as long as they persist. 'Recently the influence is less intense because we have included their perspectives' (Rwa int 18). Commonly mentioned is the selection of beneficiaries, which often follows the official *ubudehe* categorization. 'The authorities provide people from category one' (Rwa int 1). Throughout, CSOs need the authorities' approval of their activities, permission to operate in an area, and acceptance of their reports. 'If they see that something is wrong, they say: please change this!' (Rwa int 26).

Several CSO representatives also describe how their activities are geared towards meeting local authorities' goals. 'We have ten *imihigo* targets, which we contribute to at the district level' (Rwa int 37). Beneficiaries, meanwhile, note that CSOs encourage them to fulfil targets such as having a health insurance and a vegetable garden (Rwa int 14).

While most respondents do not explicitly reflect on this affiliation with national policies and adjustment to authorities' requirements, a few CSO representatives openly regret that they cannot determine their activities.

> We must align with government strategies. We are an independent organization, but that does not mean that we have our own agenda. You see, this is Rwanda.... You cannot have your own agenda.... I don't think there is a single organization which has its own agenda. (Rwa int 34)

The national representative of another organization compares the situation to other countries and points to being closely observed and possibly forced to stop.

> The government of Rwanda is very different from other governments. They register you, they give you a certificate for maybe five years, but only after a rigorous exercise. Then, there is a mechanism for monitoring what you do, and if you said that you would build five classrooms, they will not clear you until they have verified that you built five classrooms.... Some projects are very tricky in a country like Rwanda. I know projects that were closed because they were perceived as *kugumura abaturage* [inciting the population to revolt]'. (Rwa int 36)

Many CSOs are financed by foreign actors, who are seen as also promoting certain things. 'If someone gives you money, there is an agenda that they try to advance' (Rwa int 31). CSO representatives claim, though, to adjust to funders' agendas only to a limited extent: 'Once there is a call for proposals, we apply if it fits our focus areas.... We don't go for every call' (Rwa int 34).

While adjusting to foreign funders is thus apparently a choice, aligning with government policies is not open to discussion, which one CSO representative perceives as a change. 'We no longer take commands from donors.... Instead, we decide according to national guidelines' (Rwa int 1). However, the Rwandan government's external relations may affect the organizations. 'Imagine when Rwanda and France had issues. Just imagine what happened to an NGO that got funding from France. That can happen ... between Rwanda and any country. And when that happens, aid stops' (Rwa int 30). According to another respondent, the government's approach affects their access to foreign funding in yet another way.

> We have lost almost all donors. Why? Because when they compare us to our neighbours, say Congo.... We don't present needs as Congo does. In Congo it is *byacitse* [it's an emergency], give me, give me. Here it is *agaciro, kwihesha agaciro,* kwihagararaho [dignity, self-determination, self-support]. It's a language that makes people think that Rwanda is becoming a middle-income country. (Rwa int 36)

Expectations and Dynamics of Local Participation

CSO representatives are familiar with prevailing priorities and favoured approaches, including that of local participation, and recognize the benefits of engaging beneficiaries. 'We don't come and solve their problems, we involve them in the planning, they decide what they need' (Rwa int 30). Some also spontaneously point to problems of non-participation. 'Without the consent and acceptance and participation of people, the project cannot succeed' (Rwa int 18). 'If you just give them animals, the animals will die tomorrow' (Rwa int 3). Several respondents note a difference from the state of emergency when 'we were just providing things' (Rwa int 2). A national representative recalls:

> We used to sit in this office, and we would say 'Well, at this site, what are the needs? Oh, there is stunting. Okay can we do a project on stunting?' Then you made a proposal, and you waited for Denmark or Canada or whoever to say 'Oh, we have some money to fight stunting'. And then, when you got the money, you would go to that site with the assumption that there were stunted children. But either those children would not be there, or the strategies you thought you would use would not be appropriate. So, we've left that approach of top-down planning. (Rwa int 36)

Another purpose of involving the population is also mentioned. 'It helps citizens to know their rights ... to know that it's their right to receive good services, and to realise that it's their responsibility to ask' (Rwa int 25). 'We're strengthening them to advocate for what they don't have, and that the government should provide it' (Rwa int 36).

Thus aware of the potentials of local participation, respondents also identify several obstacles. One is beneficiaries' previous experiences. 'When a citizen sees a donor coming, he knows that he will be given something' (Rwa int 26). An inclination to accept what is offered and requested, rather than making suggestions, is confirmed by beneficiaries. 'My first role was to be a good child and implement everything they told me' (Rwa int 11). 'We do whatever the government asks us' (Rwa int 17). 'We must do ... and behave as they tell us' (Rwa int 29). Such experiences and expectations impede active involvement. 'It takes a lot of effort to convince them to participate' (Rwa int 2). Another problem is that beneficiaries do not trust that they will be allowed to keep what they achieve. 'Maybe there is something behind. Maybe soon they will come and say that this field is no longer yours' (Rwa int 19).

A general hindrance is lack of time. People are busy making a living and CSOs may not be able to provide enough incentives to get involved in their activities. This is highlighted by beneficiaries who are most appreciative when paid work is provided and critical when payments are not enough or stops. 'No one wants to work together for nothing.... You were paid a small sum, and worked nine hours, from morning to 3 o'clock' (Rwa int 23). 'During the project, many had jobs. Now they are unemployed' (Rwa int 21). For the organizations, too, time is a constraint. 'For government funds in Rwanda, they need a report after three months. With that timeline for conceiving a project, implementing, and reporting ... it's hard to involve the beneficiaries' (Rwa int 31).

Despite predetermined agendas and various obstacles, CSO representatives as well as beneficiaries point to instances of people having substantial influence. One example is the selection of beneficiaries. Although, as seen, the authorities may 'provide' people from a certain *ubudehe* category, sometimes people choose to join or are recruited by the community: 'anyone could vote for whomever they wanted' (Rwa int 22).

Most examples of influence, however, concern the choice of input. In a case of tree planting, farmers made the organization provide fruit trees, which had not been planned. 'We gathered to choose which species to be used in this village and how these species will be protected from animals' (Rwa int 21). Also at their suggestion, participants were allowed to sell seedlings that they produced, and when people wanted better knowledge on tree nursing and seed collection, such training was provided. In another case, people could propose what domestic animals they would receive. 'They won't give you an animal that you're not happy with' (Rwa int 5). One participant decided to not go for animals at all.

> They gave us 20,000 to buy animals, but I asked myself 'If I buy this animal, how will I take care of it? How will I feed it?' So I decided to rent land instead to grow tomatoes, expecting to buy animals after I harvest my tomatoes and raise a larger capital. They were planning to give me an animal. But I realized that buying that animal would slow my development. (Rwa int 8)

While this person's preference was accepted, there are limits to beneficiaries' alternatives. A young woman illustrates that every choice must be considered worthwhile by the CSO. She was determined to take up her studies, but others were not. 'Some think they cannot study anymore and say "Let me sell charcoal, eggs or avocadoes, and work for money." Everyone has their own choice—unless you make a bad choice, then they won't help you' (Rwa int 29).

8.3.4 The Nature and Role of Local Participation in Rwandan-Owned Development

Rwandan ownership is undisputable. The government sets the agenda, determines priorities, and formulates strategies, following an explicit development vision. It manages its aid providers, closely monitoring their performance, while playing down the importance of aid resources. Meanwhile, the government eloquently commits to and actively promotes local participation.

Our interviews show that Rwandan CSOs cautiously operate in line with government priorities. Their activities are designed to contribute to local authorities' *imihigo* targets, local officials 'provide' beneficiaries and the expected role is to help implementing national policies. While most respondents express no dissatisfaction with thus serving the government agenda, critical voices point to CSOs being constrained and controlled: 'this is Rwanda'. CSO representatives report that they only partly adjust to foreign funding, while being thoroughly affected by the government's approach to aid and aid providers, as its promotion of national self-sufficiency and downplaying of aid dependence decrease their funding opportunities.

Our interviews also show that CSO representatives are familiar with and favourable towards local participation, proficiently pointing to its benefits and to problems of non-participation. There are well-known obstacles to participation, such as experiences and expectations of hand-outs and top-down instructions, and of people preferring—or having to prioritize—paid work rather than participating in development activities. Still, there are numerous instances of substantial beneficiary influence on CSO activities. However—and though a couple of CSO representatives mention empowering and emancipatory purposes, such as knowing and claiming your rights—the examples encountered reflect participation that promotes efficiency and cost-effectiveness by making input locally or individually appropriate, and thus not a kind of participation that could promote alternative priorities and strategies or hold decision- and policy-makers to account. Instead, CSO activities make people follow the government agenda, and the limited forms of participation implied come to serve the realization of the centrally determined development model.

8.4 Cambodia

After a genocide in the late 1970s and civil war throughout the 1980s, in the 1990s Cambodia was one of the poorest countries in the world, with acute lack of essentials such as infrastructure, education, economic resources, modern judiciary, and political institutions (Curtis 1998). In parallel with Rwanda, from 1994 onwards the international development community flooded the country with aid and good will for a speedy reconstruction.

8.4.1 Political Context and the Evolution of National Ownership

The sudden and massive inflow of aid was not easy to handle for the central government, suffering from an acute deficit of human resources and institutions and harbouring many internal conflicts. Several development actors—NGOs, bilaterals, and even UN-based actors—operated in the country without government permission (cf. Bernander et al. 1995). Heavily dependent not only on aid funds, but also on technical assistance, the country has been described as 'donor-driven'; as a 'laboratory for donor trial-and-error experiments' (Ear 2013: 10); and as trapped in low ownership, with lack of state capacity and lack of donor trust reinforcing each other (Hubbard 2005: 367). A first major attempt to retake control of the development agenda came with Cambodia's First Socio-Economic Development Plan (FSEDP; RGC 1996). This was followed by a 'triangular strategy' in 1999 and a 'rectangular strategy' in 2004, which based national development (and adherent aid) on four pillars. With the Paris Declaration in 2005, the process of taking control over the development agenda was pushed further by the international ideal of national ownership.

Over time a more organized form of cooperation emerged in sequence with the aid itself becoming more structured, long-term, and sustainable. Annual donor meetings abroad in the 1990s, where bi- and multilaterals outbid each other in pledges with Cambodia as a passive recipient, were replaced by in-country, government-hosted meetings. Sector-wide approaches were developed and budget support discussed. From the early 2000s, the government became more assertive, firmly expressing its priorities and less readily accepting aid conditionalities. Moreover, from 2005 onwards, donors tried to coordinate better among themselves and await government initiatives (civil servant, Sida, field notes 2008). In 2006, the first aid strategy was adopted, stating that ownership was setting out to further strengthen government leadership (RGC 2006). A national focal point for issues related to development cooperation was established, a more coherent policy framework constructed, and ambitious development targets set (EU 2014).

The fourth 'rectangular strategy', 2018–23, places governance reform at the centre and circles that with four prioritized areas: human resource development, private sector development, inclusive and sustainable development, and economic diversification (RGC 2018). The government claims that, through the third phase, social expenditure has been boosted by a factor of almost three and asserts that virtually all social indicators in the country are pointing sharply upwards. The strategy is, furthermore, part of the 'Political Platform of the Royal Government of the Sixth Legislature of the National Assembly' and constitutes a framework for the more detailed National Strategic Development Plan, 2019–23.

This gradual, though uneven and incomplete, process from donor dominance to national ownership was largely driven by growing independence, internal capacity, reliance on 'new' donors (mainly China), and increasing ability to keep donors at arms' length. In late 2017, then, the trajectory towards a more controlling central government and increased national ownership was further emphasized when national politics returned to political authoritarianism. Since then, political control has been strengthened through the government's overall control of society and zero tolerance of activity that deviates politically from the party line (cf. Andersen et al. 2019). With a very strict approach to human rights/democracy activism, internationally funded development activities are strictly monitored, and the government has very low tolerance of any development aid that could be understood as politically oppositional.

8.4.2 National Ambitions of Local Participation

The hasty 'democratization' after the peace agreement in 1991 (Öjendal 1996) did not sit easily in Cambodia, both for historical reasons (Chandler 1983) and because of remaining deep-seated conflicts in the political community and in the societal fabric (cf. Öjendal and Ou 2013). With a liberal constitution, bottom-up processes and local participation were introduced across the board, although unevenly and sometimes in contrast to local habits (Blunt and Turner 2005). The liberal foundation for the 'new' Cambodia was in turn strengthened by the Western-based development industry. Throughout the 1990s, vast resources were spent in the name of local development, with a common request for 'local participation' attached to them, seeking to activate bottom-up processes at every level and at all sites (Plummer and Tritt 2010; World Bank/Asia Foundation 2013).

For many—officials and people in general—this was a new approach, containing uncertainties and novelty. Although 'local participation' was constantly on the agenda, there were many sceptics regarding the viability of this approach (e.g., Blunt and Turner 2005). Yet many Cambodians had survived harsh times before by being pragmatic, and at the time it 'paid off' to adopt a participatory approach to local development. 'If we have to do participation, we can do participation' (government official, field notes 1997). These processes had a massive impact on development practices in Cambodia, especially at lower levels. The outcomes, however, were not always the intended ones, and ethnographic research and donor assessments show that people's participation remained limited (Hasselskog 2009; Plummer and Tritt 2010; World Bank/Asia Foundation 2013).

As a major example, in the mid-1990s, the UN-sponsored project CARERE (Cambodian Rehabilitation and Regeneration) was pursued in parts of the country, with a grounded method for local participation and enhanced local democratization (Hasselskog 2009). This initiative grew and by 1996 had become a nationwide programme named Seila ('foundation in stone'). Eventually it was scaled up to an official reform of democratic decentralization, including commune elections and budget-controlling commune councils creating a full second layer of government (Evans 2000; Öjendal and Dellnäs 2013). In this phase, the scope of civil society grew rapidly, ranging from CBOs (community-based organizations) with localized activities to international NGOs with major operations in the country (Öjendal 2013). In a World Bank study from 2009, it was estimated that there were more than 8,000 CBOs, close to 2,000 CSOs, around 400 labour unions, including a vast number of village-based 'traditional associations' (Malena and Chhim 2009: 27–8). This was complemented by mass organizations spanning from unions to student organizations. By the mid-2010s, a subculture of sorts had evolved nationwide, fostering organization, self-management, and bottom-up work (Malena and Chhim 2009; Öjendal 2013; Ou and Kim 2014).

For the government led by the CPP (Cambodian People's Party), the broad and often progressive NGO sector has for decades represented a growing problem of (what they perceive as) illegitimate interference in politics. After an intense debate since it was first proposed in 2011, in 2015 the controversial Law on NGOs (LANGO) was established, regulating the work of NGOs. It included, inter alia, strict demands on registration, reporting of activities, and financial declarations. Moreover, there is a clause demanding that NGOs be politically neutral, making any disagreement with central or local government subject to suspicions of siding with 'the opposition'. Failure to comply with these rules may lead to withdrawal of permission to work or even prosecution. There has, predictably, been widespread critique of the LANGO, for instance visible in a 'Joint Statement' of 28 Cambodian NGOs in December 2020. The NGO community at large deems the law unconstitutional and argues that it prevents NGOs from doing their work on poverty alleviation, social improvement, and good governance (ICNL 2024b).

The government, however, refutes this perspective: 'If LANGO were restrictive, why does the number of newly registered NGOs keep rising, making the total number at nearly 6,000?' (*Khmer Times*, 9 October 2021). With the adoption of the LANGO and the re-entrance of authoritarianism in 2017, the significance of the local participatory subculture faded, funding was withdrawn, and the number of international organizations dwindled (cf. Cohen 2019; Morgenbesser 2019). Development activities by NGOs are tightly monitored, and unions, NGOs, and human rights organizations have, in phases, been challenged, pressed, or outright forbidden to do their work. As a result, the entire NGO sector has been curtailed—Human Rights Watch calling it an 'onslaught' (HRW 2023)—and gone through a process of damaging self-censorship.

8.4.3 CSO Experiences of National Ownership and Local Participation

So, given this gradual, though uneven, increase of national ownership until the pronounced step towards central control in 2017, and given the government's ambiguous approach to local participation, how does the prevailing form of national ownership play out among Cambodian CSOs?

CSO Relations with the Government and Foreign Funders

The demand to comply with the government's stricter rules tends to divide development agents at local levels. An often-repeated observation made by local development practitioners is that when working under the current government regime, you risk losing contact with and funding from the broader development community. It is cautiously explained to us that complying with the government's stricter control reduces the space to do development work in a credible way. 'After being approved by the government in 2018, I feel we are being discriminated by other organizations' (Cam int 1). Locally, the same trend is reportedly equally visible: 'The local participation has dropped significantly' (Cam int 1). Yet the same respondent notes that 'I am the one who makes crucial and final decisions ...

The government will usually follow accordingly'. Such sentiments we have heard from several sources, indicating that a certain degree of self-censorship is ongoing, allowing at least a minimum of continuation of CSOs' development work. Complying with government dictates gives space to work and offers a certain degree of security, but on the other hand leads to reduced legitimacy in the development community as well as with the local population.

Others emphasize the enhanced cooperation with local authorities: for many CSOs, relations with the authorities have become paramount. 'We need a good relationship and open communication with the [local] authorities' and, to further emphasize the significance of this, 'Without the participation of the [local] authorities, [the] project would not go forward' (Cam int 10). For some, possibly in uncontroversial sectors, this is not much of a problem but rather a source of comfort. 'When they know that [the work of the CSO] aligns with the national plan, their thoughts and actions become activated and improved' (Cam int 2). An executive director of a development-CSO observes that '[Local authorities'] participation has improved a lot in the last five years' but also that 'donors have sponsored much less' (Cam int 3; cf. Cam int 8).

In contrast, for controversial NGOs local authorities are suspicious, critical, and unwelcoming. One interviewee stated that 'the local authority did not know me well so they were not very welcoming. They kept questioning our motive and intent' (Cam int 17). Another CSO worker shared the same experience: 'The local authorities used to be [good] to work with. [They were difficult initially], but after getting to know one another, we developed a partnership' (Cam int 13). Sometimes the situation was explicitly politicized, '[local authorities] may suspect that my group is politically motivated. This creates fear in my group and discourages them from conducting the project [well]' (Cam int 18).[2]

While contacts with the local authorities have become increasingly pivotal, relations with donors have weakened. A project manager states that 'donors' and [CSOs'] behaviour does not align [any more]' (Cam int 2), presumably because the CSOs have been forced to follow government policy more closely. A director observes, 'After being approved ... by the government, we receive less funding from [foreign] NGOs' (Cam int 1). Possibly, funding agents are reluctant to keep a high profile locally because that could disturb the local CSOs' relations with local authorities, fitting the pattern of overall less presence of donors on the development scene since 2018.

Expectations and Dynamics of Local Participation

Above, we saw one interviewee claiming that local participation is harder now when the CSOs are under stricter government control, distancing them from the

[2] It should be noted that the study concerns development CSOs working locally, and may thus be inadvertently tilted towards more co-operative actors

local population. Interestingly, others report the contrary: a high and satisfying degree of local participation. '[The villagers'] participation has been very active as they seem to want to learn more' (Cam int 9; cf. Cam int 7). One local coordinator said that 'for the local participation, there is a significant number of people who join in the trainings ... the number is impressive. For example [in a recent meeting], of 50 people invited, 47 turned up' (Cam int 4). Another respondent mentioned that participation was great and '[we have] at least 40 per cent women [in our meetings], but we tend to set the number of participants beforehand [and then just call this many to the meeting]'. The same interviewee continues: 'youth participation has increased significantly. Not only the number of youths who are volunteering [are impressing], but also their commitment to the projects' (Cam int 4). This is a form of local participation where the headcount defines how many want to/should join a meeting/training and the number turning up determines the degree of success of participation. It is neither organic nor political and (definitely) not a decision-making form of participation, as is often assumed in the literature on local participation.

Another common response was that 'participation is ... more active [now] because we can have various meetings with authorities and commune councils in all projects, compared to some past projects that lack[ed] the participation from the government side' (Cam int 12), reflecting a conception of 'local participation' as cooperation between CSOs and local authorities. This conception had many variations: '[we] have developed a [new] partnership where I am invited to various commune meetings and listen to the decision-making' (Cam int 13). One development worker got so close to the commune council that she 'was invited by the local authority to join the dispute settlement committee' (Cam int 16). Another CSO worker stated that 'the local authority joins me teaching [the villagers]. Sometimes they would join fully, and sometimes they would only join half-way, but they will always encourage the villagers to join and stay for the full teaching' (Cam int 17). Unsurprisingly in an authoritarian system, the line between cooperation and control may be fine at times.

Many of the interviewed CSO workers act as educators, mediators in local conflicts, or legal advisers, appointed in random 'elections'. In one instance it was stated that 'The voters were limited to around 25–30 people from the village' and 'No criteria is set as to what the elected representative must fulfil.' Moreover, 'it is up to the village chief to select as long as they are from the village' (Cam int 4). In other cases, workers are reported to have been selected by the commune chief (Cam int 5; Cam int 7). There are seemingly very thin democratic/participatory practices involved in these selection processes, and people are rather appointed or even recruited and engaged. Hence the typical pattern is that CSO workers are appointed based on loyalty or merit, rather than being the local population's choice and representatives.

In the first decade of the 2000s, the international development community strongly emphasized the internal democracy in contracted Cambodian CSOs

(Bryld et al. 2012: 37). The contemporary environment among Cambodian CSOs is a far cry from those demands. The critique of centralized and non-democratic structures in the management of CSOs is more valid than ever. On a direct question as to whether external influence has an impact on the organization's activities, the reply was 'I am the director, therefore, I am the one who makes the project' (Cam int 3). In contrast, an interviewee further down in the hierarchy answered: '[I have] never been involved in any important decision-making and [my] team only follows what we are instructed to do [by the director]' (Cam int 6). This was followed by: '[The central CSO] has never asked for any suggestions or comments from us, so I cannot say whether our views are taken seriously or not' (Cam int 6). Another interviewee stated as a matter of fact that '[The CSO] was the one making the decision as to how the project is conducted. My group only conduct the project as instructed' (Cam int 18). A quote summarizes this well:

> The main decision-makers are the director and the donors. They are the ones who define the action plan and its activities.... For example, when the aforementioned project ends and a new proposal is submitted to continue the project, they will make changes if needed. (Cam int 14)

Centralism and top-down management seem again (or still) to be the norm politically and internally, as local CSO workers are consulted only to a limited degree.

8.4.4 The Nature and Role of Local Participation in Cambodian-Owned Development

In our review above, we see how increased national ownership and especially the recent political evolution in Cambodia has divided the local development community. It is noted how complying development agents enjoy a higher degree of cooperation with local authorities, how a certain form of 'defensive' (or shallow) local participation has arisen, and that emancipating or decision-making forms of participation are at large absent. International donors seem to commonly avoid interfering in development processes locally in the new political landscape. Moreover, we note how internal structures of CSOs have gone 'back to the future', meaning that a certain central control/top-down approach has emerged/returned. With a historical perspective, this may be the 'natural' way of pursuing local participation in Cambodia, but it is not the way that was advocated by the international donor community until recently (cf. Plummer and Tritt 2010). With stronger national ownership, a more restrictive legal framework has been introduced, including stricter political control locally. For a certain set of CSOs, in certain sectors, the increased national ownership creates a workable (or even conducive) environment.

Some segments of civil society (those complying with government policies or/and in non-controversial sectors) are thriving, whereas others (those trying to maintain an independent stance) are being curtailed in their participatory ambition and finding it hard to work locally. Participatory development activities are pursued with some success in certain sectors, especially non-political and development-oriented ones: for example, petty land issues, work against alcohol abuse, and work for local female entrepreneurship. Villagers seem to—according to our interviewees—appreciate these activities, although 'participation' is more of a headcount than organic, and more of a cooperation between stakeholders than implying grassroots involvement. CSOs continue to work locally, but ordinary people are not included in defining issues or influencing decisions.

8.5 Reflections and Conclusions

So, what can we say about the nature and role of local participation in the context of Rwandan and Cambodian national ownership?

In Rwandan policy formulation, local participation is, and has for decades been, very present. Throughout official documents its importance is proclaimed, and participatory practices are promoted. Our empirics show that CSO representatives are committed to local participation, while the practices encountered are limited to the sort of participation that helps increase efficiency and cost-effectiveness. As CSO activities are closely aligned with government policies, participants are made to work in line with those. Local participation is thus eloquently presented as part of the Rwandan development model, and participation practices are made active use of to help reach national goals.

In Cambodia, local participation was for much longer driven by aid providers, before gradually and partly taken over by the government. With shrinking aid dependency, enhanced capacity, and authoritarian rule, however, there is less room for ideals nurtured by the international aid community, and local participation has little role in the current Cambodian development model. Our empirics, meanwhile, show that CSO representatives are favourable towards local participation though their perception of the term is very broad. Their activities are tolerated by the government as long as they comply with the strict regulatory framework and are not politically challenging. As a result, the sort of participation entailed is limited to 'defensive' approaches such as inclusion of villagers in activities, cooperation with local authorities, and broad-based awareness-building.

The two countries' respective approaches to local participation partly reflect their different approaches to national ownership. Rwandan ownership is the result of a determined policy to claim policy independence and active management of aid providers, with the government skilfully navigating the aid arena and exploiting prevailing ideals (Hasselskog 2023). Cambodian ownership is more the result of striving for sovereignty, control and economic growth. So, there are different ways of reaching and exercising national ownership and different ways of relating to local participation. In both cases, however, prevailing participation practices fall short of the emancipatory and empowering forms originally envisioned and supposedly nurtured by the international aid community.

Our findings thus show that national ownership is not per se conducive to local participation. In situations of strong national ownership, it cannot be assumed that policy-makers will adhere to the ideal or promote certain participatory practices. Rather, if a country's development priorities and strategies are determined domestically—in line with national ownership—it cannot be predicted what those priorities and strategies will be. Whether local participation is valued and promoted and, if so, what sort of participation and for what purposes, will inevitably depend on what value and role national policy-makers see for it.

This may seem obvious and the common assumption that local participation goes hand in hand with national ownership may be explained by an implicit belief that democracy prevails, or is emerging, in aid recipient countries. When the ownership agenda was made explicit, democracy was the only game in town, with the 'end of history' (Fukuyama 1992) reflecting the notion that liberal democracy had 'won' and there was no going back. With that notion, a likely expectation was that, when an aid recipient government gains ownership, it will adhere to the ideal of local participation, endorsing and 'owning' participatory practices. However, the geopolitical context has drastically changed in at least two ways—the third wave of democratization has been halted and the hegemony of 'traditional' aid has been undermined. Popular influence will not be favoured by non-democratic leaders and the relationship will be tense between national ownership and local participation.

In practice, and as noted in the introduction, strong national ownership has often come to coincide with centrally controlled policy-making. This is convenient for aid providers, as it entails predictability and clarity. In some cases the ownership agenda—aimed at countering legacies of colonialism and oppression by shifting the power balance—may even have contributed to such centralization since it facilitates features favoured by the agenda, such as strong government leadership, clear development priorities, a coherent policy framework linked to budget, and coordination of aid providers. Our cases illustrate that, at least, the ownership principle allows room for centralized—even authoritarian—governance, which is likely to have negative, though highly disparate, effects on local participation, depending on policy-makers' inclinations.

So, if national ownership is the overarching aim, centrally controlled policy- and decision-making in aid recipient countries is a possible, perhaps expected, consequence. If, on the other hand, democratization is a priority, the declared principles need to be revised. The widening of the ownership concept—with pleas for deeper, democratic, substantive, inclusive, balanced, shared, multi-stakeholder, and broad-based forms of ownership (Hasselskog 2020: O98)—has not solved the problem. Such a combination of different and, as this chapter illustrates, contradictory ideals make the ownership principle—though appealing and easy to agree on—even less operationable. With continuous widening of the concept also comes a familiar sense of donor influence—there should be not only ownership, but ownership with certain characteristics.

A different way forward could be a renewed focus on aid providers' motives and rationales. Why do they provide resources, what kind of influence do they expect/require, and—not least—what accountabilities come with such influence? This would entail a long way to go from the common focus on recipients but might have a chance of revitalizing current and future forms of international development cooperation, making it clearer what it can—and cannot—achieve, in whose interests, based on whose responsibilities, and on what terms.

References

Adamczyk, C. (2012). 'Independent Actors or Silent Agents: Where to Go for Rwandan Civil Society?'. In M. Campioni and P. Noack, editors, *Rwanda Fast Forward: Social, Economic, Military and Reconciliation Prospects.* Basingstoke: Palgrave Macmillan. https://doi.org/10.1057/9781137265159_5.

Andersen, H., K.-A. Larsson, and J. Öjendal (2019). *Supporting State-Building for Democratisation? A Study of 20 Years of Swedish Democracy Aid to Cambodia.* EBA Report 2019:03. Stockholm: The Expert Group for Aid Studies (Expertgruppen för Biståndsanalys/EBA).

Arnstein, S. R. (1969). 'A Ladder of Citizen Participation'. *Journal of the American Institute of Planners,* 35(4): 216–24. https://doi.org/10.1080/01944366908977225.

Bernander, B., C. Lindahl, J. Öjendal, J. Charny, and M. Eastmond (1995). *Facing a Complex Emergency: An Evaluation of Swedish Support to Emergency Aid to Cambodia.* Stockholm: Sida.

Blunt, P., and M. Turner (2005). 'Decentralisation, Democracy and Development in a Post-Conflict Society: Commune Councils in Cambodia'. *Public Administration and Development,* 25(1): 75–87. https://doi.org/10.1002/pad.349.

Booth, D. (2012). 'Aid Effectiveness: Bringing Country Ownership (and Politics) Back In'. *Conflict, Security and Development,* 12(5): 537–58. https://doi.org/10.1080/14678802.2012.744184.

Bryld, E., H. Alffram, and S. Kim (2012). *Evaluation of Forum Syd and Diakonia's Democracy and Human Rights programmes in Cambodia.* Stockholm: Sida.

Chandler, D. (1983). *A History of Cambodia.* Boulder, CO: Westview Press.

Chemouni, B. (2014). 'Explaining the Design of the Rwandan Decentralization: Elite Vulnerability and the Territorial Repartition of Power'. *Journal of Eastern African Studies,* 8(2): 246–62. https://doi.org/10.1080/17531055.2014.891800.

Cohen, H. J. (2019). 'Unconditional Aid and "Hybrid Democracy": The Case of Cambodia'. *Asian Journal of Public Affairs,* 11(2): 1–8. https://doi.org/10.18003/ajpa.20194.

Cornwall, A. (ed.) (2011). *The Participation Reader.* London: Zed Books.

Curtis, G. (1998). *Cambodia Reborn? The Transition to Democracy and Development.* Washington, DC: Brookings Institution Press.

Desrosiers, M.-E., and H. J. Swedlund (2019). 'Rwanda's Post-Genocide Foreign Aid Relations: Revisiting Notions of Exceptionalism.' *African Affairs*, 118(472): 435–62. https://doi.org/10.1093/afraf/ady032.

Ear, S. (2013). *Aid Dependence in Cambodia: How Foreign Assistance Undermines Democracy.* New York: Columbia University Press. https://doi.org/10.7312/columbia/9780231161121.001.0001.

EU (2014). *European Development Cooperation Strategy for Cambodia 2014–2018.* Brussels: European External Action Service.

EU/GoR (Government of Rwanda) (2014). *National Indicative Programme for the Period 2014–2020.* Brussels: European External Action Service.

Evans, H. (2000). *Strategic Evaluation of CARERE.* Stockholm: Sida.

Eyben, R. (ed.) (2006). *Relationships for Aid.* London and Sterling: Earthscan.

Fukuyama, F. (1992). *The End of History and the Last Man.* Toronto and New York: Maxwell Macmillan.

Gaynor, N. (2016). 'Beneath the Veneer: Decentralisation and Post-Conflict Reconstruction in Rwanda.' *Third World Thematics: A TWQ Journal*, 1(6): 779–98. https://doi.org/10.1080/23802014.2016.1333450.

GoS (Government of Sweden) (2015). *Strategi för Sveriges utvecklingssamarbete med Rwanda 2015–2019.* Stockholm: GoS.

GoS (2020). *Strategi för Sveriges utvecklingssamarbete med Rwanda 2020–2024.* Stockholm: GoS.

GPEDC (Global Partnership for Effective Development Cooperation) (2016a). 'Monitoring Profile—October 2016: Cambodia.' Paris: GPEDC.

GPEDC (2016b). 'Monitoring Profile—October 2016: Rwanda.' Paris: GPEDC.

GPEDC (2018). *Rwanda.* Paris: GPEDC.

Grimm, S. (2013). 'Aid Dependency as a Limitation to National Development Policy? The Case of Rwanda.' In W. Brown and S. Harman, editors, *African Agency in International Politics.* Abingdon, Oxfordshire, and New York: Routledge: 81–96.

Harper-Shipman, T. (2020). *Rethinking Ownership of Development in Africa.* Abingdon and New York: Routledge. https://doi.org/10.4324/9780429330452.

Hasselskog, M. (2009). 'Development Intervention on the Ground: Inherent Rationales of Aid and Their Encounter with Local Dynamics in Three Cambodian Villages.' PhD dissertation. Gothenburg: University of Gothenburg. Available at: https://gupea.ub.gu.se/bitstream/2077/21129/1/gupea_2077_21129_1.pdf (accessed 22 April 2024).

Hasselskog, M. (2016). 'Participation or What? Local Experiences and Perceptions of Household Performance Contracting in Rwanda.' *Forum for Development Studies*, 43(2): 177–99. https://doi.org/10.1080/08039410.2015.1090477.

Hasselskog, M. (2018). 'Rwandan "Home Grown Initiatives": Illustrating Inherent Contradictions of the Democratic Developmental State.' *Development Policy Review*, 2018(36): 309–28. https://doi-org.ezproxy.ub.gu.se/10.1111/dpr.12217.

Hasselskog, M. (2020). 'What Happens to Local Participation When National Ownership Gets Stronger? Initiating an Exploration in Rwanda and Cambodia.' *Development Policy Review*, 38(51): O91–O111. https://doi.org/10.1111/dpr.12488.

Hasselskog, M. (2022). 'What Happened to the Focus on the Aid Relationship in the Ownership Discussion?' *World Development*, 155: 105896. https://doi.org/10.1016/j.worlddev.2022.105896.

Hasselskog, M. (2023). 'Exploiting International Development Ideals. The Rwandan Government's Approach to Local Participation in Light of Its Exercise of National Ownership'. *Forum for Development Studies*, 50(3): 371–95. https://doi.org/10.1080/08039410.2023.2230203.

Hasselskog, M., and I. Schierenbeck (2015). 'National Policy in Local Practice: The Case of Rwanda'. *Third World Quarterly*, 36(5): 950–66. https://doi.org/10.1080/01436597.2015.1030386.

Hasselskog, M., P. Mugume, E. Ndushabandi, and I. Schierenbeck (2017). 'National Ownership and Donor Involvement: An Aid Paradox illustrated by the Case of Rwanda'. *Third World Quarterly*, 38(8): 1816–30. https://doi.org/10.1080/01436597.2016.1256763.

Hout, W., and R. Robinson (eds) (2009). *Governance and the Depoliticisation of Development*. Abingdon, Oxfordshire, and New York: Routledge.

Hubbard, M. (2005). 'Aid Management: Beyond the New Orthodoxy'. *Public Administration and Development*, 25: 365–71. https://doi.org/10.1002/pad.372.

HRW (2023) 'Cambodia: Two Years of Relentless Onslaught on Political Opposition and Civil Society'. https://www.hrw.org/news/2023/10/10/cambodia-two-years-relentless-onslaught-political-opposition-and-civil-society (accessed 16 April 2024).

ICNL (International Center for Not-for-Profit Law) (2024a). 'Rwanda'. Available at: www.icnl.org/resources/civic-freedom-monitor/rwanda (accessed 22 April 2024).

ICNL (2024b). 'Cambodia'. Available at: https://www.icnl.org/resources/civic-freedom-monitor/cambodia (accessed 22 April 2024).

Kantengwa, O., R. Interayamahanga, and M. Mahoro (2019). *The Role of Civil Society in Enhancing Citizen Participation in Governance and Development Processes in Post-Genocide Rwanda*. Kigali: Never Again and Interpeace.

Malena, C., and K. Chhim (2009). *Linking Citizens and the State: An Assessment of Civil Society Contributions to Good Governance in Cambodia*. Phnom Penh: World Bank.

Mansuri, G., and V. Rao (2013). *Localizing Development: Does Participation Work?* Washington, DC: World Bank. https://doi.org/10.1596/978-0-8213-8256-1.

Mawdsley, E. (2019). 'South–South Cooperation 3.0? Managing the Consequences of Success in the Decade Ahead'. *Oxford Development Studies*, 47(3): 259–74. https://doi.org/10.1080/13600818.2019.1585792.

Morgenbesser, L. (2019). 'Cambodia's Transition to Hegemonic Authoritarianism'. *Journal of Democracy*, 30(1): 158–71. 10.1353/jod.2019.0012.

Newbury, M. C. (1978). 'Ethnicity in Rwanda: The Case of Kinyaga'. *Africa: Journal of the International African Institute*, 48(1): 17–29. https://doi.org/10.2307/1158708.

Nyiransabimana, V. (2018). 'Gender Equality: Key Challenges and Practical Solutions to Women Participation in Local Governance in Rwanda'. *African Journal of Public Affairs*, 10(3): 1–22.

OECD (2003). *Rome Declaration on Harmonization*. Paris: OECD.

OECD (2007). *2006 Survey on Monitoring the Paris Declaration: Overview of the Results*. Paris: OECD.

OECD (2008). *2008 Survey on Monitoring the Paris Declaration: Making Aid More Effective by 2010*. Paris: OECD.

OECD (2012). *Aid Effectiveness 2011: Progress in Implementing the Paris Declaration, Better Aid*. OECD Publishing. http://dx.doi.org/10.1787/9789264125780-en

OECD (2024). 'Official Development Assistance: Definition and Coverage'. Available at: www.oecd.org/development/financing-sustainable-development/development-finance-standards/officialdevelopmentassistancedefinitionandcoverage.htm#ODA2017 (accessed 8 March 2024).

OECD DAC (Development Assistance Committee) (2005/2008). *The Paris Declaration on Aid Effectiveness and The Accra Agenda for Action*. Paris: OECD.

OECD/UNDP (2019). *Making Development Co-operation More Effective: 2019 Progress Report*. Paris: OECD Publishing. https://doi.org/10.1787/26f2638f-en.

Ou, S., and S. Kim (2014). 'NGOs and the Illusion of a Cambodian Civil Society'. In G. Waibel, J. Ehlert, and H. Feuer, editors, *Southeast Asia and the Civil Society Gaze: Scoping a Contested Concept in Cambodia and Vietnam*. London: Routledge. https://doi.org/10.4324/9781315885407-11.

Öjendal, J. (1996). 'Democracy Lost? The Fate of the U.N.-Implanted Democracy in Cambodia'. *Contemporary Southeast Asia*, 18(2): 193–218. https://doi.org/10.1355/CS18_2E.

Öjendal, J. (2013). 'In Search of a Civil Society: Re-negotiating State–Society Relations in Cambodia'. In G. Waibel, J. Ehlert, and H. Feuer, editors, *Southeast Asia and the Civil Society Gaze: Scoping a Contested Concept in Cambodia and Vietnam*. London: Routledge. https://doi.org/10.4324/9781315885407-2.

Öjendal, J., and A. Dellnäs (2013). 'Introduction'. In J. Öjendal and A. Dellnäs, editors, *The Imperative of Good Local Governance: State of the Art of Local Governance and the Challenges for the Next Decade*. Tokyo: United Nations University Press: 3–28.

Öjendal, J., and S. Ou (2013). 'From Friction to Hybridity in Cambodia: 20 Years of Unfinished Peacebuilding'. *Journal of Peacebuilding*, 1(3): 365–80. https://doi-org.ezproxy.ub.gu.se/10.1080/21647259.2013.813178.

Plummer, J., and G. Tritt (2010). *Voice, Choice and Decision: A Study of Local Governance Processes in Cambodia*. Washington, DC: World Bank.

Protik, A. E., I. Nichols-Barrer, J. Berman, and M. Sloan (2018). 'Bridging the Information Gap between Citizens and Local Governments: Evidence from a Civic Participation Strengthening Program in Rwanda'. *World Development*, 108: 145–56. https://doi.org/10.1016/j.worlddev.2018.03.016.

RGB (Rwanda Governance Board) (2022). 'Non-Governmental Organisations'. Available at: www.rgb.rw/1/civil-society-faith-based-and-political-organisations/non-governmental-organisations (accessed 22 April 2024).

RGC (Royal Government of Cambodia) (1996). *Cambodia's First Socio-Economic Development Plan*. Phnom Penh: RGC.

RGC (2006). *Strategic Framework for Development Cooperation Management*. Phnom Penh: Royal Government of Cambodia.

RGC (2018). *Rectangular Strategy*. Phnom Penh: Royal Government of Cambodia.

RoR (Republic of Rwanda) (2000). *Rwanda Vision 2020*. Kigali: Minecofin.

RoR (2001). *National Decentralization Policy*. Kigali: Minaloc.

RoR (2006). *Rwanda Aid Policy*. Kigali: Minecofin.

RoR (2012a). *Law No. 04/2012 of 17/02/2012: Governing the Organisation and the Functioning of National Non-Governmental Organisations*. Kigali: RoR.

RoR (2012b). *National Decentralization Policy (Revised)*. Kigali: Minaloc.

RoR (2015). *Vision 2050*. Kigali: Republic of Rwanda.

RoR (2017). *7 Years Government Programme: National Strategy for Transformation (NST 1) 2017–2024*. Kigali: RoR.

RoR (2018). *Governance and Decentralization Sector Strategic Plan (2018/19–2023/24)*. Kigali: Minaloc.

RoR (2021). *External Development Finance Report. Fiscal Year 2019/2020*. Kigali: Republic of Rwanda.

Sida (2020). *Strategirapport för Sveriges utvecklingssamarbete med Rwanda 2015–2019.* Stockholm: Sida.

UN (2017). *United Nations Development Assistance Plan (UNDAP). July 2018 to June 2023 for Rwanda.* New York: UN.

Van Leeuwen, M. (2008). 'Imagining the Great Lakes Region: Discourses and Practices of Civil Society Regional Approaches for Peacebuilding in Rwanda, Burundi and DR Congo'. *Journal of Modern African Studies*, 46(3): 393–426. https://doi.org/10.1017/S0022278X08003352.

Whitfield, L. (ed.) (2009). *The Politics of Aid: African Strategies for Dealing with Donors.* Oxford: Oxford University Press.

World Bank (2024). 'Net ODA Received (% of Central Government Expense)'. Available at: https://data.worldbank.org/indicator/DT.ODA.ODAT.XP.ZS?end=2023&locations=RWandmost_recent_value_desc%3Dtrue&most_recent_value_desc=true&start=2000&view=chart (accessed 12 March 2024).

World Bank/Asia Foundation (2013). *Voice, Choice, and Decision 2: A Study of Local Basic Service Delivery in Cambodia.* Washington, DC: World Bank. https://openknowledge.worldbank.org/handle/10986/16758.

Yin, R. K. (2009). *Case Study Research: Design and Methods.* London: Sage.

Zorbas, E. (2011). 'Aid Dependence and Policy Independence: Explaining the Rwandan Paradox'. In S. Straus and L. Waldorf, editors, *Remaking Rwanda: State Building and Human Rights after Mass Violence.* Madison: University of Wisconsin Press.

Index

Tables and figures are indicated by an italic *t* and *f*.

For the benefit of digital users, indexed terms that span two pages (e.g., 52–53) may, on occasion, appear on only one of those pages.